DOMESDAY BOOK

Kent

History from the Sources

DOMESDAY BOOK

A Survey of the Counties of England

LIBER DE WINTONIA

Compiled by direction of

KING WILLIAM I

Winchester
1086

DOMESDAY BOOK

general editor

JOHN MORRIS

1

Kent

edited by
Philip Morgan

from a draft translation prepared by
Veronica Sankaran

PHILLIMORE
Chichester
1983

1983
Published by
PHILLIMORE & CO. LTD.
London and Chichester
Head Office: Shopwyke Hall,
Chichester, Sussex, England

ISBN 0 85033 153 6 (case)
ISBN 0 85033 154 4 (limp)

Printed in Great Britain by
Titus Wilson & Son Ltd.,
Kendal

KENT

Introduction

The Domesday Survey of Kent

Notes

Index of Persons

Index of Places

Map and Map Keys

Systems of Reference

Technical Terms

History from the Sources
General Editor: John Morris

The series aims to publish history
written directly from the sources
for all interested readers, both
specialists and others. The first
priority is to publish important
texts which should be widely
available, but are not.

DOMESDAY BOOK

The contents, with the folio on which each county begins, are:

Supplementary volume (35) BOLDON BOOK

Domesday Book is termed *Liber de Wintonia* (The Book of Winchester) in column 332c

INTRODUCTION

The Domesday Survey

In 1066 Duke William of Normandy conquered England. He was crowned King, and most of the lands of the English nobility were soon granted to his followers. Domesday Book was compiled 20 years later. The Saxon Chronicle records that in 1085

> at Gloucester at midwinter ... the King had deep speech with his counsellors ... and sent men all over England to each shire ... to find out ... what or how much each landholder held ... in land and livestock, and what it was worth ... The returns were brought to him.[1]

William was thorough. One of his Counsellors reports that he also sent a second set of Commissioners 'to shires they did not know, where they were themselves unknown, to check their predecessors' survey, and report culprits to the King.'[2]

The information was collected at Winchester, corrected, abridged, chiefly by omission of livestock and the 1066 population, and fair-copied by one writer into a single volume, now known as Domesday Book Volume I, or DB. The task of abridgement and codification was not complete by the time work stopped at the death of King William. The remaining material, the commissioners' circuit returns for Norfolk, Suffolk and Essex, which there had not been time to reduce, was left unabridged, copied by several writers, in a second volume, smaller than the first, usually now referred to as Domesday Book Volume II or Little Domesday Book or LDB, which states that 'the Survey was made in 1086'. The surveys of Durham and Northumberland, and of several towns, including London, were not transcribed, and most of Cumberland and Westmorland, not yet in England, was not surveyed. The whole undertaking was completed at speed, in less than 12 months, though the fair-copying of the main volume may have taken a little longer. Both volumes are now preserved at the Public Record Office. Some versions of regional returns also survive. One of them, from Ely Abbey,[3] copies out the Commissioners' brief. They were to ask

> The name of the place. Who held it, before 1066, and now?
> How many *hides*?[4] How many ploughs, both those in lordship and the men's?
> How many villagers, cottagers and slaves, how many free men and Freemen?[5]
> How much woodland, meadow and pasture? How many mills and fishponds?
> How much has been added or taken away? What the total value was and is?
> How much each free man or Freeman had or has? All threefold, before 1066,
>   when King William gave it, and now; and if more can be had than at present.

The Ely volume also describes the procedure. The Commissioners took evidence on oath 'from the Sheriff; from all the barons and their Frenchmen; and from the whole Hundred, the priests, the reeves and six villagers from each village'. It also names four Frenchmen and four Englishmen from each Hundred, who were sworn to verify the detail.

---

[1]Before he left England for the last time, late in 1086. [2]Robert Losinga, Bishop of Hereford 1079-1095 (see *E.H.R.* 22, 1907, 74). [3]*Inquisitio Eliensis*, first paragraph. [4]A land unit, reckoned as 120 acres. [5]*Quot Sochemani.*

The King wanted to know what he had, and who held it. The Commissioners therefore listed lands in dispute, for Domesday Book was not only a tax-assessment. To the King's grandson, Bishop Henry of Winchester, its purpose was that every 'man should know his right and not usurp another's'; and because it was the final authoritative register of rightful possession 'the natives called it Domesday Book, by analogy from the Day of Judgement'; that was why it was carefully arranged by Counties, and by landholders within Counties, 'numbered consecutively ... for easy reference'.[6]

Domesday Book describes Old English society under new management, in minute statistical detail. Foreign lords had taken over, but little else had yet changed. The chief landholders and those who held from them are named, and the rest of the population was counted. Most of them lived in villages, whose houses might be clustered together, or dispersed among their fields. Villages were grouped in administrative districts called Hundreds, which formed regions within Shires, or Counties, which survive today with minor boundary changes; the recent deformation of some ancient county identities is here disregarded, as are various short-lived modern changes. The local assemblies, though overshadowed by lords great and small, gave men a voice, which the Commissioners heeded. Very many holdings were described by the Norman term *manerium* (manor), greatly varied in size and structure, from tiny farmsteads to vast holdings; and many lords exercised their own jurisdiction and other rights, termed *soca*, whose meaning still eludes exact definition.

The Survey was unmatched in Europe for many centuries, the product of a sophisticated and experienced English administration, fully exploited by the Conqueror's commanding energy. But its unique assemblage of facts and figures has been hard to study, because the text has not been easily available, and abounds in technicalities. Investigation has therefore been chiefly confined to specialists; many questions cannot be tackled adequately without a cheap text and uniform translation available to a wider range of students, including local historians.

Previous Editions

The text has been printed once, in 1783, in an edition by Abraham Farley, probably of 1250 copies, at Government expense, said to have been £38,000; its preparation took 16 years. It was set in a specially designed type, here reproduced photographically, which was destroyed by fire in 1808. In 1811 and 1816 the Records Commissioners added an introduction, indices, and associated texts, edited by Sir Henry Ellis; and in 1861-1863 the Ordnance Survey issued zincograph facsimiles of the whole. Texts of individual counties have appeared since 1673, separate translations in the Victoria County Histories and elsewhere.

[6]*Dialogus de Scaccario* 1,16.

This Edition

Farley's text is used, because of its excellence, and because any worthy alternative would prove astronomically expensive. His text has been checked against the facsimile, and discrepancies observed have been verified against the manuscript, by the kindness of Miss Daphne Gifford of the Public Record Office. Farley's few errors are indicated in the notes.

The editor is responsible for the translation and lay-out. It aims at what the compiler would have written if his language had been modern English; though no translation can be exact, for even a simple word like 'free' nowadays means freedom from different restrictions. Bishop Henry emphasized that his grandfather preferred 'ordinary words'; the nearest ordinary modern English is therefore chosen whenever possible. Words that are now obsolete, or have changed their meaning, are avoided, but measurements have to be transliterated, since their extent is often unknown or arguable, and varied regionally. The terse inventory form of the original has been retained, as have the ambiguities of the Latin.

Modern English commands two main devices unknown to 11th century Latin, standardised punctuation and paragraphs; in the Latin, *ibi* ('there are') often does duty for a modern full stop, *et* ('and') for a comma or semi-colon. The entries normally answer the Commissioners' questions, arranged in five main groups, (i) the place and its holder, its hides, ploughs and lordship; (ii) people; (iii) resources; (iv) value; and (v) additional notes. The groups are usually given as separate paragraphs.

In both volumes of the MS, chapters were numbered 'for easy reference'. In the larger volume, sections within chapters are commonly marked, usually by initial capitals, often edged in red. In LDB (representing an earlier stage of the Inquiry's codification) sections are at first usually introduced by a paragraph mark, while red edging is reserved for chapter and Hundred headings; further on, however, the system of paragraphing the text becomes more haphazard and it is thus not always followed in the present translation. Owing to the less tabulated nature of the entries in LDB for Norfolk and Suffolk it is not possible to maintain throughout the translation of these two counties the sub-paragraphing that the late John Morris employed in the translation of other counties in the series. Maps, indices and an explanation of technical terms are also given. Later, it is hoped to publish analytical and explanatory volumes, and associated texts.

The editor is deeply indebted to the advice of many scholars, too numerous to name, and especially to the Public Record Office, and to the publisher's patience. The draft translations are the work of a team; they have been co-ordinated and corrected by the editor, and each has been checked by several people. It is therefore hoped that mistakes may be fewer than in versions published by single fallible individuals. But it would be Utopian to hope that the translation is altogether free from error; the editor would like to be informed of mistakes observed.

The maps are the work of Nell Bowen.

The preparation of this volume has been greatly assisted by a generous grant from the Leverhulme Trust Fund.

This support, originally given to the late Dr. J. R. Morris, has been kindly extended to his successors. At the time of Dr. Morris's death in June 1977, he had completed volumes 2, 3, 11, 12, 19, 23, 24. He had more or less finished the preparation of volumes 13, 14, 20, 28. These and subsequent volumes in the series were brought out under the supervision of John Dodgson and Alison Hawkins, who have endeavoured to follow, as far as possible, the editorial principles established by John Morris.

Conventions

★   refers to note on discrepancy between MS and Farley text

[ ]   enclose words omitted in the MS   ( ) enclose editorial explanation

CHENTH.

DOVERE Tēpore regis EDWARDI reddebat . xviii . libras. de quibus. denariis habebat rex . E . duas partes. 7 comes Goduin terciā. Contra hoc habebant canonici de ſčo Martino medietatē aliam. Burgenſes dedeř . xx . naues una uice in anno ad . xv . dies. 7 in una quaqᵩ naui erant hōēs . xx 7 uñ. Hoc faciebant pro eo qđ eis pdonauerat ſaccā 7 ſocā. Quando miſſatici regis ueniebant ibi: dabant pro caballo tranſducendo . iii . denarios in hieme . 7 ii . in eſtate. Burgenſes ū inueniebaɴ ſtiremannū 7 unū aliū adjutorē . 7 ſi plus opus . eet: de pecunia ej conducebat . A feſtiuitate Š Michaelis uſqᵩ ad feſtū Sči Andreæ: treuua regis erat in uilla. Siɋs eam infregiſſet: inde ppoſit regis accipiebat cō munē emendationē. Quicunqᵩ manens in uilla aſſiduus . reddebat regi čſuetudinē: quietus erat de theloneo p totā Angliā. Oɱs hæ conſuetudi nes erant ibi . quando Wiłłs rex in Angliā uenit. In ipſo pmo Aduentu ej in Angliā . fuit ipſa uilla cōbuſta . 7 idō pčiū ej non potuit cōputari quantū ualebat quando eps baiocenſis eā recepit . Modo appčiat . xl . lib . 7 tam ppoſit inde reddit . l . iiii . lib . Regi ɋdē . xxiiii . lib de denar qui ſuɴ xx . in ora: comiti ū . xxx . lib ad numerū.

KENT

D **DOVER**

1 before 1066 paid £18, of which pence King Edward had two parts and Earl Godwin the third. Against this, the Canons of St. Martin's had the other half.

2 The burgesses gave 20 ships to the King once a year for 15 days. In each ship were 21 men. They did this because he had given over to them full jurisdiction.

3 When the King's messengers came there, they gave 3d in winter and 2d in summer for horse passage. The burgesses found a steersman and 1 other assistant. If there was more labour, it was hired with his own money.

4 From the Feast of St. Michael until the Feast of St. Andrew the King's truce, that is peace, was in the town. If anyone broke it, the King's reeve received the common fine for it.

5 Whoever lived permanently in the town and paid customary dues to the King was exempt from toll throughout the whole of England.

6 All these customs were there when King William came to England.

7 At his first arrival in England the town was burnt. Its valuation could not therefore be reckoned, what its value was when the Bishop of Bayeux acquired it. Now it is assessed at £40; however, the reeve pays £54, that is £24 of pence, which are 20 to the *ora*, to the King and £30 at face value to the Earl.

In Douere funȝ . XXIX . manfuræ . de qᵇȝ rex p̄dit c̄fue
tudinē . De his habet Roƀt de romenel duas.
Radulf⁹ de curbefpine . III . Wiłłs fili⁹ Tedaldi . I.
Wiłłs fili⁹ Ogeri . I . Wiłłs fili⁹ Tedoldi 7 Roƀtus
niger . VI . Wiłłs filius Goisfridi . III . in qᵇȝ erat
gihałła burgenfiũ . Hugo de montfort . I . domũ.
Durand⁹ . I . Rannulf⁹ de colũbels . I . Wadard⁹ . VI.
Filius Modƀti unā . Et hi om̄s de his domiƀȝ reuo
cant eꝑm baiocenfē ad ꝓtectorē 7 liberatorem.

De illa mafura quā tenet Rannulf⁹ de colũbels quæ
fuit cujdā exulis: c̄cordant qd dimidia tra eſt
regis . 7 Rannulf⁹ ipfe habet utrunqᷓ . Hunfridus
tenet . I . mafurā . de qua erat forisfactura dimidia
regis . Roger⁹ de Oſtrehā fecit quandā domũ fuꝑ
aquā regis . 7 tenuit huc ufqᷓ c̄fuetudinē regis . Nec
dom⁹ fuit ibi T.R.E. In introitu portus de Douere
eſt unū molendiñ . qd om̄s pene naues confringit
ꝓ magnā turbationē maris . 7 maximũ dānũ fa
cit regi 7 hominiƀȝ . 7 non fuit ibi . T.R.E . De hoc dicit
Nepos Herberti . qd eꝑs baiocenfis conceſſit illũ
fieri Auunculo fuo Herberto filio Iuonis.

1 b
Has infra fcriptas leges regis c̄cordant hōes
de . IIII . Leſtis . hoc . ē Boruuar Leſt . 7 Eſtreleſt.
7 Linuuartleſt . 7 Wiuuartleſt . Siqᷓs fecerit
fepē uel foſſatū pro quo ſtrictior fiat publica
uia regis . aut arborē ſtantē extra uiā intra pro
ſtrauerit . 7 inde ramū uel frondē portauerit:
pro una quaqᷓ harũ forisfactur⁷ foluet regi . c . foł.

8 In Dover are 29 dwellings whose customary dues the King
   has lost. Of these, Robert of Romney has 2, Ralph of
   Courbépine 3, William son of Theodwald 1, William son
   of Odger 1, William son of Theodwald and Robert Black 6,
   William son of Geoffrey 3, including the burgesses' guild-hall,
   Hugh de Montfort 1 house, Durand 1, Ranulf of
   Colombières 1, Wadard 6, and Modbert's son 1.
   For these houses they all cite the Bishop of Bayeux as
   protector and deliverer, that is donor.

9 For the dwelling which Ranulf of Colombières holds, which
   was an exile's, that is an outlaw's, they agree that half the land
   is the King's; Ranulf has both (halves) himself. Humphrey
   Strapfoot holds 1 dwelling, half of which was forfeit to the
   King. Roger of Westerham made a house on the King's
   waterway, and has hitherto kept the King's customary dues.
   The house was not there before 1066.

10 At the entrance to Dover harbour is a mill, which wrecks almost
   all ships, through its great disturbance of the sea; it does very
   great harm to the King and his men; it was not there before 1066.
   Of this, Herbert's nephew says that the Bishop of Bayeux gave
   permission for it to be made by his uncle, Herbert son of Ivo.

11 The men of four Lathes, that is Borough Lathe, Eastry Lathe,   1 b
   Lympne Lathe and Wye Lathe, agree upon the following
   royal laws.

12 If anyone has made a fence or ditch whereby the King's
   public road is narrowed, or has felled into the road a tree
   that stood outside the road, and has carried off branch or
   foliage from it; for each of these offences he shall pay 100s
   to the King.

Et fi abierit domũ non apꝑhenſus uel diuadi
atus ꞈ tamen miniſter regis eũ ſequet᷎. 7 c . ſolid
emdabit. De gribrige ũ ſiꝗs eā fecerit 7 calũ
niat | aut diuadiat fuerit ꞈ viii . liƀ regi emda
bit. Sin autē ꞈ quiet erit erga regē . non erga
dñm cuj᷉ homo fuerit . de aliis forisfaꝛturis ſicuti
de gribrige . ſed p . c . ſoꞏl emdabit. Has forisfac
turas hꞇ rex ſuꝑ oñs alodiarios toti᷉ comitatus
de Chent . 7 ſuꝑ hōes ipſoꝝ . Et quando morit᷎
alodiarius ꞈ rex inde habet releuationē trǣ.
excepta tra ꞏS̃ ꝁINITATIS 7 ꞏS̃ Auguſtini . 7 ꞏS̃ mar
tini . 7 Exceptis his . Godric de Burnes . 7 Godric
carleſone . 7 Alnod cilt . 7 Eſber biga . 7 Siret de
cillehā . 7 Turgis 7 Norman . 7 Azor. Suꝑ iſtos
hꞇ rex forisfaꝛturā . de capitibꝝ eoꝝ tantũ m̃.
7 de terris eoꝝ hꞇ releuamen . qui hñt ſuā ſaca
7 ſocā. Et de his tris ſcilicet Goſlaches . 7 Boche
land . 7 aliũ Bocheland . 7 tꝛciũ Bocheland . 7 Herſle .
. i . jugũ de ora . 7 i . jugũ de Herte.
Schildrichehā . Macheheue . Ernulfitone . Oſla
chintone . Piria . 7 alia Piria . Brulege . Oſpringes.
Hortone . hꞇ rex . has forisfaꝛturas . Handſocā.
Gribrige . Foriſtel. De Adulterio ũ p totũ cheꝗᷓ
hꞇ rex hominē . 7 Archieꝑs mulierē . excepta
tra ꞏS̃ ꝁINITATIS . 7 ꞏS̃ Auguſtini . 7 ꞏS̃ Martini . de
quibꝝ rex nichil hꞇ . De latrone qui judicat᷉ eſt ad
mortē . hꞇ rex medietatē pecuniæ ej᷉ . Et qui exulē re
cepit ſine licentia regis ꞈ inde hꞇ rex forisfaꝛturā.

13   If he has gone away from home without being apprehended or attached, nevertheless the King's officer should follow him and he shall be fined 100s.

14   On breach of the peace, if anyone commits it and is charged on the road or attached he shall pay a fine of £8 to the King. But if he is exempt towards the King he shall not be so for the Lord whose man he is.

15   For other offences it as for breach of the peace, but he shall pay a fine of 100s.

16   The King has (the fines for) these penalties over all freeholders of the whole of the County of Kent.

17   When a freeholder dies then the King has the death duty on the land, apart from the land of Holy Trinity, of St. Augustine's and of St. Martin's, and with these exceptions; Godric of Bishopsbourne, Godric Karlson, Young Alnoth, Esbern Big, Sired of Chilham, Thorgils, Norman and Azor. Over these the King has only the capital penalty even now, and he has the death duty on the lands of those who have full jurisdiction.

18   And over these lands, namely *Goslaches,* Buckland, the other Buckland, the third Buckland, Hurst, 1 yoke of Oare, 1 yoke of Harty, *Schildricheham,* Macknade, Arnolton, *Oslachintone,* Perry, the other Perry, Throwley, Ospringe and Horton the King has these penalties: house-breaking, breach of the peace, highway robbery.

19   On adultery, over the whole of Kent the King has the (fine from) the man and the Archbishop (from) the woman, apart from the land of Holy Trinity, of St. Augustine's and of St. Martin's, from which the King has nothing.

20   On theft, the King has half the goods of whoever is condemned to death.

21   Whoever receives an exile without the King's permission, the King has the fine from him.

De terris ˢᶸˑpra nominatis Alnodi 7 ſimiliū eꝯ̃ ꞓ ht̄ rex

cuſtodiā . vi . diebₜ apud cantuariā . uel apud Sanuuic ꞓ

7 ibi hn̄t de regē cibū 7 potū . Si non habuerint ꞓ ſine

forisfaƈtura recedunt . Si fuerint p̄moniti ut c̄ueniaꞃ̃

ad ſcirā ꞓ ibunt uſꝗ ad pinnedennā . non longius . Et ſi

non uenerint ꞓ de hac forisfaƈtura 7 de aliis om̄ibₜ rex

. c . ſot habebit . excepta Gribrige quæ . viii . lib em̄dat́ .

7 de callibₜ ſic̄ ſupius ſcriptū . e̅ .

In Linuuartleſt in briſeuuei ht̄ rex c̄ſuetudinē . ſcilicet.

. ii ꞉ caretas . 7 ii . ſticas anguillaꝝ ꝑ uno Ineuuardo . 7 in

tra ſophis ht̄ xii . den̄ ꝑ uno Ineuuardo . 7 de uno jugo

de northburg . xii . den̄ aut unū Ineuuard́ . 7 de dena

xviii . den̄ . 7 de Gara unū Ineuuard́ . He træ jacent in Wiꞓ

7 hōes de his tris cuſtodiebaꞃ̃ regē apud cantuariā

ɫ apud Sanuuic ꝑ . iii . dies . ſi rex illuc ueniſſet .

¹c
In ᴸeſt de Sudtonc 7 in Leſt de Ailesford habuer̄

iſti fachā 7 Socā . Brixi cilt . Adelold de Eltehā .

Anſchil de Bechehā . Azor de Leſneis . Aluuinus ʰᵒʳ

Wluuard Wit . Ordinc de hortone . Eſbern de

cillesfclle . Leuenot de Sudtone . Eduuard de Eſtan .

Vleſtan 7 Leuric de Otrinberge . Oſuuard de Nord

tone . Edid de Aiſiholte . Alret de Ellinges .

Terra Canonicoꝝ ꞩ Martini de Dovre.

In Leſt de Eſtrede habebant canonici de ſco

Martino . T . R . E . xxi . folin In hund́ de Cornely

7 in hund́ de Beuſberge . In Leſt de Linuuarlet

habebant . iii . folins . unū in Eſtret hund́ . aliū in

Beliſſolt hund́ . 7 tc̄iū in Blacheborn hund́ .

T . R . E . eraꞃ̃ p̄bendæ cōmunes . 7 reddeƀ . lxi . liƀ .

int̄ totū . Modo ſunt diuiſæ ꝑ ſingulos . ꝑ ep̄m Baioć .

22 From the aforenamed lands of Young Alnoth and others like him, the King has a body-guard for 6 days at Canterbury or at Sandwich. They have food and drink from the King; if they have not had it they withdraw without penalty.

23 If they are summoned to meet at the Shire they go as far as Pennenden, not further. If they do not come, the King has 100s for this offence and for all others, with the exception of breach of the peace for which the fine is £8; and from the roads, as written above.

24 In Lympne Lathe, in *Briseuuei* the King has a customary due, namely 2 carts and 2 sticks of eels, for one Escort; and in the land of *Sophis* he has 12d for one Escort; and from 1 yoke of 'Northborough' 12d for one Escort; and from Dean 18d, and from *Gara* one Escort. These lands lie in Wye. Men from these lands guard the King at Canterbury or at Sandwich for 3 days if the King comes there.

25 In the Lathe of Sutton and in the Lathe of Aylesford, these had   1 c
full jurisdiction: Young Brictsi, Aethelwold of Eltham, Askell of Beckenham, Azor of Lessness, Alwin Horn, Wulfward White, Ording of Horton, Esbern of Chelsfield, Leofnoth of Sutton, Edward of Stone, Wulfstan and Leofric of Wateringbury, Osward of Norton, Edith of Asholt and Alfred of Yalding.

M   LAND OF THE CANONS OF ST. MARTIN'S OF DOVER

1 In the Lathe of Eastry the Canons of St Martin's had 21 sulungs before 1066 in Cornilo Hundred and Bewsborough Hundred. In the Lathe of Lympne they had 3 sulungs, one in Street Hundred, another in Bircholt Hundred, and a third in Blackburn Hundred. Before 1066 they were prebends in common; and paid £61 in total. Now they have been distributed individually by the Bishop of Bayeux.

Radulf de S Sansone ten . 1 . (m) in p̄benda . Cerlen
tone uocat . 7 defd se .p . i . solin . Ibi hr . III . uillos
7 IIII . bord cū . I . car . Int tot ual LXX . sol . T.R.E:́
c . sol . Leuuin tenuit in p̄benda.

In ead uilla ten Wills fili Ogerii . I . solin . 7 ibi hr
I . uill 7 . VII . bord cū dim car . 7 I . molin de . XL . sol.
Ibi qdā francig hr . I . car . Isd Wills ten . I . monast
in Dovere de ep̄o . 7 redd ei . XI . sol . Canonici calūn.
Hoc tot ual . VI . lib . T.R.E:́ XII . lib . Sired tenuit.

In Bochelande ten Aluui . I . solin . 7 ibi hr . VI . uill
7 . X . bord cū . I . car 7 dimid . Int tot ual . IIII . lib.
T.R.E:́ c . sol . Iste ide tenuit in p̄benda.

In Gocistone ten Vlric . I . jug . 7 ibi hr . II . uillos
7 I . bord cū . I . car . Ad hanc tram ptin . XXV . ac træ
in Corneli hund . 7 ibi sunt . V . bord cū dim car.
Int tot ual . XX . sol . T.R.E:́ X . sol . Elric tenuit in

IN HOC EOD HVND JACET S MARGARITA. ꜰ p̄benda.

Ibi hr Sired . I . solin . 7 I . car in dn̄io . 7 VI . bord
cū . IIII . seruis . Val . c . sol . T.R.E:́ IIII . lib . Pat ejd
Sired tenuit in p̄benda.

Ibide ten Radulf . I . solin . 7 hr . I . car in dn̄io.
7 VII . bord . Val . LX 7 IX . sol . 7 II . den . T.R.E:
IIII . lib . Alric tenuit in p̄benda similit.

Ibide ten Alred . I . solin . 7 hr in dn̄io . I . car.
7 II . uill 7 II . bord cū dim car . Val . LX . sol . T.R.E:́
XX . sol . Pat huj tenuit in p̄benda.

In BEWSBOROUGH Hundred

2   Ralph of St. Samson holds 1 manor in prebend. It is called
CHARLTON, and answers for 1 sulung. He has
    3 villagers and 4 smallholders with 1 plough.
In total, value 70s; before 1066, 100s.
    Leofwin held it in prebend.

3   In the same village William son of Odger holds 1 sulung. He has
    1 villager and 7 smallholders with ½ plough.
    1 mill at 40s.
    A Frenchman has 1 plough.
    William also holds 1 monastery in Dover from the Bishop; it
        pays him 11s; the Canons claim it.
Value of all this £6; before 1066, £12.
    Sired held it.

4   In BUCKLAND Alwin holds 1 sulung. He has
    6 villagers and 10 smallholders with 1½ ploughs.
In total, value £4; before 1066, 100s.
    He held it himself in prebend.

5   In GUSTON Wulfric holds 1 yoke. He has
    2 villagers and 1 smallholder with 1 plough.
To this land belongs 25 acres of land in Cornilo Hundred;
    5 smallholders with ½ plough.
In total, value 20s; before 1066, 10s.
    Alric held it in prebend.

6   In this same Hundred lies ST. MARGARET'S (at Cliffe). Sired
has 1 sulung and 1 plough in lordship and
    6 smallholders with 4 slaves.
Value 100s; before 1066, £4.
    Sired's father held it in prebend.

7   There Ralph also holds 1 sulung. He has 1 plough in lordship
and
    7 smallholders.
Value 60s and 9s 2d; before 1066, £4.
    Alric held it in prebend likewise.

8   There Alfred also holds 1 sulung. He has 1 plough in lordship
and
    2 villagers and 2 smallholders with ½ plough.
Value 60s; before 1066, 20s.
    His father held it in prebend.

Ibiđ teñ Roƀt niger . ı . ſolin . 7 hƮ ibi . ııı . uiƚƚos

7 vı . borđ cū . ı . car̷ . Vaƚ . xxx . ſoƚ . T . R . E ꞏ́ xx . ſoƚ.

Eſmeƚƚt tenuit capeƚƚañ . R . E.

Ibiđ teñ Walter . ı . ſolin . 7 ibi hƮ . ııı . uiƚƚ . 7 v . borđ.

cū . ı . car̷ 7 dim̃ . Vaƚ . ʟx . ſoƚ . T . R . E ꞏ́ ʟxx . ſoliđ.

Sigar tenuit in p̄benda.

1 d

Ibiđ teñ Turbat dimiđ ſolin . 7 ibi hƮ . ıı . uiƚƚos 7 ı . borđ

cū dimiđ car̷ . 7 iſđē Roƀt̷ haƀ dimiđ ſolin in *CORNILAI HĐ.*

7 ibi dimiđ car̷ in dñio . 7 v . borđ . Int̷ tot̄ uaƚ . ııı . liƀ.

T . R . E ꞏ́ ıııı . liƀ . Golđſtan tenuit.

Ibiđē teñ Eduuine dimiđ ſolin . 7 adhuc . xxv . aĉs . tr̷æ.

In dñio ƚƮ dimiđ car̷ . 7 ı . uiƚƚm cū dimiđ car̷ . *IN CORNILAI HĐ*

hƮ iſđ Eduin⁹ q̃t̷ xx . 7 v . aĉs . 7 ibi . ı . uiƚƚm cū . ı . car̷.

Vaƚ . ııı . liƀ . T . R . E ꞏ́ ıııı . liƀ . Ipſemet tenuit . T . R . E . De hac

p̄benda ſūpſit ep̃s Baioĉ . vııı . aĉs . 7 dedit Alan clerico ſuo.

Modo hƮ Vƚric de Oxeneforđ . *IN CORNELAI HⱯNĐ.*

In Addeƚā ten Anſchitil . ı . ſolin . 7 ibi hƮ in dñio . ıı . car̷.

cū . vı . borđ . hanc tr̄a tenuit Stigand Archiep̃s.

Huic eiđ Anſchitillo deđ ep̃s baioĉ . ʟ . aĉs tr̷æ Ad deƚā.

7 alias . ʟ . aĉs ap̃ ſcām Margaritā . ubi hƮ . ı . uiƚƚm

7 dim̃ car̷ . Hæ . c . acræ erant de p̄bendis ut teſtificant.̃

Int̷ tot̄u ualet . vııı . liƀ . T . R . E ꞏ́ vıı . liƀ . *IN BEⱯSBERG HĐ.*

1 c, d

9   There Robert Black also holds 1 sulung. He has
      3 villagers and 6 smallholders with 1 plough.
    Value 30s; before 1066, 20s.
      Smelt, King Edward's Chaplain, held it.

10   There Walter also holds 1 sulung. He has
      3 villagers and 5 smallholders with 1½ ploughs.
    Value 60s; before 1066, 70s.
      Sigar held it in prebend.

11   There Thorbert also holds ½ sulung. He has   1 d
      2 villagers and 1 smallholder with ½ plough.

    In Cornilo hundred Robert also has ½ sulung and ½ plough
    in lordship, and 5 smallholders.
    In total, value £3; before 1066, £4.
      Goldstan held it.

12   There Edwin also holds ½ sulung and a further 25 acres of land.
    He has ½ plough in lordship, and
      1 villager with ½ plough.

In CORNILO Hundred
13   Edwin also has 85 acres, and
      1 villager with 1 plough.
    Value £3; before 1066, £4.
      He held it himself before 1066. The Bishop of Bayeux took
    8 acres from this prebend and gave them to his clerk Alan.
    Now Wulfric of Oxford has it.

In CORNILO Hundred
14   In DEAL Archdeacon Ansketel holds 1 sulung.
      He has 2 ploughs in lordship, with
      6 smallholders.
      Archbishop Stigand held this land. The Bishop of Bayeux also
    gave Ansketel 50 acres of land at Deal and another 50 acres
    at St. Margaret's (at Cliffe), where he has
      1 villager and ½ plough.
    These 100 acres were from the prebends, as they testify.
    In total, value £8; before 1066, £7.

In Sibertesuualt ten Wills pictau dimid solin
7 XII . acs . 7 in Addela dimid solin . XII . acs min . 7 ibi
ht . II . uittos 7 III . bord . cu . I . car 7 dim . Totu hoc valet
LV . sol . T.R.E. IIII . lib.   IN CORNELAI HVND.
🖙 In Addelam ten Adelold . III . uirg . 7 ibi ht . III . uittos
7 VIII . bord cu . I . car . Val 7 ualuit sep . LX . sol . Istemet
tenuit T.R.E.   IN BEVSBERG HD 7 IN CORNELAI HD..
In Addela ten abb S Augustini . I . solin . 7 ibi ht . III . uittos
7 VII . bord cu . I . car 7 dimid . Val . xxx . sol . T.R.E. XL . sol.
Antecessor ej tenuit in pbenda similit.
In Addela ten Wills filius Tedaldi dimid solin 7 dimid
jugu . 7 ibi ht in dnio . I . car . 7 II . uittos 7 II .. bord . Val
LX . sol . T.R.E. XL . sol . Derinc tenuit.
fili' Sired
In Sibertesuualt ten Sigar . I . jugu 7 dimid . 7 ibi ht
in dnio dimid car . 7 II . uittos 7 I . bord . Val . xxv . sol.
T.R.E. xxxv . sol . Pat ipsius tenuit in pbenda.
Nigellus medicus ap scam Margarita ten . I . jugu.
7 dimid . 7 ibi ht . I . uittm cu . II . bobz . Val . xx . sol . T.R.E.
xxv . sol . Spirites tenuit in pbenda .   IN BEVSBERG HD.
In Ferlingelai ten Wills fili Gaufridi . I . solin . 7 ibi ht
in dnio . I . car . 7 IIII . uittos cu . I car . Val . IIII . lib . T.R.E.
vi . lib . Sired tenuit in pbenda.

In BEWSBOROUGH Hundred
15 In SIBERTSWOLD William of Poitou holds ½ sulung and 12 acres,
and in DEAL ½ sulung less 12 acres. He has
    2 villagers and 3 smallholders with 1½ ploughs.
Value of the whole, 55s; before 1066 £4.

16 *Added at the foot of the column and directed to its proper place by transposition signs.*

In CORNILO Hundred
17 In DEAL Aethelwold holds 3 virgates. He has
    3 villagers and 8 smallholders with 1 plough.
The value is and always was 60s.
He held it himself before 1066.

In BEWSBOROUGH Hundred and in CORNILO Hundred
18 In DEAL the Abbot of St Augustine's holds 1 sulung. He has
    3 villagers and 7 smallholders with 1½ ploughs.
Value 30s; before 1066, 40s.
His predecesssor held it in prebend likewise.

19 In DEAL William son of Theodwold holds ½ sulung and ½ yoke.
He has in lordship 1 plough, and
    2 villagers and 2 smallholders.
Value 60s; before 1066, 40s.
Dering son of Sired held it.

20 In SIBERTSWOLD Sigar holds 1½ yokes. He has in lordship ½
plough, and
    2 villagers and 1 smallholder.
Value 25s; before 1066, 35s.
His father held it in prebend.

21 Nigel the Doctor holds 1½ yokes at St. Margaret's (at Cliffe).
He has 1 villager with 2 oxen.
Value 20s; before 1066, 25s.
Spirites held it in prebend.

In BEWSBOROUGH Hundred
22 In FARTHINGLOE William son of Geoffrey holds 1 sulung.
He has in lordship 1 plough, and
    4 villagers with 1 plough.
Value £4; before 1066, £6.
Sired held it in prebend.

In Hichā ten Balduin . i . folin . 7 ibi hт .iiii. uillos . 7 v.

borđ cū . ii . car . Val . iiii . liƀ . T . R . E ℣ o . fol . Eduin tenuit.

In Bocheland ten Godric . i . folin . 7 ibi hт . ii . car in dnio.

7 iii . uillos 7 iiii . borđ cū . i . car . 7 una æccla . Val . vi . liƀ.

T . R . E ℣ viii . liƀ.

☞ In Siƀtefuuald ten Vlſtan . f . Vluuin . i . folin 7 ibi hт dimiđ car .

7 iii . uillos 7 ix . borđ cū . i . car . T . R . E . ualƀ . c . fol . modo . lx . fol.

Pat ej tenuit.

2 a

In CIVITATE CANTVARIA habuit Rex EDWARD

L . 7 i . burgens . reddentes gablū . 7 alios . cc 7 xii.

ſup quos habebat faca 7 foca . 7 iii . molenđ de . xl . fol.

Modo burgens gablū reddentes funt . xix . De . xxxii.

alijs qui fueraɴ ℣ funt uaſtati . xi . in foſſato ciuitatis.

7 archieps hт ex eis . vii . 7 abƀ S Auguſtini alios . xiiii.

p excābio caſtelli . 7 adhuc funt . cc . 7 xii . burgs . fup .

quos hт rex faca 7 foca . 7 molenđ redđ . c 7 viii . fol.

7 theloneū redđ . lxviii . fol . Ibi . viii . acræ pti quæ

folebant . ee . legatoɀ regis . m̄ redđ de cenfu . xv . fol.

7 mille acræ filuæ infructuofæ . de qua exeuɴ . xxiiii.

folidi . Int totū . T . R . E . ualuit . li . liƀ . 7 tntđ qđo uicec

recep . 7 m̄ . L . liƀ app̄ciat . Tam qui ten n̄c reddit . xxx.

liƀ arfas 7 penfatas . 7 xxiiii . liƀ ad numerū . Sup h̄ onia

hт uicecom . c 7 x . fol.

Duas dom duoɀ burgfiu . unā foris aliā int cicuitatē . qđa

monachus æcclæ cantuar abſtulit . Hæ eraɴ pofitæ in calle

23   In HOUGHAM Baldwin holds 1 sulung. He has
     4 villagers and 5 smallholders with 2 ploughs.
  Value £4; before 1066, 100s.
     Edwin held it.

24   In BUCKLAND Godric holds 1 sulung. He has 2 ploughs in
  lordship, and
     3 villagers and 4 smallholders with 1 plough.
     A church.
  Value £6; before 1066, £8.

Directed to its proper place by transposition signs.

16   In SIBERTSWOLD Wulfstan son of Wulfwin holds 1 sulung.
  He has ½ plough, and
     3 villagers and 9 smallholders with 1 plough.
  Value before 1066, 100s; now 60s.
     His father held it.

C 1   In the City of Canterbury King Edward had 51 burgesses   2 a
  who paid tribute and another 212 over whom he had full
  jurisdiction; and 3 mills at 40s. Now there are 19 burgesses
  who pay tribute. (The houses) of 32 others who were there
  have been destroyed, 11 in the city ditch, the Archbishop has
  7 of them, the Abbot of St. Augustine's another 14 in exchange
  for the castle. There are still 212 burgesses over whom the
  King has full jurisdiction; and the 3 mills pay 108s. The toll
  pays 68s; 8 acres of meadow which used to be the King's
  messengers' now pay 15s in tribute; 1000 acres of unproductive
  woodland which produce 24s.
  In total, value before 1066, £51; as much when Hamo the Sheriff
  acquired it; now assessed at £50. However the present holder pays
  £30 assayed and weighed, and £24 at face value. Over and above
  all this the Sheriff has 110s.

2   A monk of Canterbury Church took away two houses of two
  burgesses, one outside, the other inside, the City. These were
  situated on the King's road.

Burgſes habuer̄ . XLV . manſur̄ ext̄ ciuitatē . de q̄bƷ
ipſi habeƀ gablū 7 c̄ſuetud ⁊ rex aut̄ haƀ ſacā 7 ſocā.
Ipſi q̄q̄ burgſes habebant de rege .XXX.III. ac̄s tr̄æ
in gildā ſuā. Has dom̄ 7 hanc tr̄a ten̄ Rannulf̄ de Colū
bels . Habet etiā q̄t̄ XX . ac̄s tr̄æ ſuƥ hæc . quas tenebaɴ
burgens̄ in alodia de rege. Tenet quoq̄ . V . ac̄s tr̄æ.
quæ juſte ƥtinent uni æcclæ. De his om̄ibƷ reuocat
iſdē Rannulf̄ ad ƥtec̄torē epm Baiocenſein.

Radulf̄ de Curbeſpine ht̄ .IIII. manſuras in ciuitate.
quas tenuit quædā c̄cubina heraldi . de quibƷ eſt ſaca
7 ſoca regis. ſed ſuſq̄ n̄c non habuit.
Iſdē Radulf̄ ten̄ alias . XI . maſuras de epo in ipſa ciuitate. baioc⁹
Que fuer̄ Sbern biga . 7 reddt̄ XI . ſolid̄ 7 II . den̄ . 7 I . obolū

Per totā ciuitatē cantuariæ ht̄ rex ſacā 7 ſocā . excepta
tr̄a æcclæ S̄ ꝃIN.7 S̄ Auguſtini . 7 Eddeuæ reginæ . 7 Alnod
cild . 7 Esber biga . 7 Siret de Cillehā.
Corcordatū eſt de rec̄tis callibƷ quæ habeɴ ƥ ciuitatē
introitū 7 exitū . quicunq̄ in illis forisfecerit ⁊ regi
em̄dabit . Similit̄ de callibƷ rec̄tis extra ciuitatē⁊
uſq̄ ad unā leugā . 7III. ƥticas . 7 III . pedes. Siq̄s ḡ
infra has publicas uias intus ciuitatē uel ext̄ foderit
uel palū fixerit ⁊ ſequit⁓ illū p̄poſit regis ubicunq̄ abierit.
7 emendā accipiet ad opus regis.
Archieps̄ calūniat⁓forisfac̄turā in uiis ext̄ ciuitatē ex utq̄ parte.
ubi terra ſua . ē . ꝉ Quidā p̄poſit̄ Brumañn n̄ōe T.R.E. cepit c̄ſue
tudines de extraneis mercatoribƷ in tr̄a S̄ ꝃINITATIS 7 S̄ Auguſtini.
Qui poſtea T.R.W. ante archiepm Lanfranc̄ 7 epm baiocenſē recog
nouit ſe injuſte accepiſſe . 7 ſacram̄to fac̄to jurauit qd̄ ipſæ æcclæ
ſuas c̄ſuetudines q̄etas habuer̄ . R.E. tēpore. Et exinde utreq̄ æcclæ
in ſua tr̄a habuer̄ c̄ſuetud ſuas . judicio baronū regis q̄ placitū tenuer̄.

3   The burgesses had 45 dwellings outside the City, from which they had tribute and customary dues; the King however had full jurisdiction. These burgesses also had from the King 33 acres of land for their tax. Ranulf of Colombières holds these houses and this land. He also has 80 acres of land over and above these, which the burgesses held in freehold from the King. He also holds 5 acres of land which rightly belong to a church. For all these Ranulf appeals to the Bishop of Bayeux as his protector.

4   Ralph of Courbépine has 4 dwellings in the City, which Harold's concubine held; of which the full jurisdiction is the King's, but up to the present he has not had it.

5   Ralph also holds another 11 dwellings from the Bishop of Bayeux in the City itself; they belonged to Esbern Big, and paid 11s 2½d.

6   The King has full jurisdiction throughout the whole City of Canterbury, apart from the land of Holy Trinity Church, of St. Augustine's, of Queen Edith, of Young Alnoth, of Esbern Big and of Sired of Chilham. It was agreed about the straight roads which have entry and exit through the City, that whoever does wrong on them shall pay the fine to the King; likewise regarding the straight roads outside the City as far as 1 league, 3 perches and 3 feet. If anyone digs or fixes a post within these public roads within the City or outside it, the King's reeve follows him wherever he has gone, and receives the fine for the King's works.

7   The Archbishop claims the fine on roads outside the City on both sides where the land is his.

8   A reeve, named Brunman, took the customs from foreign merchants before 1066 in the land of Holy Trinity and of St. Augustine's; after 1066 he acknowledged before Archbishop Lanfranc and the Bishop of Bayeux that he had received them wrongfully; he swore on the sacrament that these Churches had their customs exempt before 1066. From then on both Churches had their customs in their land, by the judgement of the King's barons, who tried the case.

Ciuitas *ROVECESTRE* T.R.E. ualebat . c . folid . Q̃do cᵉⁱˢ recep̃ fimilit.
Modo ꝰ uat . xx . lib . tamen ille qui ten̄ reddit . xl . lib.

ITEM POSSESSIO S̃ MARTINI.

De cõmunitate Sc̃i *MARTINI* hn̄t fimul iii . canonici
unū folin 7 xvi . acras . ideft Sired . Godric 7 Seuuen.
In hac tra funt . iiii . uilli 7 ix . bord cū una car̃ . Reddunt
.xxii. folid. ꝼDe Left *LIMWARLET* . unū foliñ In Blache
burne hund . 7 ibi funt . ix . uilti cū . ii . car̃ . Reddt̄ .xvi. fot
7 viii . den̄. ꝼIn *STRET* hund jacet uñ folin de Stanetdefte.
Ibi . vii . uilti hn̄t . ii . car̃ 7 dimid . 7 vii . bord . 7 uñ pratū reddt̄
xvi . fot 7 viii . den̄. ꝼIn *BILESOLD* hurd uñ foliñ de
Staneftede . ibi funt . vii . uilti 7 vii . bord 7 hn̄t . iiii . car̃.
7 Reddt̄ . xx fot . ii den min. Ad ifta . iii . folina funt
.v . denæ . 7 vi . uilti 7 v . bord . 7 reddt̄ . ix . fot . iii . denar̃
min . hn̄t . iii . car̃ 7 dimid. In *BRenfete* paululū terræ
funt , ii . uilti 7 iii . bord 7 hn̄t dim̃ car̃ . Reddunt . l . denar̃.
Illa . iiii . folina fup̃dicta hn̄t canonici S̃ Martini in cõmu
nitate int̄ nem̃ 7 planū . T.R.E. ualb̄ . x . lib . modo fimilit.
Terra Nordeuuode 7 tra Ripe . 7 tra Brandet reddt̄ xx . fot.
7 vi . den̄ ad S̃ Martin̄ in elemofina.
In inland S̃ Martini maneꝰ . vii . bord . cū dimid car̃ . Redd
lx . folid ad calciam̃ta canonicoꝛ . Ibi . ẽ un' rufticus. S̃ Margarita redd . viii . lib.
Theloneū de doure T.R.E. ualb̄ . viii . lib . modo ꝰ xxii . lib.
Tres æcclæ ap̃ Douerā reddt̄ . xxxvi . folid . 7 viii . denar̃.

R

1   The City of Rochester was valued at 100s before 1066; when the Bishop acquired it, the same; value now £20; however the holder pays £40.

P   **LIKEWISE THE POSSESSIONS OF ST. MARTIN'S**   2 b

1   Three Canons of the community of St. Martin's together have 1 sulung and 16 acres, that is Sired, Godric and Sewen. In this land are
     4 villagers and 9 smallholders with 1 plough.
They pay 22s.

2   Of the Lathe of Lympne, 1 sulung in Blackburn Hundred.
     9 villagers with 2 ploughs.
They pay 16s 8d.

3   In Street hundred lies 1 sulung of STANSTED.
     7 villagers have 2½ ploughs and 7 smallholders.
     A meadow which pays 16s 8d.

4   In Bircholt hundred 1 sulung of STANSTED.
     7 villagers and 7 smallholders have 4 ploughs.
They pay 20s less 2d.
     To these 3 sulungs belong 5 pig pastures, and
     6 villagers and 5 smallholders.
They pay 9s less 3d. They have 3½ ploughs.

5   In BRENZETT a small piece of land.
     2 villagers and 3 smallholders have ½ plough.
They pay 50d.
     The Canons of St. Martin's have those 4 said sulungs in common, wood and open land.
Value before 1066, £10; now the same.

6   The land of NORWOOD, the land of RIPE and the land of BRENZETT pay 20s 6d to St. Martin's in alms.

7   In the *inland* of St. Martin's live 7 smallholders with ½ plough; they pay 60s for the Canon's footwear.

8   St. Margaret's (at Cliffe) pays £8. 1 countryman there.

9   Value of the tolls from Dover before 1066, £8; now £22.

10   Three churches at Dover pay 36s 8d.

De paſtura Medrediue 7 de hortis douere exeuɲ . ix . ſoł

7 iiii . denar̅. Vna paſtura in Siberteſuualt꞉ xvi . den̅ redd̅.

S̅c̅s Martin͂ h̅t̅ . x . molend̅ 7 dimid̅ . redd̅ vii . lib̅ . T.R.E.

tantd̅ reddider̅ . Modo app̅ciant͂ . xii . lib̅ . ſed n̅ ad ꝓſicuū

canonicoꝛ̗ . Sub illis molinis manent . viii . h̅o̅es . Apud

ſcortebroc una paſtura redd̅ . ii . ſolid̅.

De hac c̅o̅munitate h̅t̅ Archieps̅ ſingulis annis . lv . ſoł꞉

Ibi ſunt . vi . h̅o̅es cū . i car̅ 7 dimid̅.

In c̅o̅muni t͡ra S̅ Martini ſ̅u̅nt .cccc. acræ . 7 dimid̅ . quæ

fiunt . ii . ſolinos 7 dimid̅.H̅ t͡ra nunꝗ reddid̅ aliꝗd c̅ſue

tudinis uel ſcoti . ꝗa . xx.iiii . ſolini H̅ o̅m̅ia adꝗetant.

Ap̅ Ripā ſunt . c . acræ . quæ ſe adꝗetat ubi T.R.E . ſe

adꝗetabat . Ap̅ Nordeude ſunt . l . acræ . 7 c . ap̅ Brand.

que adꝗetant ſe ubi 7 ſupiora . In hac t͡ra ſunt . iii . uiłłi

7 ix . bord̅ . h̅n̅t . i . car̅ 7 dimid̅ . H̅ o̅m̅a ſi canonici ha

berent ſicuti jus . e̅c̅t꞉ ualeret iłł . lx . lib̅ ſinguł annis.

modo n̅ h̅n̅t niſi . xlvii . lib̅ . 7 vi . ſoł . 7 iiii . denar̅.

⌐ Rannulf̅ de Colūbels aufert eis un̅ p̅t̅ū . Rotb̅t de rome

nel aufert eis ſinguł annis . xx . denar̅.7 unā ſalinā 7 unā

piſcariā Herb̅tus fili͂ Juonis ded̅ ep̅o baioc̅ſi mark̅ auri

ꝓ uno molino eoꝛ̗ . nolentib̗ illis . Lanb̅t͂ un̅ . Wadard . un̅. ͫ ͦ ͪ ͮ

Radulf̅ de curbeſpine un̅.

⌐ Alnod p̅ uiolentiā Heraldi abſtulit S̅ Martino Mercleſhā.

7 Hauocheſten . ꝓ quib̗ ded̅ canonicis iniquā c̅o̅mutati̅o̅n̅e̅.

Modo ten̅ Rob̅tus de Romenel . qd̅ ei canonici calūni

antur ſemp̅.

11 From the pasture at MEDERCLIVE and from the gardens in
DOVER come 9s 4d.

12 A pasture in SIBERTSWOLD pays 16d.

13 St. Martin's has 10½ mills; they pay £7; before 1066 they paid
as much; now they are assessed at £12, but not for the Canon's
profit. Under those mills 8 men live.

14 At *SCORTESBROC* a pasture pays 2s.

15 From this community the Archbishop has every year 55s.
    6 men with 1½ ploughs.

16 In the community of St. Martin's are 400½ acres, which make
2½ sulungs. This land never paid any customary due or levy
because 24 sulungs meet the tax for the whole.

17 At RIPE are 100 acres which meet their tax where they did
before 1066.

18 At NORWOOD are 50 acres and 100 at BRENZETT which meet
their tax as the above do. In this land are 3 villagers and
9 smallholders. They have 1½ ploughs. If the Canons had all
these as rightly they should, the value would be £60 each year;
now they have only £47 6s 4d.

19 Ranulf of Colombières takes away from them a meadow and
Robert of Romney takes away from them each year 20d, a
salt-house and a fishery. Herbert son of Ivo gave the Bishop of
Bayeux a mark of gold for 1 of their mills, against their will;
Lambert 1 mill, Wadard 1 mill, and Ralph of Courbépine 1 [mill].

20 Young Alnoth, through Harold's violence took away from
St. Martin's *MERCLESHAM* and HAWKHURST, for which he
granted the Canons an unfair exchange. Now Robert of Romney
holds them; the Canons continue to claim it from him.

HIC ANNOTANT TENENTES TERRAS IN CHENT.

.I. REX WILLELMVS.

.II. Archieps Cantuar.

.III. 7 Monachi 7 hōes ej.

.IIII Eps Rofeceſtrens.

.V. Eps Baiocenſis.

.VI. Abbatia de Batailge.

.VII. Abbatia S Auguſtini.

.VIII. Abbatia de Gand.

.IX. Hugo de montford.

.X. Comes Euſtachius.

.XI. Ricardus de Tonebrige.

.XII. Haimo uicecomes.

.XIII. Albertus capellanus.

2 c

TERRA REGIS.

IN DIMIDIO LEST DE SVDTONE. IN ACHESTAN HD.

.I. REX WILLELMVS ten *TARENTEFORT.*

ꝓ uno ſolino 7 dimidio ſe defd. Tra.ē.xl.

caruc. In dñio ſunt .ii. car. 7 cxlii. uilli

cū .x. bord hñt. liii. car. Ibi ſunt .iii. ſerui. 7 i. mold.

pti .xx.ii. acræ.paſturæ.xl.ac. De ſilua.viii. denæ

paruæ . 7 iii. magnæ. Ibi .ii. hedæ. id eſt .ii. port.

T.R.E. ualuit. lx . lib. 7 tntd qdo haimo recepit.

Modo apꝑciat ab anglis . lx . lib. Ppoſit ū francig

qui ten ad firmā. dicit qa ual qt xx. lib. 7 x . lib.

Ipſe tam reddit de iſto ꝏ . lxx. lib penſatas. 7 cxi.

ſolid de den.xx. in ora. 7 vii . lib 7 xxvi . den ad numer.

Sup hæc reddit uicec.c.ſol.

LIST OF LANDHOLDERS IN KENT

1 King William	8 Ghent Abbey
2 The Archbishop of Canterbury	9 Hugh de Montfort
3 His monks and his men	10 Count Eustace
4 The Bishop of Rochester	11 Richard of Tonbridge
5 The Bishop of Bayeux	12 Hamo the Sheriff
6 Battle Abbey	13 Albert the Chaplain
7 St. Augustine's Abbey	

LAND OF THE KING

1   In the Half-Lathe of SUTTON   2 c

In AXTON Hundred

1   King William holds DARTFORD. It answers for 1½ sulungs. Land for 40 ploughs. In lordship 2 ploughs.
    142 villagers with 10 smallholders have 53 ploughs.
    3 slaves; a mill; meadow, 22 acres; pasture, 40 acres;
        from the woodland 8 small and 3 large pig pastures;
        2 hythes, that is 2 harbours.
Value before 1066, £60; as much when Hamo the Sheriff acquired it; now it is assessed by the English at £60; but the French reeve who holds at a revenue says that its value is £90. However, he pays from this manor £70 weighed and 111s of pence at 20d to the *ora,* and £7 and 26d at face value. In addition to this it pays the Sheriff 100s.

Homines de hund teſtificant̃ . q̃d de iſto Ⓜ regis

ablatū . ē unū p̃tū . 7 uñ alnetū . 7 uñ mold . 7 xx. acræ

træ . 7 adhuc tant̃ p̃ti quantū ptiñ ad . x . ac̃s træ.

quæ oīa eraɴ in firma regis . E . dū uiueret . ħ uał . xx.

ſoł.   Dicunt aut̃ q̃d Oſuuard r̃c uicecom̃ præſtitit ea

Aleſtan p̃poſito Lundoñ . 7 m̃ teñ helt dapifer 7 nepos

Teſtant̃ quoq̃ q̃d HAGELEI de iſto Ⓜ ablata . ē.

quæ ſe defd̃ p̃ dim̃ ſolin . Hanc tr̃a tenebat uicecom̃.

7 q̃do uicecomitatū amittebat: in firma regis remaneb̃.

Ita p̃manſit 7 poſt morte R.E. Modo teñ Hugo de

port . cū . L.IIII. acris træ plus . Totū hoc uał . xv . liƀ.

De eod̃ Ⓜ regis adhuc ſunt ablatæ . VI. acræ træ.

7 quædā ſilua quā iſd̃ Oſuuard poſuit ext̃ Ⓜ.

p̃ q̃dd̃a uadimon . XL . ſolidoꝝ.

Æccłam huj̃ Ⓜ teñ eps de Roueceſtre . 7 uał . LX . ſoł.

Extra hanc ſuɴ adhuc ibi . III . æccleſiolæ.

IN LEST DE ELESFORD . IN LAVROCHESFEL HVND̃.

Rex . W . teñ *ELESFORD* . p̃ uno ſolin ſe defd̃ . Tr̃a

ē . xv . car̃ . In dñio ſunt . III . car̃ . 7 XL . uilłi cū

.v. bord̃ h̃nt . xv . car̃ . Ibi . VIII . ſerui . 7 I . mold̃ . XL.

deñ . 7 XLIII . ac̃ p̃ti . Silua . LXX . porc̃.

Int̃ tot ualeƀ . T.R.E. xv . liƀ . 7 t̃nt̃d q̃do haĩmo recep̃.

m̃ uał . xx . liƀ . Tam̃ redd̃ . xxxI . liƀ . 7 uicec̃ inde h̃ꝝ

III . liƀ . De hoc Ⓜ teñ Anſgot̃ juxta roueceſtre

tantū træ . q̃d app̃ciat̃ . VII . liƀ.

Eps etiā de Rouecest̃ p̃ excãbio tr̃e in qua caſtellū

ſedet . tantū de hac tr̃a teñ . q̃d . xVII . ſoł 7 IIII . deñ uał.

The men of the Hundred testify that from this manor of the King's have been taken 1 meadow, 1 alder grove, 1 mill and 20 acres of land and furthermore as much meadow as belongs to 10 acres of land. All of these were in King Edward's revenue while he was alive. Value of this, 20s. However, they say that Osward, then Sheriff, leased them to Alstan, Reeve of London. Now Helto the Steward and his nephew hold them.

They also testify that Hawley has been taken from this manor. It answered for ½ sulung. The Sheriff held this land. When he lost the Sheriffdom, it stayed in the King's revenue. It remained so after King Edward's death. Now Hugh of Port holds it with 54 acres of land more.
Value of the whole, £15.

Further from the same manor of the King 6 acres of land have been taken and a wood which Osward the Sheriff also placed outside the manor through a pledge of 40s.

The Bishop of Rochester holds the church of this manor.
Value 60s.

As well as this there are a further 3 small churches.

In AYLESFORD Lathe
In LARKFIELD Hundred
2 King William holds AYLESFORD. It answers for 1 sulung. Land for 15 ploughs. In lordship 3 ploughs.
40 villagers with 5 smallholders have 15 ploughs.
8 slaves; a mill at 40d; meadow, 43 acres;
woodland, 70 pigs.
Total value before 1066, £15; as much when Hamo the Sheriff acquired it; value now £20; however it pays £31; the Sheriff has £3 from it. Ansgot holds as much of the land of this manor as is assessed at £7 near Rochester. The Bishop of Rochester also holds as much of this land as is valued at 17s 4d in exchange for the land on which the castle is situated.

Rex . W . teñ *MIDDELTVNE* . p quat . xx . ti . folins fe
defđ. Extra hos : funt in dñio . iiii . folins . 7 ibi . iii .
car in dñio. In hoc ꝳ . ccc . 7 ix . uitti cū . lxxiiii . borđ.
hñt . clx.vii . car . Ibi funt . vi . molđ de . xxx . foliđ.
7 xviii . ac pti. Ibi . xxvii . falinæ de . xxvii . folidis.

2 d
Ibi . xxxii . pifcariæ de . xxii . fol 7 viii . deñ. De theloneo
xl . fol. De paftura . xiii . fol 7 iiii . deñ. Silua . cc.xx . porc.
7 hões de Walt reddunt . l . fol pro Ineuuarđ 7 Aueris.
In hoc ꝳ funt . x . ferui . Int totū . T.R.E. ualeb . cc . lib
ad numerū . 7 tntđ qdo Haimo receptum. uicecom' 7 m̃ fimiliter.

⌐ De hoc ꝳ teñ hugo de port . viii . folins 7 unū jugū.
qui T.R.E. erant cū alijs folins in cfuetudine . Ibi hт . iii . car
in dñio.

Н tra quā teñ Hugo de port . uat . xx . lib . æ cõputant in . cc . lib tis
toti ꝳ *MIDDELTVN*. qui teñ reddit . cxl . lib ad igñe
7 ad penfa . 7 infup . xv . lib 7 vi . fol . ii . denar min ad nu
merū. Haimoni dat ppofit . uicec' xii . lib.

⌐ De filua regis hт Wadard tant qđ redđ xvi . deñ p añn.
7 dimidiā denā tenet quā T.R.E. qđa uillan tenuit . 7 Alnod
cild duas partes cuidā uitto p uim abftulit.

⌐ Æcctas 7 decimas huj ꝳ teñ abb S Auguftini . 7 xl .
fot de . iiii . folins regis exeunt ei.

Rex . W . teñ *FAVRESHANT* . p . vii . folins de defđ . Tra . ē
xvii . car . In dñio funt . ii . Ibi . xxx . uitti cū . xl . borđ.
hñt . xxiiii . car . Ibi . v . ferui . 7 i . molin de . xx . fol . 7 ii . ac
pti . Silua . c . porc. 7 de paftura filuæ . xxxi fol . 7 ii . deñ.

In the Half-Lathe of MILTON

In MILTON Hundred

3   King William holds MILTON (Regis). It answers for 80 sulungs. As well as these, there are 4 sulungs in lordship. In lordship 3 ploughs. In this manor

> 309 villagers with 74 smallholders have 167 ploughs.
>
> 6 mills at 30s; meadow, 18 acres. 27 salt-houses at 27s.
>
> > 32 fisheries at 22s 8d; from the tolls, 40s; from the   2 d pasture, 13s 4d; woodland, 220 pigs.
> >
> > Walter's men pay 50s for Escorts and cartage.
> >
> > In this manor, 10 slaves.

Total value before 1066, £200 at face value; as much when Hamo the Sheriff acquired it; now the same.

> Hugh of Port holds 8 sulungs and 1 yoke of this manor, which were with the other sulungs before 1066 in customary payment. He has 3 ploughs in lordship.

Value of this land which Hugh of Port holds, £20, which are accounted in the £200 of the whole manor of Milton. Its holder pays £140 fired and weighed, and in addition £15 6s less 2d at face value. The reeve gives Hamo the Sheriff £12.

> Wadard has as much of the King's woodland as pays 16d a year. He holds ½ a pig pasture which a villager held before 1066. Young Alnoth took away 2 parts from a villager by force.
>
> The Abbot of St. Augustine's holds the churches and tithes of this manor; 40s from 4 sulungs of the King go to him.

In WYE Lathe

In FAVERSHAM Hundred

4   King William holds FAVERSHAM. It answers for 7 sulungs. Land for 17 ploughs. In lordship 2.

> 30 villagers with 40 smallholders have 24 ploughs.
>
> 5 slaves; a mill at 20s; meadow, 2 acres; woodland, 100 pigs;
>
> > from woodland pasture, 31s 2d;
> >
> > a market at £4.

Mercatū . de . iiii . liƀ . 7 ĩi . falinæ de . iii . foliđ 7 ii .deń. 7 in
cantuar ciuitate . iii . hagæ | ad hoc ꝏ ptiń . In totis ualent
T.R.E. ualeƀ . lx . liƀ . v . foliđ miń. 7 poſt: ix . liƀ. Modo uaſ
ꝗter . xx . liƀ.

TERRA ARCHIEPĪ CANTVARIENSIS.

.II. *IN CIVITATE CANTVARIA* habet Archieps .xii . buŕ
genfes. 7 xxxii. manfuras quas tenent clerici de uilla
in gildā fuā . 7 reddunt . xxxv . foſ . 7 uń molđ de . v . foſ.

SANDWICE jacet in fuo pprio *HVND* . hoc burgū teń
archieps . 7 eſt de ueſtitu monachoꝝ . 7 reddit fimile
feruitiū regi ficut *DOVERE* . 7 hoc teſtificant homines
de iſto burgo . qđ antequā rex EDw dediſſet illū ꝺ ꝑin.
reddeƀ regi . xv . liƀ. Tēpore | R . E ꝰ non erat ad firmam.
Qđo receꝓ archieps ꝰ reddeƀ . xl . liƀ . de firma . 7 xl.
milia allecibꝫ ad uictū monachoꝝ . In anno quo facta
eſt hæc defcriptio ꝰ reddidit | l . liƀ de firma . 7 alleces
ficut prius . T.R.E ꝰ erant ibi . ccc . 7 vii. manfuræ hos
pitatæ. modo funt plus . lxxvi. ideſt fimul. ccc.lxxx.iii.

IN *ACHESTAN HVND*.

Archieps cantuar teń in dńio. *TARENT* . p . ii . folins
fe defđ . Tra . ē   In dńio . ē una car . 7 xxii . uilli
cū . vii. cot hñt. vii. car. Ibi . vi . ferui. 7 ii. molđ de . l . foſ.
Ad hoc ꝏ ptiń . v . burgſes in rouecest. redđ . vi. foſ 7 viii. deń.
Ibi . viii. ač ꝑti. Silua . xx . porc. In totis ualent T.R.E. ualuit
xiiii. liƀ. Qđo receꝓ ꝰ x. liƀ. m̄ .xv. liƀ 7 x. foſ. Tam qui
tenet ꝏ redđ . xviii. liƀ.

2 salt-houses at 3s 2d; in the City of
Canterbury 3 sites at 20d belong to this manor.
Total value before 1066, £60 less 5s; later £60; now £80.

2   LAND OF THE ARCHBISHOP OF CANTERBURY   3 a

1   In the City of CANTERBURY the Archbishop has 12 burgesses
and 32 dwellings which the clergy of the town hold in their
guild; they pay 35s.
    A mill at 5s.

2   SANDWICH lies in its own Hundred. The Archbishop holds
this Borough. It is for the clothing of the monks. It pays the
same service to the King as Dover. The men of this borough
testify this, that before King Edward gave it to Holy Trinity,
it paid £15 to the King. In 1066 it was not in the revenue.
When the Archbishop acquired it, it paid £40 in revenue and
40,000 herrings for the supplies of the monks. In the year in
which this Survey was made Sandwich paid £50 in revenue and
herrings as before. Before 1066 there were 307 habitable
dwellings; now there are 76 more; that is, 383 altogether.

In AXTON Hundred
3   The Archbishop of Canterbury holds DARENTH, in lordship.
It answers for 2 sulungs. Land for ... In lordship 1 plough.
    22 villagers with 7 cottagers have 7 ploughs.
    6 slaves; 2 mills at 50s.
    To this manor belong 5 burgesses in Rochester who
    pay 6s 8d.
    Meadow, 8 acres; woodland, 20 pigs.
Total value before 1066, £14; when acquired, £10; now
£15 10s. However the holder of the manor pays £18.

Ipſe Archieps ten̄ *OTEFORT* in dn̄io. p. VIII. | folins ſe defđ. Tra. ē

XL. II. car̄. In dn̄io ſunt. VI. car̄. Ibi. c. 7 un̄ uiłłs cū. XVIII.

borđ hn̄t. XLV. car̄. Ibi. VIII. ſerui. 7. VI. molini de. LXXII.

ſoliđ. 7 L. ac̄ p̄ti. Silua. C.L. porc̄.

De hoc m̄ ten̄. III. teigni. I. ſolin 7 dimiđ. 7 ibi hn̄t in dn̄io

. III. car̄. 7 XVI. uiłłos cū. XI. borđ hn̄tes. IIII. car̄. Ibi. V. ſerui

7 II. molđ de. XXIIII. ſoł. 7 XXVIII. ac̄s p̄ti. Silua. XXX. porc̄.

In totis ualent T.R.E. 7 poſt ualeƀ · · · · Modo

ap̄p̄ciat dn̄iū arch̄. LX. liƀ. Teignoʒ. XII. liƀ. Ricarđ de

Tonebrige qđ in ſua leuga ten̄: ap̄p̄ciat. X. liƀ.

Ipſe archieps ten̄ *SONDRESSE*. p uno ſolin 7 dim̄ ſe defđ.

Tra. ē · · · In dn̄io ſunt. III. car̄. 7 XXVII. uiłłi cū. IX.

borđ hn̄t. VIII. car̄. Ibi. VIII. ſerui. 7 III. molđ 7 dim̄ de

. XIII. ſoliđ I.VI.đ 7 dim̄. Ibi. VIII. ac̄ p̄ti. Silua. LX. porc̄. Ibi æcc̄la.

In totis ualent T.R.E. ual. XII. liƀ. Qdo recep: XVI. liƀ. 7 modo

XVIII. liƀ. Tam̄ reddit. XXIII. liƀ. 7 unū militē in ſeruitio Arch̄.

IN *HELMESTREI HVND*.

Ipſe Archieps ten̄. *BIX*. p. IIII. folins ſe defđ T.R.E. 7 m̄ p. II. ł

Tra. ē · · · In dn̄io ſunt. II. car̄. 7 XLI. uiłł cū. XV. borđ

hn̄t. X. car̄. Ibi æcc̄la. 7 III. molđ de. XLVIII. ſoliđ. 7 VIII. ac̄

p̄ti. Silua. C. porc̄. In totis ualent. T.R.E. 7 poſt ual. XII. liƀ

7 m̄. XX. liƀ. 7 tam̄ reddit. XXX. liƀ. 7 VIII. ſoł.

IN *LITELAI HVND*.

Ipſe archieps ten̄ *ERHEDE*. p. IIII. folins ſe defđ. Tra. ē. VIII.

car̄. In dn̄io ſunt. II. 7 XXVII. uiłłi cū. II. borđ hn̄t. VIII. car̄.

3 b

Ibi æcc̄la. 7 III : molđ de. L. ſoliđ 7 VI. den̄. Ibi. V. ſeruī:

7 X. ac̄ p̄ti. Silua. XL. porc̄. In totis ualent T.R.E. ual

XII. liƀ. 7 tn̄tđ qdo recep̄. Modo. XVI. liƀ. 7 tam̄ redđ

XXI. liƀ.

The Archbishop himself holds

4   OTFORD, in lordship. It answers for 8 sulungs. Land for
42 ploughs. In lordship 6 ploughs.
>101 villagers with 18 smallholders have 45 ploughs.
>8 slaves; 6 mills at 72s; meadow, 50 acres; woodland,
>>150 pigs.

Of this manor 3 thanes hold 1½ sulungs. They have 3 ploughs
in lordship, and
>16 villagers with 11 smallholders, who have 4 ploughs.
>5 slaves; 2 mills at 24s; meadow, 28 acres; woodland, 30 pigs.

Total value before 1066 and later ...; now the Archbishop's
lordship is assessed at £60; the thanes' at £12.
What Richard of Tonbridge holds in his territory is assessed at £10.

5   SUNDRIDGE. It answers for 1½ sulungs. Land for ... In lordship
3 ploughs.
>27 villagers with 9 smallholders have 8 ploughs.
>8 slaves; 3½ mills at 13s 6d; meadow, 8 acres;
>>woodland, 60 pigs. A church.

Total value before 1066 £12; when acquired, £16; now £18;
however, it pays £23 and a man-at-arms for the Archbishop's
service.

in RUXLEY Hundred

6   BEXLEY.   It answered for 3 sulungs before 1066; now for 2.
Land for ... In lordship 2 ploughs.
>41 villagers with 15 smallholders have 10 ploughs.
>A church; 3 mills at 48s; meadow, 8 acres; woodland,
>>100 pigs.

Total value before 1066 and later £12; now £20; however it
pays £30 8s.

in LITTLE Hundred

7   CRAYFORD. It answered for 4 sulungs. Land for 8 ploughs.
In lordship 2.
>27 villagers with 2 smallholders have 8 ploughs.
>A church; 3 mills at 50s 6d; 5 slaves; meadow, 10 acres;   3 b
>>woodland, 40 pigs.

Total value before 1066 £12; as much when acquired; now £16;
however, it pays £21.

Ipfe archieps teñ in dñio M*etlinges* . ꝑ .ii. folins

fe defd . Tra . ē . vii . car. In dñio funt . iii. car. 7 xxx.viii.

uilli cū . xii. bord hñt . v. car. Ibi æccla 7 v. ferui . 7 ii.

mold de . x . fol . 7 xxi. ač p̃ti . Silua . lx. porc . In totis

ualent . T.R.E. ual . ix. lib . Similit q̃do recep̃ . 7 m̃ tñtd

7 tam redd . xv. lib.   I*n Tollentrev hvnd*.

Ipfe archieps teñ in dñio N*orflvet* . ꝑ . vi. folins

defd fe . T.R.E. 7 iñ ꝑ . v. Tra . ē . xiiii . car. In dñio fuᶰ

. ii . 7 xxxvi . uilli hñt . x. car. Ibi æccla 7 vii. ferui

7 i. moliñ de x . fol cū una pifcar. 7 xx . ač p̃ti . Silua

xx. porc. In totis ualent. T.R.E. ual . x. lib . Q̃do recep̃ ꞓ

xii . lib . 7 m̃ . xxvii . lib . 7 tam redd xxxvii . lib 7 x. fol.

Ricard de tonebrige q̃d teñ in fua leuga de hoc ꝳ̃.ual

   I*n Broteha hvnd*. ⌐ xxx. fol.

Ipfe archieps teñ B*roteham* . ꝑ . viii . folins fe defd.

Tra . ē . xx . car. In dñio funt . iii . car. 7 lxxvi. uilli

cū . xviii. bord hñt . xiiii . car. Ibi æccla 7 x. ferui.

7 iii. mold de . xv. folid . 7 . ix . ač p̃ti . Silua q̃do fructific: ꞓ

q̃ngent porc.

De hoc ꝳ̃ teñ Willts difpenfat . i. folin . 7 ibi hĩ . i . car

in dñio . 7 ii. uillos cū dim car.

De eod ꝳ̃ teñ Goisfr de archiepo . i. folin . 7 ibi hĩ . i . car.

7 vi . uillos cū . i. bord hñtes . ii . car.

De ipfo ꝳ̃ teñ Farman . i. jug 7 dim de archiepo . 7 ibi hĩ

iii . car. 7 vi uillos cū xii . cot hñtes . ii . car Ibi . x . ferui.

In totis ualent. T.R.E. ual hoc ꝳ̃ . xv. lib. 7 poft . xvi.

lib . Modo appciat dñiũ arch: xxiiii . lib . 7 tam redd

xxxv. lib . Militū: xi . lib . Ricard de Tonebrige

q̃d teñ in fua leuga: appciat xv . lib.

in the Lathe of AYLESFORD

in LARKFIELD Hundred

8 (? East) MALLING in lordship. It answers for 2 sulungs. Land
for 7 ploughs. In lordship 3 ploughs.
38 villagers with 12 smallholders have 5 ploughs.
A church; 5 slaves; 2 mills at 10s; meadow, 21 acres;
woodland, 60 pigs.
Total value before 1066 £9; the same when acquired; now as much;
however, it pays £15.

in TOLTINGTROUGH Hundred

9 NORTHFLEET, in lordship. It answered for 6 sulungs before 1066;
now for 5. Land for 14 ploughs. In lordship 2.
36 villagers have 10 ploughs.
A church; 7 slaves; 1 mill at 10s, with a fishery;
meadow, 20 acres; woodland, 20 pigs.
Total value before 1066 £10; when acquired, £12; now £27;
however, it pays £37 10s. What Richard of Tonbridge holds in
his territory from this manor, value 30s.

in WROTHAM Hundred

10 WROTHAM. It answers for 8 sulungs. Land for 20 ploughs.
In lordship 3 ploughs.
76 villagers with 18 smallholders have 14 ploughs.
A church; 10 slaves; 3 mills at 15s; meadow, 9 acres;
woodland, when fruitful, 500 pigs.
William the Bursar holds 1 sulung of this manor; he has
1 plough in lordship, and
2 villagers with ½ plough.
Geoffrey holds 1 sulung of the same manor from the
Archbishop; he has 1 plough, and
6 villagers with 1 smallholder who have 2 ploughs.
Farman holds 1½ yokes of this manor from the Archbishop;
he has 3 ploughs, and
6 villagers with 12 cottagers who have 2 ploughs.
10 slaves.
The total value of this manor before 1066 £15; later £16; now the
Archbishop's lordship is assessed at £24; however, it pays £35;
the men-at-arms' £11; what Richard of Tonbridge holds in his
territory is assessed at £15.

Ipſe archieps ten *Meddestane* . p x . ſoliñs ſe defđ.
Tra . ē . xxx . caŕ. In dñio ſunt . iii . caŕ. 7 xxv . uiłłi cū
xxi . borđ hñt . xxv . caŕ. Ibi æccła 7 x . ſerui . 7 v . moliñ
de . xxxvi . ſoliđ 7 viii . deñ. Ibi . ii . piſcariæ . de cclxx . anguiłł.
Ibi . x . ač p̄ti . Silua . xxx . porč.
De hoc m̃ ten de archiepo . iii . milit. iiii . ſoliñs . 7 ibî
hñt . iii . caŕ 7 dim in dñio . 7 xxxii . uiłłos cū . x . borđ
hñtes . vi . caŕ. 7 x . ſeru . 7 hñt . i . moliñ de . v . ſoliđ . 7 xiii.
ač̃s p̄ti . 7 ii . piſcaŕ 7 dimiđ de . clxxx . anguiłł 7 . ii . ſaliñ.
Siluã . xxiii . porč.
In totis ualent T . R . E ual hoc m̃ . xiiii . liƀ . Qdo recep̄
xii . liƀ . 7 m̃ dñiũ archiep̄i ual . xx . liƀ . Militū . xv.
liƀ 7 x . ſoł. Monachi cantuaŕ hñt om̃i anno de
duobʒ hõibʒ huj m̃ . xx . ſoł.

In Cetehã Hvnd.

Ipſe archieps ten *Gelingehã* . p . vi . ſoliñs ſe defđ.
Tra . ē . xv . caŕ. In dñio ſunt . ii . caŕ. 7 xlii . uiłłi cū
xvi . borđ hñt . xv . caŕ. Ibi æccła . 7 iii . ſerui . 7 iii . pis
cariæ de . xl . ii . ſoliđ 7 viii . deñ. 7 i . moliñ de . xvi.
ſoliđ 7 viii . deñ. 7 xiiii . ač p̄ti . Silua . xx . porč.
De hõc m̃ ten q̃dã franciġ trã ad . i . caŕ . 7 ibi h̃t
ii . borđ . In totis ualent T . R . E . ual hoc m̃ . xv . liƀ.
Qdo recep̄ xii . liƀ . 7 m̃ xxiii . liƀ . 7 tam redđ
xxvi . liƀ . xii . deñ miñ . Qđ ten franciġ . xl . ſoł.

In Rocvlf Hvnd.

Ipſe Archieps ten *Rocvlf* . p . viii . ſoliñs ſe
defđ . Tra . ē . xxx . caŕ. In dñio ſunt . iii . caŕ.
7 q̃t xx . 7 x . uiłłi cū . xxv . borđ hñt . xxvii . caŕ.

in MAIDSTONE Hundred
11 MAIDSTONE. It anwers for 10 sulungs. Land for 30 ploughs.
In lordship 3 ploughs.
25 villagers with 21 smallholders have 25 ploughs.
A church; 10 slaves; 5 mills at 36s 8d; 2 fisheries at
270 eels. Meadow, 10 acres; woodland, 30 pigs.
Of this manor 3 men-at-arms hold 4 sulungs from the
Archbishop; they have 3½ ploughs in lordship, and
32 villagers with 10 smallholders who have 6 ploughs.
10 slaves. They(also) have 1 mill at 5s; meadow, 13 acres;
2½ fisheries at 180 eels; 2 salt-houses; woodland, 23 pigs.
Total value of this manor before 1066 £14; when acquired £12;
now the value Archbishop's lordship £20; the men-at-arms' £15 10s.
The monks of Canterbury have 20s from 2 men of this manor
every year.

in CHATHAM Hundred   3 c
12 GILLINGHAM. It answers for 6 sulungs. Land for 15 ploughs.
In lordship 2 ploughs.
42 villagers with 16 smallholders have 15 ploughs.
A church; 3 slaves; 3 fisheries at 42s 8d; 1 mill at 16s 8d;
meadow, 14 acres; woodland, 20 pigs.
Of this manor a Frenchman holds land for 1 plough. He
has 2 smallholders.
Total value of this manor before 1066 £15; when acquired, £12;
now £23; however, it pays £26 less 12d; what the Frenchman
holds 40s.

in RECULVER Hundred
13 RECULVER. It answers for 8 sulungs. Land for 30 ploughs.
In lordship 3 ploughs.
90 villagers with 25 smallholders have 27 ploughs.

Ibi æccła 7 1 . moliñ de xxv . deñ. 7 xxx.iii. ać p̃ti.

Silua . xx . porć . 7 v . falinæ de lxiiii . deñ . 7 una

pifcaria . In totis ualent . T.R.E. ualuit hoc m̄ . xiiii .

lib̄ . Q̈do recep̃ ꞓ fimilit . 7 m̄ .xxxv. lib̄ . Suꝑ hæc

ht archieꝑs . vii . lib̄ 7 vii . foliđ.

Iꝑfe Archieꝑs teñ NORTONE in dñio . ꝑ xiii . fo

lins fe defđ . Tra . ē . xxvi . car̄ . In dñio funt . ii .

car̄ . 7 q̈t xx. 7 xii . uiłłi cū . xl borđ . hñt . lix.

car̄ 7 dimiđ . Ibi æccła . 7 x . ać p̃ti . Silua . l . porć .

In totis ualent . T.R.E. ualuit hoc m̄ . xxiiii . lib̄

7 v . foł . 7 poft tñtđ . 7 m̄ redđ archieꝑo . l . lib̄ .

7 xiiii . foł 7 ii . deñ . 7 archidiacono . xx . foł.

De hoc m̄ teñ Vitalis de archieꝑo . iii . folins.

7 uñ juḡ 7 xii . ać tr̄æ . 7 ibi ht . v . car̄ . 7 xxix.

borđ 7 v . feruos . 7 vii . falinas de . xxv . foł 7 iiii . deñ.

Ibi . ē æccła 7 una parua dena filuæ . Int̄ totū uał

xiiii . lib̄ . 7 vi . foł 7 vi . deñ.

IN BOROWART LEST . IN PITEHĀ HVND.

Iꝑfe archieꝑs teñ PITEHAM . ꝑ .vii. folins fe defđ.

Tra . ē ad xx . car̄ . In dñio funt . iii . car̄ . 7 xxxii.

uiłłi cū xxi . borđ hñt . xix . car̄ . Ibi . ii . æcclæ.

Ibi . ii . ferui . 7 xiii . ać p̃ti . Silua . xx . porć.

In totis ualent T.R.E. ualuit hoc m̄ . xvii . lib̄.

7 vi . foł 7 iii . deñ . 7 poft tñtđ . 7 m̄ uał . xx . lib̄.

De hoc m̄ teñ Godefriđ 7 Nigełł de archieꝑo

uñ folin 7 dim̄ . 7 jugū . 7 ibi hñt . iiii . car̄.

7 iiii . uiłłos cū . viii . borđ hñtes . iii . car̄ . Int̄ tot̄

uał . ix . lib̄ . De his hñt monachi . viii . foł ꝑ anñ.

A church; a mill at 25d; meadow, 33 acres; woodland
20 pigs; 5 salt-houses at 64d; a fishery.
Total value of this manor before 1066 £14; when acquired,
the same; now £35. In addition to these the Archbishop
has £7 7s.

14   WHITSTABLE, in lordship. It answers for 13 sulungs. Land for
26 ploughs. In lordship 2 ploughs.
92 villagers with 40 smallholders have 59½ ploughs.
A church; meadow, 10 acres; woodland, 50 pigs.
Total value of this manor before 1066 £24 5s; later as much;
now it pays £50 14s 2d to the Archbishop and 20s to the
Archdeacon.
Vitalis holds 3 sulungs 1 yoke and 12 acres of land of this
manor from the Archbishop. He has 5 ploughs and
29 smallholders and 5 slaves.
7 salt-houses at 25s 4d. A church; a small pig pasture
of woodland.
In total, value £14 6s 6d.

in BOROUGH Lathe
in PETHAM Hundred

15   PETHAM. It answers for 7 sulungs.. Land for 20 ploughs.
In lordship 3 ploughs.
32 villagers with 21 smallholders have 19 ploughs.
2 churches. 2 slaves; meadow, 13 acres; woodland, 20 pigs.
Total value of this manor before 1066 £17 6s 3d; later as much;
value now £20.
Godfrey and Nigel hold 1½ sulungs and 1 yoke of this manor
from the Archbishop. They have 4 ploughs and
4 villagers with 8 smallholders who have 3 ploughs.
In total, value £9. Of these the monks have 8s a year.

Ipse archieps teñ *ESTVRSETE* in dñio . p VII . ſo
lins ſe defd . Tra . ē . xx . caŕ . In dñio ſunt . IIII . caŕ.
7 XVII . uiłłi cū q̃t xx . 7 III . bord hñt . XVI . caŕ.
Ibi . XII . molins de . IIII . liƀ 7 v . ſoł . 7 c . ać p̃ti . Silua
. L . porć . Ad hoc m̃ ptinueŕ T.R.E. in ciuitate
LII . maſuræ . 7 m̃ non ſunt niſi . xxv . q̃a aliæ
ſunt deſtructæ Inoua hoſpitatione archiep̃i.

In totis ualent T.R.E. 7 poſt ualeƀ XXIIII . liƀ . 7 XII . ſoł 7 VI.
den . Modo uał XL . liƀ.
De hoc m̃ hñt . v . hõēs archiep̃i . unū ſolin 7 VI . juga.
7 ibi hñt . v . caŕ 7 dimid in dñio . 7 VIII . uiłłos cū . XXVI.
bord hñtes . II . caŕ . 7 III . mold 7 XXXIIII . aćs p̃ti . Silua . x.
porć . Int totū uał . IX . liƀ.
De ipſo m̃ teñ Haimo uicec̃ . dimid ſolin de arch̃ . 7 ibi hŕ
II . caŕ . cū . v . bord 7 uno ſeruo . 7 II . mold de . xv . ſoł . Vał

∫ c.ſolid.

Ipse archieps teñ in dñio *BVRNES* . p . VI . ſolins ſe defd.
Tra . ē . L . caŕ . In dñio ſunt . v . caŕ . 7 LXIIII . uiłłi cū . LIII.
bord hñt xxx caŕ 7 dim . Ibi æccła 7 II . mold de . VIII . ſoł
7 VI . den . 7 xx ać p̃ti . Silua . xv . porć . De herbagio . XXVII.
den . In totis ualent . T.R.E. 7 poſt ualeƀ . xx . liƀ . m̃ . xxx . liƀ.

Ipse archieps teñ in dñio *BOLTVNE* . p . v . ſolins 7 dim
ſe defd . Tra . ē   In dñio ſunt . II . caŕ . 7 XXXI . uiłłs
cū . XXXI . bord hñtes xv . caŕ . Ibi . IIII . ać p̃ti . 7 piſcaria
de . x . den . Salina de . xvi . den . Silua . XLV . porć . In
totis ualent T.R.E. 7 poſt ualeƀ . xv . liƀ 7 XVI . ſoł 7 III . den.
7 I . obołū . Modo uał xxx . liƀ . 7 XVI . ſoł 7 III . den 7 I . obołū.

in WESTGATE Hundred

16   WESTGATE in lordship. It answers for 7 sulungs. Land for 20
ploughs. In lordship 4 ploughs.
    17 villagers with 83 smallholders have 16 ploughs.
    A church; 12 mills at £4 5s; meadow, 100 acres;
        woodland, 50 pigs.
    To this manor belonged 52 dwellings before 1066; now there
are only 25 because the rest were destroyed for the Archbishop's
new lodging.
Total value before 1066 and later £24 12s 6d; value now £40.   3 d
    Of this manor 5 of the Archbishop's men have 1 sulung
and 6 yokes. They have 5½ ploughs in lordship, and
    8 villagers with 26 smallholders who have 2 ploughs.
    3 mills; meadow, 34 acres; woodland 10 pigs.
In total, value £9.
    Hamo the Sheriff holds ½ sulung of this manor from the
Archbishop. He has 2 ploughs, with
    5 smallholders and 1 slave.
    2 mills at 15s.
Value 100s.

in BARHAM Hundred

17   BISHOPSBOURNE in lordship. It answers for 6 sulungs. Land
for 50 ploughs. In lordship 5 ploughs.
    64 villagers with 53 smallholders have 30½ ploughs.
    A church; 2 mills at 8s 6d; meadow, 20 acres; woodland,
        15 pigs; from grazing, 27d.
Total value before 1066 and later £20; now £30.

in BOUGHTON Hundred

18   BOUGHTON [under Blean] in lordship. It answers for 5 sulungs.
Land for ...   In lordship 2 ploughs, and
    31 villagers with 31 smallholders who have 15 ploughs.
    Meadow, 4 acres; a fishery at 10d; a salt-house at 16d;
        woodland, 45 pigs.
Total value before 1066 and later £15 16 3½d; value now
£30 16 3½d.

Ipſe archieṕs teń in dñio CHERINGES . ꝑ . VIII . ſoł ſe defđ.

Tra . ē . XL . caŕ . In dñio . ē uń ſolin 7 ibi . IIII . caŕ 7 dim̄ . Ibi . XXVI.

uiłłi cū . XXVII . borđ hñt . XXVII . caŕ . Ibi . XII . ſerui . 7 uñ

molin̄ de XL . deń . Ibi . XXV . ãc p̄ti . Silua . XXVI . porc̄.

In totis ualent T . R . E . ualeƀ . XXIIII . liƀ . Q̇do receṕ꞉ tn̄tđ.

Modo apꝑciat̄ . XXXIIII . liƀ . 7 tam̄ reddit . LX . liƀ.

Ipſe archieṕs teń in dñio PLVCHELEI . ꝑ uno ſolin ſe defđ.

Tra . ē . XII . caŕ . In dñio . II . caŕ 7 dim̄ . 7 XVI . uiłłi cū . VII.

borđ hñt . XI . caŕ . Ibi . VIII . ſerui . 7 XII . ãc p̄ti 7 dim̄ . Silua

CXL . porc̄ . Int tot̄ T . R . E . ualeƀ XII . liƀ . Q̇do receṕ꞉

VIII . liƀ . 7 modo . XV . liƀ . 7 tam̄ redđ . XX . liƀ.

In LEST DE ESTREI.   *In* WINGEHA HVND.

Ipſe archieṕs teń. WINGEHEHA . in dñio . ꝑ . XL . ſolins ſe

defđ . T . R . E . 7 m̄ ꝑ XXXV . Tra . ē   In dñio ſunt

VIII . caŕ . 7 q̇ter XX. 7 V . uiłłi cū . XX . borđ . hñtes . LVII.

caŕ . Ibi . VIII . ſerui . 7 II . molđ de . XXX . IIII . ſoł . Silua . V.

porc̄ . 7 ii̅ . ſiluulæ ad clauſuſā . In totis ualent T . R . E . ual

LXXVII . liƀ . Q̇do receṕ꞉ ſimilit̄ . 7 m̄ . c . liƀ.

De hoc m̃ teń Wiłłs de arcis . I . ſolin In Fletes . 7 ibi h̄ in

dñio . I . caŕ . 7 IIII . uiłłos 7 uñ milite cū . I . caŕ . 7 unā piſcaŕ

cū ſalina de . XXX . deń . Tot̄ ual . XL . ſoł.

De ipſo m̃ teń . V . hōes archieṕi . V . ſolins 7 dim̄ . 7 iij . juga.

7 ibi hñt in dñio . VIII . caŕ . 7 XXII . borđ 7 VIII . ſeru̅ . Int tot̄

ual XXI . liƀ.   *In* LANGEBRIGE HVND.

Ipſe archieṕs teń in dñio MERSEHAM . ꝑ VII . ſolins ſe defđ.

T . R . E . 7 m̄ ꝑ . III . Tra . ē . XII . caŕ . In dñio ſunt . III . caŕ.

7 XXXIX . uiłłi cū . IX . borđ hñtes . XVI . caŕ . Ibi æccła . 7 II . molđ

de V . ſoł . 7 II . ſalinæ de . V . ſoł . 7 XIII . ãc p̄ti . Silua . XXX . porc̄.

4 a
In totis ualent T . R . E . ual 7 poſt . X . liƀ . Modo . XX . liƀ.

in CALEHILL Hundred

19 CHARING in lordship. It answers for 8 sulungs. Land for 40 ploughs. In lordship 1 sulung. 4½ ploughs.
    26 villagers with 27 smallholders have 27 ploughs.
    12 slaves; a mill at 40d. Meadow, 25 acres; woodland, 26 pigs.
Total value before 1066 £24; when acquired, as much; now it is assessed at £34; however, it pays £60.

20 PLUCKLEY in lordship. It answers for 1 sulung. Land for 12 ploughs. In lordship 2½ ploughs.
    16 villagers with 7 smallholders have 11 ploughs.
    8 slaves; meadow, 12½ acres; woodland, 140 pigs.
Total value before 1066 £12; when acquired, £8; now £15; however, it pays £20.

in the Lathe of EASTRY
in WINGHAM Hundred

21 WINGHAM in lordship. It answered for 40 sulungs before 1066; now for 35. Land for ... In lordship 8 ploughs, and
    85 villagers with 20 smallholders who have 57 ploughs.
    8 slaves; 2 mills at 34s; woodland, 5 pigs; 2 small woods for fencing.
Total value before 1066 £77; when acquired the same; now £100.
    William of Arques holds 1 sulung of this manor in Fleet. He has 1 plough in lordship, and
    4 villagers and 1 man-at-arms with 1 plough.
    A fishery with a salt-house at 30d.
Value of the whole 40s.
    Of the manor itself 5 of the Archbishop's men hold 5½ sulungs and 3 yokes. In lordship they have 8 ploughs.
    22 smallholders and 8 slaves.
In total, value £21.

in LONGBRIDGE Hundred

22 MERSHAM in lordship. Before 1066 it answered for 6 sulungs; now for 3. Land for 12 ploughs. In lordship 3 ploughs.
    39 villagers with 9 smallholders who have 16 ploughs.
    A church. 2 mills at 5s; 2 salt-houses at 5s; meadow, 13 acres; woodland, 30 pigs.
Total value before 1066 and later £10; now £20.   4 a

Ipfe archiep̃s ten̄ *Aldintone* in dñio . ꝑ xxi . folin fe

defð . T . R . E . 7 m̃ ꝑ . xv . folins . Tra . c . car̄ . In dñio funt . xiii .

car̄ . 7 ducenti uiłłi x . min̄ cū . l . borð hn̄t lxx . car̄ .

Ibi æccła . 7 xiii . ferui . 7 iii . molð de xvi . foł . 7 iii . pifcar̄

de . xxi . den̄ . Ibi . clxx . ãc p̃ti . Silua . lx . porc̃ .

In totis ualent̄ T . R . E . ualeb̄ . lxii . lib̄ . 7 tn̄tð q̃do recep̃ .

Modo redð . c . lib̄ 7 xx . foł .

Ipfe archiep̃s ten̄ uilłā quæ uocat̄ S̃ Martin̄ 7 p̃tin̄ ad

Efturfete . 7 jacet in ipfo hund . 7 defð | ꝑ uno folin 7 dim̄

Tra . ē　　In dñio funt . ii . car̄ . 7 xxxvi . borð .

Ad hanc trā p̃tin̄ . vii . burg̃fes in cantuaria . reddñes

viii . foł 7 iiii . den̄ . Ibi . v . molð de . xx . foł . 7 parua filua .

In hac uilla ten̄ Radulf̄ dim̄ folin de archiep̃o . 7 ibi h̃t

ii . car̄ in dñio . 7 v . uiłłos cū . iii . borð hñtes . ii . car̄ 7 dimid̄ .

T . R . E . ualeb̄ . vii . lib̄ dim̄ folin S̃ Mart̃ . 7 aliud dim̄ folin

uał femp . iiii . lib̄ .

In *Romenel* funt q̃t xx . 7 v . burg̃fes qui p̃tin̄ ad *Aldint̄*

M̃ archiep̃i . 7 ualuer̄ 7 m̃ ualent dño . vi . lib̄ .

De ipfo M̃ Aldinton jacet in Limes dimid̄ jugū 7 dimið

uirga . Archiep̃s ten̄ in dñio . 7 ibi h̃t . i . car̄ . 7 uñ uiłłm

cū xviii . borð hñtes . i . car̄ . 7 dimid̄ . Ibi funt . vii . p̃bri qui

reddunt . vii . lib̄ 7 v . foł . Tra . ē . ii . car̄ . Vał 7 ualuit . xii . lib̄ .

7 tam̄ reddit . xv . lib̄ .

De eoð M̃ ten̄ comes de Ow . Eftotinghes ꝑ . i . M̃ .

ꝑ uno folin 7 dim̄ fe defð T . R . E . 7 m̃ ꝑ uno folin tantū .

Tra . ē . viii . car̄ . In dñio funt . ii . 7 xxvii . uiłłi cū . xiii . borð .

hñtes . vii . car̄ . 7 i . molin de . xxv . den̄ . Ibi æccła . 7 xx . ãc p̃ti .

Silua . x . porc̃ . 7 viii . ferui . T . R . E : 7 poft : uał . viii . lib̄ . M : x . lib̄ .

in LYMPNE Lathe
in BIRCHOLT Hundred

23   ALDINGTON, in lordship. Before 1066 it answered for 21 sulungs;
      now for 15 sulungs. Land for 100 ploughs. In lordship 13 ploughs.
        200 villagers less 10 with 50 smallholders have 70 ploughs.
        A church; 13 slaves; 3 mills at 16s; 3 fisheries at 21d.
            Meadow, 170 acres; woodland, 60 pigs.
      Total value before 1066 £62; as much when acquired; now it
      pays £100 20s.

24   the village which is called ST. MARTINS. It belongs to Westgate;
      lies in this Hundred and answers for 1½ sulungs. Land for ...
      In lordship 2 ploughs;
        36 smallholders.
      To this land belong 7 burgesses in Canterbury who pay 8s 4d.
      5 mills at 20s; a small wood.
      In this village Ralph holds ½ sulung from the Archbishop. He
      has 2 ploughs in lordship, and
        5 villagers with 3 smallholders who have 2½ ploughs.
      Value before 1066 of ½ sulung of St. Martins' £7; value of
      another ½ sulung always £4.

25   In ROMNEY 85 burgesses who belong to Aldington, the Archbishop's
      manor. The value to the lordship was and now is £6.
        Of this manor of Aldington ½ yoke and ½ virgate lie in Lympne.
      The Archbishop holds in lordship. He has 1 plough, and
        1 villager with 18 smallholders who have 1½ ploughs.
        7 priests who pay £7 5s.
      Land for 2 ploughs.
      The value is and was £12; however, it pays £15.
        Of this manor the Count of Eu held Stowting as 1 manor
      Before 1066 it answered for 1½ sulungs; now for only 1 sulung.
      Land for 8 ploughs. In lordship 2, and
        27 villagers with 13 smallholders who have 7 ploughs.
        1 mill at 25d; a church; meadow, 20 acres; woodland.
            10 pigs; 8 slaves.
      Value before 1066 and later £8; now £10.

Ipfe Archieps ten in dñio *Leminges* . ꝓ .vii. folins fe defđ.

Tra . ē .lx. car . In dñio funt . iiii . 7 c. 7 uñ uitts cū . xvi. borđ

hñtes .lv. car . Ibi æccła 7 x. ferui . 7 i. moliñ de.xxx. deñ.

7 i. pifcar de xl. anguitt . 7 xxx. ac pti . Silua . c . porc.

Ibi ptiñ .vi. burgens in *Hede* . T.R.E. ualeb .xxiiii. lib.

7 poftea .xl. lib . 7 m̃ fimilit . 7 tam̃ reddit .lx. lib.

De hoc ꟽ ten. iii. hões archiepi .ii. folins 7 dim̃ . 7 dimiđ

jugū . 7 ibi hñt .v. car in dñio . 7 xx. uittos cū . xvi . borđ.

hñtes .v. car 7 dimiđ . 7 i. feruū . 7 ii. moliñ de .vii. fot 7 vi. deñ.

7 xl . acs pti . Silua .xi. porc. Ibi .ii. æcclæ. Inł tot uał .xi. lib.

Ipfe Archieps ten *Newedene* . ꝓ uno folin fe defđ . Tra . ē

Ibi funt .xxv. uitti cū .iiii. borđ. hñtes .v. car . Ibi . ē mer

catū de xl . fot .v . deñ miñ. Silua .xl. porc. Inł totū

T.R.E. ualeb .c. fot . Qdo recep̃ xii. lib . 7 m̃ . x . lib. 7 tam̃

p̄pofit redđ .xviii. lib . 7 x . foliđ.

4b TERRA MILITVM EJUS. *In Achestan Hvnd.*

Anfgotus ten de archiepo . *Forningeham*.

꙼p uno folino fe defđ . Tra . ē   In dñio funt

ii . car . 7 xiii . uitti cū . v . borđ hñtes .iii. car 7 dim̃.

Ibi . vi . ac pti . Silua .xx. porc . 7 Ricard de Tonebrige

de eađ filua tntđ hr̃ in fua leuua . T.R.E. ualebat

hoc ꟽ .vii. lib . 7 m̃ . xi . lib . De his hñt monachi

cantuar .iiii. lib. ad ueftitū fuū . 7

In LONINGBOROUGH Hundred

26 The Archbishop holds LYMINGE himself, in lordship. It answers
for 7 sulungs. Land for 60 ploughs. In lordship 4, and
 101 villagers with 16 smallholders who have 55 ploughs.
 A church; 10 slaves; a mill at 30d; a fishery at 40 eels;
  meadow, 30 acres; woodland, 100 pigs.
 6 burgesses belong in Hythe.
Value before 1066 £24; later £40, now the same; however,
it pays £60.
 Of this manor 3 of the Archbishop's men hold 2½ sulungs and
½ yoke. They have 5 ploughs in lordship, and
 20 villagers with 16 smallholders who have 5½ ploughs.
 1 slave; 2 mills at 7s 6d; meadow, 40 acres; woodland, 11 pigs.
 2 churches.
In total, value £11.

In SELBRITTENDEN Hundred

27 The Archbishop holds NEWENDEN himself. It answers for 1 sulung.
Land for ...
 25 villagers with 4 smallholders who have 5 ploughs.
 A market at 40s less 5d; woodland, 40 pigs.
In total, value before 1066, 100s; when acquired, £12; now £10;
however, the reeve pays £18 10s.

2   LAND OF HIS MEN-AT-ARMS   4 b

In AXTON Hundred

28 Ansgot holds FARNINGHAM from the Archbishop. It answers for
1 sulung. Land for ... In lordship 2 ploughs, and
 13 villagers with 5 smallholders who have 3½ ploughs.
 Meadow, 6 acres; woodland, 20 pigs.
 Richard of Tonbridge has as much of the same woodland
in his territory.
Value of this manor before 1066 £7; now £11; of these the
monks of Canterbury have £4 for their clothing.

Radulſ fili Vnſpac teñ Elesford de archiepo.

p̄. vi. ſolins ſe defđ. Tra. ē   In dñio ſunt

.v. car̄. 7 xxix. uiłłi cū. ix. borđ h̄nt. xv. car̄. Ibi

ii. æccłæ. 7 ix. ſerui. 7 ii. molđ de. xl.iii. ſol. 7 xxix. ac̄

p̄ti. Silua. xx. porc̄. T.R.E. ualeb. xvi. lib. 7 m̄ uał

.xx. lib. De hoc m̄ teñ Ricarđ de Tonebrige. tantū

ſiluæ unde exire poſſ. xx. porc̄. 7 i. moliñ de. v. ſoliđ.

7 unā piſcariā in ſua leuua.

Malgeri teñ de archiepo. iii. juga. in Orpinton.

7 pro tanto ſe defđ ext Orpinton. T.R.E. Modo ſuĵ

ii. juga int Orpint. 7 tciū extra. Tra. ē   In dñio

.i. car̄. 7 iiii. uiłłi cū. i. borđ. 7 iiii. ſeru. 7 dimiđ car̄. 7 iii.

ac̄ p̄ti. 7 ſilua. xi. porc̄. T.R.E. ualeb xl. ſol. Q̄do

recep̄. xx. ſol. 7 m̄. l. ſol.

Haimo uicec teñ de archiepo BRIESTEDE. p̄ uno

ſolin 7 dimiđ ſe defđ. Tra. ē. x. car̄. In dñio ſunt. ii.

7 xxiiii. uiłłi cū. xvi. borđ h̄nt xii. car̄. Ibi æccła 7 xv.

ſerui. 7 ii. molđ de xxiiii. ſol. Silua q̄t xx. porc̄. 7 de

herbagio. ix. ſoliđ 7. vi. den. Int tot̄ T.R.E. ualebat

x. lib. 7 tntđ q̄do recep̄. 7 m̄ xvii. lib. Hoc m̄ tenuit

Alnod abb de archiepo cantuar.

Comes de Ow teñ de Archiepo OLECVBE. p̄. ii.

ſolins ſe defđ. T.R.E. 7 m̄ p̄. ii. tant. Tra. ē. ix. car̄ In dñio

ſunt. ii. car̄. 7 xxiii. uiłłi cū. viii. borđ h̄nt. vii. car̄.

Ibi æccła 7 uñ molđ de. iiii. ſol. 7 viii. ac̄ p̄ti. Silua

quat xx. porc̄. Int tot̄. T.R.E. ualeb. x. lib. Q̄do recep̄.

viii. lib. Modo. xi. lib. Hoc m̄ tenuit Alfer de arcħ.

29 Ralph son of Ospak holds EYNSFORD from the Archbishop. It
answers for 6 sulungs. Land for ... In lordship 5 ploughs.
    29 villagers with 9 smallholders have 15 ploughs.
    2 churches; 9 slaves; 2 mills at 43s; meadow, 29 acres;
        woodland, 20 pigs.
Value before 1066 £16; value now £20.
    Of this manor Richard of Tonbridge holds as much woodland
as can support 20 pigs; 1 mill at 5s and 1 fishery in his territory.

30 Mauger holds 3 yokes in ORPINGTON from the Archbishop. Before
1066 it answered for as much outside Orpington. Now there are
2 yokes inside Orpington and a third outside. Land for ...
In lordship 1 plough.
    4 villagers with 1 smallholder and 4 slaves; ½ plough.
    Meadow, 3 acres; woodland, 11 pigs.
Value before 1066, 40s; when acquired, 20s; now 50s.

31 Hamo the Sheriff holds BRASTED from the Archbishop. It answers
for 1½ sulungs. Land for 10 ploughs. In lordship 2.
    24 villagers with 16 smallholders have 12 ploughs.
    A church; 15 slaves; 2 mills at 24s; woodland, 80 pigs;
        from grazing, 9s 6d.
In total, value before 1066 £10; as much when acquired; now £17.
    Abbot Alnoth held this manor from the Archbishop of Canterbury.

32 The Count of Eu holds ULCOMBE from the Archbishop. It answered
for 2½ sulungs before 1066; now for only 2. Land for 9 ploughs.
In lordship 2 ploughs.
    23 villagers with 8 smallholders have 7 ploughs.
    A church; a mill at 4s; meadow, 8 acres; woodland, 80 pigs.
In total, value before 1066 £10; when acquired, £8; now £9.
    Alfhere held this manor from the Archbishop.

Radulf filius turaldi ten BOLTONE de archiepo.

.p dimid folin fe defd 7 jacet in . VI . folins de Holinge

borne . Tra . ē . I . car 7 dim . Idnio . ē una car . 7 III . uitti

cū . II . bord hnt . I . car . Ibi æccta . 7 II . ac pti . 7 filua

XVI . porc . Int totū uat 7 ualuit fep . XL . folid.

Ricard hō archiepi ten de eo LEVELANT . .p uno folin

fe defd . Tra . ē   In dnio . I . car . 7 II . uitti cū . I . bord

hnt . I . car . Silua . v . porc . T.R.E. 7 poft uat . XXX . fot.

Ifdē Ricard ten de arch IN BOLTONE HVND. ₤ m̄ . XX . fot.

GRAVENEL . .p uno folin fe defd . Tra . ē

In dnio . ē . I . car . 7 VIII . uitti cū . X . bord . hnt . II . car.

Ibi . v . ferui . 7 X . ac pti . 7 IIII . falinæ de . IIII . fot . T.R.E.

7 poft: ualuit . c . fot . m̄ . VI . lib . De his hnt monachi cant

₤ XX . fot.

4 c

Godefrid dapifer ten de archiepo . LERHĀ . .p . II . folin

fe defd . Tra . ē   In dnio funt . II . car . 7 XV . uitti

cū . II . bord . hnt . IIII . car . Ibi . IIII . ferui . 7 VI . ac pti . 7 I . molin

de . VII . fot . 7 filua de . X . porc . Int tot uat . VIII . lib . 7 tam

reddit . XII . lib 7 X . fot.

Ifdē Godefrid ten de archiepo in SCAPE . dimid folin . Tra . ē

    In dnio . I . car . cū . II . bord 7 IIII . ferui . T.R.E. 7 poft:

ualuit . XXX . fot . Modo: IIII . lib . 7 tam reddit . c . fot.

Ofbn filius Letard ten . I . jugū

de archiepo in BOCOLAND . 7 ibi ht in dnio . I . car . 7 uat . X . fot.

In EYHORNE Hundred

33   Ralph son of Thorold holds BOUGHTON (Malherbe) from the
Archbishop. It answers for ½ sulung, and lies in 6 sulungs of
Hollingbourne. Land for 1½ ploughs. In lordship 1 plough.
   3 villagers with 2 smallholders have 1 plough.
   A church; meadow, 2 acres; woodland, 16 pigs.
In total, the value is and always was 40s.

In FAVERSHAM Hundred

34   Richard, one of the Archbishop's men, holds LEAVELAND (Court)
from him. It answers for 1 sulung. Land for ... In lordship 1 plough.
   2 villagers with 1 smallholder have 1 plough.
   Woodland, 5 pigs.
Value before 1066 and later 30s; now 20s.

In BOUGHTON Hundred

35   Richard also holds GRAVENEY from the Archbishop. It answers for
1 sulung. Land for ... In lordship 1 plough.
   8 villagers with 10 smallholders have 2 ploughs.
   5 slaves; meadow, 10 acres; 4 salt-houses at 4s.
Value before 1066 and later 100s; now £6; of these the monks of
Canterbury have 20s.

In CALEHILL Hundred   4 c

36   Godfrey the Steward holds (East) LENHAM from the Archbishop.
It answers for 2 sulungs. Land for ... In lordship 2 ploughs.
   15 villagers with 2 smallholders have 4 ploughs.
   4 slaves; meadow, 6 acres; 1 mill at 7s; woodland at 10 pigs.
In total, value £8; however, it pays £12 10s.

In TEYNHAM Hundred

37   Godfrey also holds ½ sulung in SHEPPEY from the Archbishop.
Land for ... In lordship 1 plough, with
   2 smallholders and 4 slaves.
Value before 1066 and later 30s; now £4; however it pays 100s.

In EASTRY Hundred

38   Osbern son of Ledhard holds 1 yoke in BUCKLAND from the
Archbishop. He has 1 plough in lordship.
Value 10s.

Wilts Folet ten de Archiepo *FLENGVESSA*. ꝓ dim̄ ſolin

ſe defđ. Ibi h̄t. vi. uilł. cū. i. car̄ 7 dim̄.

Iſđ Wilts ten Eſtenberge de Archiepo. 7 ꝓ dim̄ ſolin ſe

defđ. 7 ibi h̄t. xii. uilłos cū. i. car̄ 7 dimiđ.   *∫* xxx. ſoł.

He træ ualeb T.R.E. xl. ſoł. Qdo arch recep᷄.᷄ x. ſoł. Modo

Hugo de Montfort ten de Archiepo *IN HEN HVNĐ.*

SALTEODE. ꝓ. vii. ſolins ſe defđ T.R.E. 7 m̄ ꝓ. iii. ſolins.

Tra. ē. xv. car̄. In dn̄io ſunt. ii. car̄. 7 xxxiii. uilli cū. xii. borđ

h̄ntes. ix. car̄. 7 dimiđ. Ibi æccła 7 ii. ſerui. 7 ix. molđ de. xx.

ſoliđ. 7 xxxiii. ac̄ pti. Silua q̄t xx. porc̄.

Ad hoc m̄ ptin̄. cc. xxv. burgſes in Burgo hedæ

Int burgū 7 m̄ uał T.R.E. xvi. lib̄. Qdo recep᷄.᷄ viii. lib̄

m̄ int totū xxix. lib̄. 7 vi. ſoł 7 iiii. den̄. *IN ESKAITES HĐ.*

Wilts de Eddeſhā ten de Archiepo *BEREWIC* ꝓ uno m̄.

ꝓ dimiđ ſolin ſe defđ. Tra. ē. iii. car̄. In dn̄io ſunt. ii. 7 ix.

uilti cū. ix. borđ h̄nt. i. car̄ 7 dim̄. Ibi. xviii. ac̄ pti. 7 Silua

xx. porc̄. T.R.E.᷄ ualeb. lx. ſoł. 7 poſt᷄.᷄ xx. ſoł. Modo. vii.

lib̄. 7 tam̄ redđ xi. lib̄.   *IN LAMPORT HVNĐ.*

Robᵗ de Romenel ten de Archiepo *LAMPORT*.

ꝓ uno ſolin 7 dim̄ ſe defđ. Tra. ē. vi. car̄. In dn̄io ſunt. ii.

7 xxix. uilti cū. ix. borđ. h̄nt. ix. car̄. Ibi. vii. ſalinæ

de. viii. ſoł 7 ix. den̄.

Ad hoc m̄ ptin̄. xxi. burgſ. qui ſunt in Romenel. de

quib᷈ h̄t archiepſ. iii. forisfactas. Latrociniū. pacē

fractā. foriſtellū. Rex ů h̄t om̄e ſeruitiū ab eis. 7 ipſi

h̄nt om̄s c̄ſuetudines 7 alias forisfactas ꝓ ſeruitio ma

ris. 7 ſunt in manu regis. T.R.E. 7 poſt ualuit. x. lib̄.

7 m̄. xvi. lib̄.

39 William Follet holds FINGLESHAM from the Archbishop. It
answers for ½ sulung. He has
    6 villagers with 1½ ploughs.
    William also holds Statenborough from the Archbishop.
It answers for ½ sulung. He has
    12 villagers with 1½ ploughs.
Value of these lands before 1066, 40s; when the Archbishop
acquired them 10s; now 30s.

(40 entered after 2,43 and directed to its proper place by transpositions signs.)

In HAYNE Hundred

41 Hugh de Montfort holds SALTWOOD from the Archbishop. Before
1066 it answered for 7 sulungs; now for 3 sulungs. Land for 15
ploughs. In lordship 2 ploughs, and
    33 villagers with 12 smallholders who have 9½ ploughs.
    A church; 2 slaves; 9 mills at 20s; meadow, 33 acres;
        woodland, 80 pigs.
To this manor belong 225 burgesses in the Borough of Hythe.
Between the Borough and manor, value before 1066 £16; when
acquired, £8; in total, now £29 6s 4d.

In STREET Hundred

42 William of Adisham holds BERWICK from the Archbishop as 1 manor.
It answers for ½ sulung. Land for 3 ploughs. In lordship 2.
    9 villagers with 9 smallholders have 1½ ploughs.
    Meadow, 18 acres; woodland, 20 pigs.
Value before 1066, 60s; later 20s; now £7; however, it pays £11.

In LANGPORT Hundred

43 Robert of Romney holds LANGPORT from the Archbishop. It
answers for 1½ sulungs. Land for 6 ploughs. In lordship 2.
    29 villagers with 9 smallholders have 9 ploughs.
    7 salt-houses at 8s 9d.
    To this manor belong 21 burgesses who are in Romney from whom
the Archbishop has 3 forfeitures; robbery, breach of the peace and
highway robbery. But the King has all the service from them; they
themselves have all the customary dues and other forfeitures for
service at sea; they are in the hands of the King.
Value before 1066 and later £10; now £16.

☞ Wilts ten̍ de Archiepo *TILEMANESTONE* . p uno folin fe
fe defend . In dñio ſt . ii . car̍ . 7 v . bord.
Olī . xx . ſol . Modo ual̍ . xxx . ſolid̍.

.III. TERRA MONACHOȝ ARCHIEPI *IN HELMESTREI HVND̍.*

Archieps cantuar̍ ten̍ *ORPINTVN* . p . iii . folins fe defd̍.
T.R.E. 7 m̍ p . ii . folins 7 dim̍ . Tra . ē   In dñio funt
ii . car̍ . 7 xlvi . uilti cū . xxv . bord hñtes . xxiii . car̍ . Ibi . iiii.
mold̍ de xvi . ſolid̍ 7 iiii . den̍ . 7 x . ac pti . 7 v denæ ſiluæ de . l.
porc̍ . In totis ualent̍ . T.R.E. ualeb̍ . xv . lib̍ . Qdo recep̍ viii . lib̍.
7 modo . ẋxv . lib̍ . 7 tam̍ reddit . xxviii . lib̍ . Ibi funt . ii . æcclæ.

IN LEST DE ELESFORD.   *IN LITEFELLE HVND̍.*
Ipſe Archieps ten̍ *PECHEHA̅* . p . vi . folins fe defd̍ . T.R.E. 7 m̍
p . v . folins 7 uno jugo . Tra . ē . x . car̍ . In dñio funt . ii . 7 xvi . uilti
cū . xiiii . bord hñt . iiii . car̍ . 7 dim̍ . Ibi | . x . ſerui . 7 i . mold̍ 7 vi.
ac pti . Silua . x . porc̍.
De tra huj m̍ ten̍ un̍ hō archiepi dimid̍ folin . 7 cū his . vi . folins
geldabat . T.R.E. quis n̍ ptineret m̍ niſi de ſcoto . qa liba tra erat.
De eod̍ m̍ ten̍ Ricard̍ de Tonebrige . ii . folins 7 un̍ jugū . 7 ibi hr̍
xxvii . uiltos hñtes . vii . car̍ . 7 ſiluā . x . porc̍ . 7 tot ual̍ . iiii . lib̍.
T.R.E. ualeb̍ m̍ . xii . lib̍ . Qdo recep̍ archieps̍ viii . lib̍ . 7 m̍ qd
habet ualet . viii . lib̍.   *IN AIHORDE HVND̍.*
Ipſe Archieps̍ ten̍ *HOILINGEBORDE* . p . vi . folins fe defd̍ . Tra . ē
xxiiii . car̍ . In dñio funt . ii . 7 lxi . uilts cū . xvi . bord hñt . xxiii.
car̍ . Ibi æccla 7 xii . ſerui . 7 ii . mold̍ . 7 viii . ac pti . Silua . xl . porc̍.
Int̍ tot̍ T.R.E. 7 poſt . ualeb̍ . xx . lib̍ . 7 m̍ ual xxx . lib̍.

40   William holds TILMANSTONE from the Archbishop. It answers
for 1 sulung. In lordship 2 ploughs.
     5 smallholders.
Value formerly 20s; now 30s.

3   **LAND OF THE ARCHBISHOP'S MONKS**   4 d

In RUXLEY Hundred
1   The Archbishop of Canterbury holds ORPINGTON. Before 1066 it
answered for 3 sulungs; now for 2½ sulungs. Land for ...
In lordship 2 ploughs, and
     46 villagers with 25 smallholders who have 23 ploughs.
     3 mills at 16s 4d; meadow, 10 acres; 5 pig pastures of woodland
        at 50 pigs.
Total value before 1066 £15; when acquired, £8; now £25;
however, it pays £28.
     2 churches.

The Archbishop himself holds
in AYLESFORD Lathe
in LITTLEFIELD Hundred
2   (East) PECKHAM. Before 1066 it answered for 6 sulungs; now for 5
sulungs and 1 yoke. Land for 10 ploughs. In lordship 2.
     16 villagers with 14 smallholders have 4½ ploughs.
     A church; 10 slaves; 1 mill; meadow, 6 acres; woodland, 10 pigs.
     One of the Archbishop's men holds ½ sulung of the land of this
manor; before 1066 it paid tax with these 6 sulungs although it did
not belong to the manor except for (payment of) a levy, because it
was free land.
     Richard of Tonbridge holds 2 sulungs and 1 yoke of this manor.
He has
     27 villagers who have 7 ploughs.
     Woodland, 10 pigs.
Value of the whole £4.
Value of the manor before 1066 £12; when the Archbishop
acquired it £8; value of what he now has £8.

in EYHORNE Hundred.
3   HOLLINGBOURNE. It answers for 6 sulungs. Land for 24 ploughs.
In lordship 2.
     61 villagers with 16 smallholders have 23 ploughs.
     A church; 12 slaves; 2 mills; meadow, 8 acres; woodland, 40 pigs.
In total, value before 1066 and later £20; now £30.

Huic M adjacet dimid folin . q̄d nunꝗ reddid ſcot . Hunc
ten eps baioc de archiepo ad gablū .   *IN TOLLENTREV HD̄.*

Ipſe Archieps ten *MEPEHA* . ꝑ . x . ſolins ſe defd T.R.E. m̄ ꝑ . vii .
Tra ē . xxx . car . In dn̄io ſunt . iiii . 7 xxv . uiłłi cū . lxxi . bord
hn̄t . xxv . car . Ibi æccła 7 xvii . ſerui . 7 xvi . ac̄ pti . Silua
x . porc̄ . In totis ualent T.R.E. ualeb xv . lib 7 x . ſoł . Q̄do
recep̄ꝰ xv . lib̄ . Modoꝰ xxvi . lib̄ . Ricard de Tonebrige hī
in ſua leuga q̄d ual . xviii . ſoł 7 vi . den̄ . Siluā . xx . porc̄ .

Ipſe Archieps ten *FERLAGA* .   *IN MEDESTAN HVND̄.*
ꝑ . vi . ſolins ſe defd . Tra . ē . xxvi . car . In dn̄io ſunt . iiii . 7 xxxᵗᵃ .
uiłłi cū . lvi . bord hn̄t . xxx . car . Ibi æccła . 7 iii . mołd de
xxvii . ſolid 7 viii . den̄ . Ibi . viii . ſerui . 7 vi . piſcarie . de mille
cc . anguiłł . Ibi . xii . ac̄ pti . Silua . c . xv . porc̄ .
De tra hujꝰ M ten Godefrid in feuo dimid ſolin . 7 ibi hī . ii .
car . 7 vii . uiłłos cū x . bord hn̄tes . iii . car . 7 iiii . ſeruos . 7 i . mołd
de . xx . den̄ . 7 iiii . ac̄s pti . 7 Siluā . xxx . porc̄ .
Totū M T.R.E. ualeb xvi . lib . 7 poſt tn̄td . 7 m̄ꝰ xxii . lib .
Q̄d abel m̄ ten̄ꝰ vi . lib . Q̄d Godefridꝰ ix . lib̄ . Q̄d Ricard
in ſua leugaꝰ iiii . lib̄ .   *IN ESSAMELE HVND̄.*

Ipſe Archieps ten *CLIVE* . ꝑ iii . ſolins 7 dimid ſe defd . Tra . ē
vi . car̄ . In dn̄io . ē una car 7 dim . 7 xx . uiłłi cū . xviii . bord
hn̄t . v . car 7 dim̄ . Ibi æccła . 7 ii . ſerui . 7 xxx . vi . ac̄ pti .
Silua de . xii . den̄ . T.R.E. ualeb tot M . vi . lib . 7 poſt ꝰ vii . lib .

IN BOROWART LEST .   *IN TANET HVND̄.*   ⌐ 7 m̄ . xvi . lib̄ .

Ipſe Archieps ten *MONOCSTVNE* . T.R.E . ꝑ xx . ſolins
ſe defd . 7 m̄ ꝑ . xviii . Tra . ē . xxxi . car̄ . In dn̄io ſunt . iiii .
7 q̄t xx . 7 ix . uiłłi cū . xxi . bord hn̄t . xxvii . car̄ . Ibi
ii . æcclæ . 7 unū mołd de . x . ſolid . Ibi noua piſcaria . 7 una
⁵ᵃ
ſalina de . xv . denar . Silua . x . porc̄ .
In totis ualent ualeb T.R.E. 7 poſt ꝰ xx . lib . 7 m̄ . xl . lib .

To this manor is attached ½ sulung which has never paid a levy. The Bishop of Bayeux holds this from the Archbishop on payment of tribute.

in TOLTINGTROUGH Hundred

4　MEOPHAM. Before 1066 it answered for 10 sulungs; now for 7. Land for 30 ploughs. In lordship 4.
　　25 villagers with 71 smallholders have 25 ploughs.
　　A church; 17 slaves; meadow, 16 acres; woodland, 10 pigs.
　Total value before 1066 £15 10s; when acquired, £15; now £26.
　　Richard of Tonbridge has in his territory what is valued at 18s 6d. Woodland, 20 pigs.

in MAIDSTONE Hundred

5　(East) FARLEIGH. It answers for 6 sulungs. Land for 26 ploughs. In lordship 4.
　　35 villagers with 56 smallholders have 30 ploughs.
　　A church; 3 mills at 27s 8d. 8 slaves; 6 fisheries at 1,200 eels.
　　　Meadow, 12 acres; woodland, 115 pigs.
　　Godfrey holds ½ sulung of the land of this manor as a holding. He has 2 ploughs, and
　　　7 villagers with 10 smallholders who have 3 ploughs and 4 slaves.
　　1 mill at 20d; meadow, 4 acres; woodland, 30 pigs.
　Value of the whole manor before 1066 £16; later as much; now £22. What Abel now holds £6; what Godfrey (holds) £9; what Richard (holds) in his territory £4.

in SHAMWELL Hundred

6　CLIFFE. It answers for 3½ sulungs. Land for 6 ploughs. In lordship 1½ ploughs.
　　20 villagers with 18 smallholders have 5½ ploughs.
　　A church; 2 slaves; meadow, 36 acres; woodland at 12d.
　Value of the whole manor before 1066 £6; later £7; now £16.

in BOROUGH Lathe
in THANET Hundred

7　MONKTON. Before 1066 it answered for 20 sulungs; now for 18. Land for 31 ploughs. In lordship 4.
　　89 villagers with 21 smallholders have 27 ploughs.
　　2 churches; a mill at 10s. A new fishery; 1 salt-house at 15d;　5 a woodland, 10 pigs.
　Total value before 1066 and later £20; now £40.

Ipſe archieps ten̄ GECHAM   IN DVNEHĀFORT HĎ.

p̄.IIII.ſolins ſe defđ . T́ra.ē.XII.cár.In dn̄io ſunt.III.

7 XXIX.uiłłi cū.LX.cot́ hn̄t XVI.cár 7 dim̄.Ibi æccła.

7 IIII.molđ de.c.ſoliđ.7 XXXV.ãc p̂ti.7 Silua.XXX.porć.

Tot̄ ᴍ́ ualeb̄ T.R.Ĕ.7 poſt:́ XXII.lib̄.Modo:́ XXXII.lib̄.

De t́ra huj᾿ ᴍ́ ten̄ Wiłłs hō ſuus tantū qđ uał.VII.lib̄.

Ipſe archieps ten̄ NORDEVDE.   IN CANTVARIE HVND́.

p̄ uno ſolin ſe defđ.T́ra.ē.   In dn̄io.I.cár 7 dim̄.

7 VII.uiłłi cū.XXVI.borđ hn̄t.II.cár.Huic ᴍ́ p̄tinent

in ciuitate cantuaria.c.burǵſes.III.min᾿.reddentes

VIII.lib̄ 7 IIII.ſoł.Ibi.VIII.molđ de.LXXI.ſoł.XXIIII.

ãc p̂ti.Silua.XXX.porć.Int́ tot̄ uał 7 ualuit.XVII.lib̄.

In eođ BOROWART LEST.jacet paruū burgū nōe

SESELTRE qđ.p̄pe p̄tin̄ coq̇næ archiepi.Quidā nōe

Bĺize ten̄ de monachis.In dn̄io.ē una cár.7 XLVIII.

borđ cū.I.cár.Ibi æccła.7 VIII.pi cariæ de xxv.ſoł.
                                        c̄ı gablo

Silua.X.porć.T.R.E.7 poſt:́ ualuit.xx.v.ſoł.

IN WIWARLET LEST. IN FAVRESHANT HĎ ⌠ 7 m̊.c.ſoł.

Ipſe archieps ten̄ PRESTETONE.p̄ uno ſolin de defđ.

T́ra.ē.VI.cár.In dn̄io ſunt.III.7 XIII uiłłi cū XIIII.borđ

hn̄t.III.cár.Ibi æccła 7 I.ſeruus.7 I.molđ ſine cenſu.7 una

piſcaria de.cc.L.anguillis.Ibi.II.ãc p̂ti.Silua.V.porć.

T.R.E.7 poſt:́ ualuit.x.lib̄.Modo:́ xv.lib̄.

Ipſe archieps ten̄ CERTEHAM. IN FELEBERG HVND́.

p̄.IIII.ſolins ſe defđ.T́ra.ē.XIIII.cár.In dn̄io ſunt.ii̋.

5 a

in DOWNHAMFORD Hundred

8   ICKHAM. It answers for 4 sulungs. Land for 12 ploughs. In lordship 3.
29 villagers with 60 cottagers have 16½ ploughs.
A church; 4 mills at 100s; meadow, 35 acres; woodland, 30 pigs.
Value of the whole manor before 1066 and later £22; now £32.
William, one of his men, holds as much of the land of this manor as is valued at £7.

in CANTERBURY Hundred

9   NORTHGATE. It answers for 1 sulung. Land for ... In lordship 1½ ploughs.
7 villagers with 26 smallholders have 2 ploughs.
To this manor belong 100 burgesses less 3 in the City of Canterbury who pay £8 4s.
8 mills at 71s; meadow, 24 acres; woodland, 30 pigs.
In total, the value is and was £17.

10   In the same Borough Lathe lies a small Borough called SEASALTER, which belongs to the Archbishop's own kitchen. A man called Blize holds from the monks. In lordship 1 plough;
48 smallholders with 1 plough.
A church; 8 fisheries with (payment of) tribute at 25s; woodland, 10 pigs.
Value before 1066 and later 25s; now 100s.

The Archbishop himself holds
in WYE Lathe
in FAVERSHAM Hundred

11   (South) PRESTON. It answers for 1 sulung. Land for 6 ploughs. In lordship 3.
13 villagers with 14 smallholders have 3 ploughs.
A church; 1 slave; 1 mill without dues; a fishery at 250 eels.
Meadow, 2 acres; woodland, 5 pigs.
Value before 1066 and later £10; now £15.

in FELBOROUGH Hundred

12   CHARTHAM. It answers for 4 sulungs. Land for 14 ploughs. In lordship 2.

7 LX . uilli cū . xv . cot hñt xv . car 7 dim . Ibi æccła 7 I . feru.

7 v . molđ 7 dim de . LXX . fol . 7 XXX . ac p̄ti . 7 filua . xxv .

porc. T.R.E. 7 qdo recep̄: ualuit XII . lib . Modo: xxv . lib.

7 tam̄ reddit . xxx . lib.

Ipfe archieps ten GOMERSHAM . p̄ . VIII . folins fe defđ.

Tra . ē . XII . car . In dñio funt . II . 7 LX . uilli cū . VIII . cot

hñt . XVII . car . Ibi æccła 7 II . ferui . 7 I . molđ de . xxv . fol.

7 XII . ac p̄ti . Silua . XL . porc. T.R.E. 7 qdo recep̄: ualuit

XII . lib . Modo: xx . lib . 7 tam̄ reddit . xxx . lib.

Ipfe archieps ten CERTH . p̄ . III . folins IN CERT HVND.

fe defđ . Tra . ē . XII . car . In dñio funt . II . 7 XXXVI . uilli cū

XI . cot hñt . XXII . car 7 dim . Ibi . v . ferui . 7 II . molđ de . VI .

folid . 7 falina de . VI . den . 7 XXVII . ac p̄ti . 7 Silua . c . porc.

T.R.E. 7 qdo recep̄: ualuit . XII . lib . Modo . xx . lib . 7 tam̄ redđ

Ipfe archieps ten IN CALEHELLE HVND.   Ӷ xxvII . lib.

LITELCERT . T.R.E. fe defđ p̄ . III . folins . 7 m̄ p̄ . II . hid 7 dim̄.

Tra . ē   In dñio funt . II . 7 XIX . uilli cū . v . borđ hñt

VII . car . Ibi . II . molđ de . v . fol 7 x . den . 7 XI . ac p̄ti . 7 filua

xv . porc.

De tra huj̄ M̄ ten Witts de archiepo dimiđ folin . 7 ibi h̄t

in dñio . I . car . cū . IIII . feruis . 7 x . acs p̄ti . 7 filuā . xx . porc.

Totū M̄ ualeb T.R.E. 7 poft: c . fol. Modo . VIII . lib . 7 VIII . fol

7 IIII . den . Q̄đ Witts ten: ap̄pciat . XL . fol.

5 b

Ipfe archieps ten WELLE . T.R.E. fe defđ p̄ . VII . folins.

7 m̄ p̄ . v . Tra . ē . XVIII . car . In dñio funt . IIII . 7 q̄t xx .

7 un uitts cū . v . borđ hñt . XII . car 7 dim . Ibi . VII . ferui.

7 un̄ molđ de xxx . den . 7 xx . ac p̄ti . Silua . q̄t xx . porc.

T.R.E: ualeb xvII . lib 7 XI . fol 7 IIII . den . Q̄do recep̄:

tntđ . Modo: XXIIII . lib . 7 IIII . den . 7 tam̄ redđ . XL . lib.

5 a, b

60 villagers with 15 cottagers have 15½ ploughs.
A church; 1 slave; 5½ mills at 70s; meadow, 30 acres;
   woodland, 25 pigs.
Value before 1066 and when acquired £12; now £25; however,
it pays £30.

13   GODMERSHAM. It answers for 8 sulungs. Land for 12 ploughs.
In lordship 2.
   60 villagers with 8 cottagers have 17 ploughs.
   A church; 2 slaves; 1 mill at 25s; meadow, 12 acres;
      woodland, 40 pigs.
Value before 1066 and when acquired £12; now £20; however it
pays £30.

in CHART Hundred
14   (Great) CHART. It answers for 3 sulungs. Land for 12 ploughs.
In lordship 2.
   36 villagers with 11 cottagers have 22½ ploughs.
   5 slaves; 2 mills at 6s; a salt-house at 6d; meadow, 27 acres;
      woodland, 100 pigs.
Value before 1066 and when acquired £12; now £20; however
it pays £27.

in CALEHILL Hundred
15   (Little) CHART. Before 1066 it answered for 3 sulungs; now for 2½
hides. Land for ... In lordship 2.
   19 villagers with 5 smallholders have 7 ploughs.
   2 mills at 5s 10d; meadow, 11 acres; woodland, 15 pigs.
   William holds ½ sulung of the land of this manor from the
Archbishop. He has 1 plough in lordship, with 4 slaves.
   Meadow, 10 acres; woodland, 20 pigs.
Value of the whole manor before 1066 and later 100s; now £8 8s 4d;
what William holds is assessed at 40s.

16   WESTWELL. Before 1066 it answered for 7 sulungs; now for 5.   5 b
Land for 18 ploughs. In lordship 4.
   81 villagers with 5 smallholders have 12½ ploughs.
   7 slaves; a mill at 30d; meadow, 20 acres; woodland, 80 pigs.
Value before 1066 £17 11s 4d; when acquired, as much;
now £24 4d; however, it pays £40.

In Lest de Estreia.   *In Estrei Hvnd.*

Ipſe archieps teñ *Estrei*. p . vii . ſolins ſe defđ.

Tra . ē.   In dñio ſunt . iii . car . 7 lxxii . uitti

cū . xxii . borđ hñt . xxiiii . car . Ibi . i . moliñ 7 dimiđ

de . xxx . ſoliđ . 7 iii . ſalinæ de . iiii . ſoliđ . 7 xviii . ac p̃ti.

Silua : x . porc.

Et in Getinge teñ monachi cantuar dimiđ ſolin

7 unū jugū . 7 v . acs . 7 ibi hñt . vi . uittos cū . ii . car 7 dim.

Int totū T.R.E. 7 poſt ualeɓ . xxvi . liɓ 7 x . ſot

7 iiii . deñ . 7 i . ferding . Modo : xxxvi . liɓ . 7 x . ſoliđ

7 iiii . deñ 7 i . ferding.

Ipſe Archieps teñ *Edesham* . p xvii . ſolins ſe deſđ.

Tra . ē   In dñio . ii . car ſunt 7 dim . 7 c . uitti cū

xiiii . borđ hñt . xxxvi . car . Ibi . xiii . ac p̃ti . 7 iii . ſerui.

Silua ad clauſurā.

De tra huj M teñ . ii . milites de archiepo . iii . ſolins . 7 ibi

hñt in dñio . iiii . car . 7 xviii . uitti cū . v . borđ hñt . i . car .

Totū M . T.R.E. ualeɓ . xl . liɓ . Qdo recep : ſimiliter.

Modo redđ xlvi . liɓ 7 xvi . ſoliđ 7 iiii . deñ . 7 archiepo

. c . ſot de Garſunne.

Qđ milites teñ uat . xi . liɓ . 7 tam redđ . xiii . liɓ.

Ipſe Archieps teñ *Werahorne*.   *In Hame Hvnd.*

p uno ſolin ſe defđ . Tra . ē . ii . car . In dñio . ē . i . car .

7 vi . uitti cū . iii . borđ hñt . i . car . Ibi xii . ac p̃ti . 7 ſilua

vi . porc . T.R.E. 7 poſt . uat . xx . ſot . 7 m̃ . lx . ſot.

In Limowart Lest.   *In Blacheborne Hvnd.*

Ipſe Archieps teñ *Apeldres* . T.R.E. ſe defđ p . ii . ſolins.

7 m̃ p uno . Tra . ē . viii . car . In dñio ſunt . iii . car . 7 xxxvii .

uitti cū . xli . borđ hñt . xi . car . Ibi æccta . 7 vi . piſcariæ

de . iii . ſot . 7 iiii . deñ . Ibi . ii . ac p̃ti . 7 ſilua . vi . porc.

T.R.E. 7 poſt : ualeɓ . vi . liɓ . Modo : xvi . liɓ 7 xvii . ſot

in EASTRY Lathe
in EASTRY Hundred

17   EASTRY. It answers for 7 sulungs. Land for ... In lordship 3 ploughs.
    72 villagers with 22 smallholders have 24 ploughs.
    1½ mills at 30s; 3 salt-houses at 4s; meadow, 18 acres;
      woodland, 10 pigs.
    The monks of Canterbury also hold ½ sulung, 1 yoke and 5 acres
in Giddinge. They have
    6 villagers with 2½ ploughs.
In total, value before 1066 and later £26 10s 4¼d; now £36 10s 4¼d.

18   ADISHAM. It answers for 17 sulungs. Land for ... In lordship
2½ ploughs.
    100 villagers with 14 smallholders have 36 ploughs.
    Meadow, 13 acres; 3 slaves; woodland for fencing.
    2 men-at-arms hold 3 sulungs of the land of this manor from the
Archbishop. They have 4 ploughs in lordship.
    18 villagers with 5 smallholders have 1 plough.
Value of the whole manor before 1066 £40; when acquired, the same;
now it pays £46 16s 4d; and 100s as a premium to the Archbishop.
Value of what the men-at-arms hold £11; however it pays £13.

in HAM Hundred

19   WAREHORNE. It answers for 1 sulung. Land for 2 ploughs.
In lordship 1 plough.
    6 villagers with 3 smallholders have 1 plough.
    Meadow, 12 acres; woodland, 6 pigs.
Value before 1066 and later 20s; now 60s.

in LYMPNE Lathe
in BLACKBURN Hundred

20   APPLEDORE. Before 1066 it answered for 2 sulungs; now for 1.
Land for 8 ploughs. In lordship 3 ploughs.
    37 villagers with 41 smallholders have 11 ploughs.
    A church; 6 fisheries at 3s 4d. Meadow, 2 acres; woodland, 6 pigs.
Value before 1066 and later £6; now £16 17s 6d.

Ipſe Archieps̄ ten̄ *IN HVND DE WI*　　　Ⅼ 7 ⅵ . den̄.

unū m̄ qđ ſe defđ ᵱ uno ſolin T.R.E. 7 m̄ ᵱ dimidio.

Tra . ⅱ . car̄ . In dn̄io . ē una . 7 ⅲ . uiłłi cū . ⅳ . borđ hn̄t

ⅱ . car̄ 7 dimiđ . Ibi æcc̄ła . 7 ⅰ . molin̄ de . ⅱ . ſoł . 7 ⅱ . ſerui .

7 ⅶ . ac̄ p̄ti . Silua . x . porc̄ . T.R.E. 7 poſt.́ Ⅼ . ſoł . m̄ . ⅳ . liƀ.

Ipſe archieps̄ ten̄ *ASMESLANT* . *IN MARESC DE ROMEN̄* .

ᵱ uno ſolin ſe defđ . Tra . ē . ⅲ . car̄ . Ibi ſunt xxⅰ . uiłłs .

hn̄tes ⅶ . car̄ . Vał 7 ualuit ſēp . Ⅼⅲ . ſoł.

De hac tra h̄ Wiłłs ſołet . ⅰ . jugū . 7 uał ei ᵱ annū . x . ſoł.

SANDWIC ſup̄ſcript̄ eſt . ptin̄ ad dn̄iū monacho᷑ .

ⅢⅠ. TERRA EP̄I ROVECESTRE.

Ēps̄ Rofenſis ten̄ *SVDFLETA* . ᵱ . ⅵ . ſolins ſe

defđ . Tra . ē . xⅲ . car̄ . In dn̄io . ē una car̄ . 7 xxⅴ . uiłłi

cū . ⅸ . borđ hn̄tes . xⅱ . car̄ . Ibi . ⅶ . ſerui . 7 xx . ac̄ p̄ti .

Silua . x . porc̄ . Modo ſe defđ ᵱ . ⅴ . ſolins . Ibi . ē æcc̄ła .

T.R.E. 7 poſt ualuit . xⅰ . liƀ . Modo xxⅰ . liƀ . 7 tam̄ redđ

xxⅳ . liƀ 7 unciā auri .　　　Ⅼ ap̄p̄ciaꞇ . xx . ſoł.

De iſto m̄ eſt in Tonebrige tantū de ſilua 7 de tra . qđ

Iſdem eps̄ ten̄ *ESTANES* . T.R.E. defđ ᵱ ⅵ . ſolins . 7 m̄

ᵱ . ⅳ . ſolins . Tra . ē . xⅰ . car̄ . In dn̄io ſunt . ⅱ . 7 xx . uiłłi

cū . xⅱ . borđ hn̄t . xⅰ . car̄ . Ibi . æcc̄ła 7 ⅳ . ſerui . 7 ⅬxxⅡ .

ac̄ p̄ti . 7 un̄ mołđ de . ⅵ . ſoliđ 7 ⅷ . den̄ . 7 una piſcaria

de . ⅲ . ſoł 7 ⅳ . den̄ . Silua . Ⅼx . porc̄ . T.R.E. 7 poſt .

ualeƀ . xⅲ . liƀ . 7 m̄ xⅵ . liƀ . 7 tam̄ redđ . xx . liƀ .

7 unā unciā Auri . 7 un̄ Marſum . Ricarđ de Tonebrige

ten̄ de iſto m̄ tant̄ ſiluæ qđ uał . xⅴ . ſoł.

in WYE Hundred

21 One manor which answered for 1 sulung before 1066; now for ½.
Land for 2 ploughs. In lordship 1.
   3 villagers with 4 smallholders have 2½ ploughs.
   A church; 1 mill at 2s, 2 slaves; meadow, 7 acres; woodland, 10 pigs.
[Value] before 1066 and later 50s; now £4.

in ROMNEY MARSH

22 Alms-land. It answers for 1 sulung. Land for 3 ploughs.
   21 villagers who have 7 ploughs.
The value is and always was 53s.
   Of this land William Follet has 1 yoke.
Value to him 10s a year.

23 SANDWICH has been entered above. It belongs to the lordship of
the monks.

4   LAND OF THE BISHOP OF ROCHESTER

5 c

1 The Bishop of Rochester holds SOUTHFLEET. It answered for 6
sulungs. Land for 13 ploughs. In lordship 1 plough, and
   25 villagers with 9 smallholders who have 12 ploughs.
   7 slaves; meadow, 20 acres; woodland, 10 pigs. ·
Now it answers for 5 sulungs.
   A church.
Value before 1066 and later £11; now £21; however, it pays £24
and an ounce of gold.
   In Tonbridge there is as much woodland and land from this
manor as is assessed at 20s.
The Bishop also holds

2 STONE. Before 1066 it answered for 6 sulungs; now for 4 sulungs.
Land for 11 ploughs. In lordship 2.
   20 villagers with 12 smallholders have 11 ploughs.
   A church; 4 slaves; meadow, 72 acres; a mill at 6s 8d;
      a fishery at 3s 4d; woodland, 60 pigs.
Value before 1066 and later £13; now £16; however it pays £20,
an ounce of gold and a porpoise.
   Richard of Tonbridge holds as much woodland from this manor
as is valued at 15s.

Isdē eps ten̄ FACHESHAM . p̄ . II . solins se defđ . Tra . ē

In dn̄io . ē una car̄ . 7 xv . uiłłi cū . III . borđ

hn̄t . IIII . car̄ . Ibi æccła 7 III . serui . 7 II . molini de . xv .

soł . 7 IIII . ac̄ p̄ti . Silua . xxx . porc̄ . T.R.E. 7 poſt: ua

lebat . VII . lib̄ . Modo . VIII . lib̄ .

Isdē eps ten̄ LANGAFEL . 7 Anchitill de eo . p̄ uno

solin se defđ . Tra . ē   In dn̄io . ē una car̄ . 7 IX . uiłłi

cū . VII . borđ hn̄t . II . car̄ . Valuit . LXX . soł . 7 m̄ . c . soliđ .

Isdē eps ten̄ BRONLEI . p̄ . VI .   IN BRONLEI HVND.

solins se defđ . T.R.E. 7 m̄ p̄ . IIII . Tra . ē . XIII . car̄ . In dn̄io

sunt . II . car̄ . 7 xxx . uiłłi cū . xxvi . borđ hn̄t . xi . car̄ .

Ibi . I . molđ de . IIII . soliđ . 7 II . ac̄ p̄ti . Silua . c . porc̄ .

T.R.E. 7 poſt: ualuit . xii . lib̄ 7 x . soł . Modo . xviii .

lib̄ . 7 tam̄ reddit . xxi . lib̄ . ii . soliđ minus .

Isdē eps ten̄ OLDEHAM . p̄ . VI . solins se defđ . T.R.E.

7 m̄ p̄ tribȝ . Tra . ē . v . car̄ . In dn̄io sunt . II . 7 xviii . uiłłi

cū xvi . borđ hn̄t . vi . car̄ . Ibi . vi . serui . 7 i . piscaria .

7 Lx . ac̄ p̄ti . Silua . xx . porc̄ . Ibi æccła . T.R.E. 7 poſt:

ualuit . viii . lib̄ . Modo . xii . lib̄ .

Isdē eps ten̄ MELLINGETES . p̄ . III . solins se defđ

T.R.E. 7 m̄ p̄ uno 7 dimiđ . Tra . ē . iii . car̄ . In dn̄io . ē

una . 7 v . uiłłi cū . vi . borđ hn̄t . ii . car̄ . Ibi æccła .

7 un̄ molđ de . ii . soliđ . Silua . xx . porc̄ . T.R.E. 7 poſt:

ualuit . xL . soł . 7 m̄ . iiii . lib̄ .

Isdē eps ten̄ TOTESCLIVE . T.R.E. . p̄ . iii . solins se

defđ . 7 m̄ p̄ uno solin . Tra . ē . iii . car̄ . In dn̄io . ē un̄

solin 7 una car̄ ibi . 7 x . uiłłi cū . ii . car̄ . Ibi æccła .

7 i . seruus . 7 . ii . ac̄ p̄ti . 7 Silua . x . porc̄ . T.R.E. 7 poſt:

ualuit . Lx . soł . 7 m̄ . vii . lib̄ .

3   FAWKHAM. It answers for 2 sulungs. Land for ...
In lordship 1 plough
    15 villagers with 3 smallholders have 4 ploughs.
    A church; 3 slaves; 2 mills at 15s; meadow, 4 acres; woodland, 30
      pigs.
Value before 1066 and later £7; now £8.

4   LONGFIELD and Ansketel the priest from him. It answers for 1 sulung.
Land for ... In lordship 1 plough.
    9 villagers with 7 smallholders have 2 ploughs.
The value was 70s; now 100s.

  in BROMLEY Hundred
5   BROMLEY. Before 1066 it answered for 6 sulungs; now for 3.
Land for 13 ploughs. In lordship 2 ploughs.
    30 villagers with 26 smallholders have 11 ploughs.
    A mill at 4s; meadow, 2 acres; woodland, 100 pigs.
Value before 1066 and later £12 10s; now £18; however,
      it pays £21 less 2s.

6   WOULDHAM. Before 1066 it answered for 6 sulungs; now for 3.
Land for 5 ploughs. In lordship 2.
    18 villagers with 16 smallholders have 6 ploughs.
    6 slaves; 1 fishery, meadow, 60 acres; woodland, 20 pigs.
    A church.
Value before 1066 and later £8; now £12.

7   (? West) MALLING. Before 1066 it answered for 3 sulungs; now for
1½. Land for 3 ploughs. In lordship 1.
    5 villagers with 6 smallholders have 2 ploughs.
    A church; a mill at 2s; woodland, 20 pigs.
Value before 1066 and later 40s; now £4.

8   TROTTISCLIFFE. Before 1066 it answered for 3 sulungs; now for 1
sulung. Land for 3 ploughs. In lordship 1 sulung; 1 plough.
    10 villagers with 2 ploughs.
    A church; 1 slave; meadow, 2 acres; woodland, 10 pigs.
Value before 1066 and later 60s; now £7.

Iſdē eps ten̄ _ESNOILAND_ . T . R . E . ſe deſđ ꝓ . vi . ſolins.

7 m̄ ꝓ . iii . Tra . ē . vi . car̄ . In dn̄io ſunt . ii . car̄ . 7 x.

uiłłi cū . vi . borđ hn̄t . vi . car̄ . Ibi æccła 7 v . ſerui.

7 iii . molđ de . xl . ſoliđ . 7 xxx . ac̄ p̄ti . Silua . iiii , porc̄.

T . R . E . 7 poſt ꞉ ualeb̄ . vi . lib̄ . 7 m̄ . ix . lib̄.

5 d

Iſdē eps ten̄ _COCLESTANE_ . _IN ESSAMELE HVND._

ꝓ . ii . ſolins 7 dimiđ ſe deſđ T . R . E . 7 m̄ ꝓ . ii . tan̄t . Tra . ē

vi . car̄ . In dn̄io ſunt . ii . 7 xv . uiłłi cū . ix . borđ hn̄t v . car̄.

Ibi æccła 7 ii . ſerui . 7 i . molin̄ de xxx . den̄ . 7 xx . ac̄ p̄ti.

T . R . E . 7 poſt ꞉ ualeb̄ . iiii . lib̄ 7 x . ſoł . 7 m̄ x . lib̄ 7 x . ſoliđ.

Iſdē eps ten̄ _DANITONE_ . ꝓ . ii . ſolins ſe deſđ T . R . E . 7 m̄

ꝓ dimiđ ſolin . Tra . ē . ii . car̄ . In dn̄io . ē una . 7 vi . uiłłi hn̄t

ibi . i . car̄ . Ibi æccła 7 iiii . ſerui . 7 iiii . ac̄ p̄ti . Silua . xv . porc̄.

T . R . E . 7 poſt ꞉ ualeb̄ . c . ſoł . 7 m̄ . vii . lib̄ 7 xv . ſoliđ.

Iſdē eps ten̄ _HALLINGES_ . T . R . E . ſe deſđ ꝓ . vi . ſolins . 7 m̄

ꝓ . ii . 7 dimiđ . Tra . ē . vii . car̄ . In dn̄io ſunt . iii . car̄ . 7 xv . uiłłi

cū . ix . borđ hn̄t . vi . car̄ . Ibi æccła 7 ii . ſerui . 7 xxx . ac̄ p̄ti.

7 ſilua . v . porc̄ . T . R . E . 7 poſt ualeb̄ . vii . lib̄ . M xvi . lib̄ . Qđ Ricard ten̄ in ſua leu꞉ ual . vii . ſoł . 7

Iſdē eps ten̄ _FRANDESBERIE_ . ꝓ . x . ſolins ſe deſđ T . R . E.

7 m̄ ꝓ . vii . Tra . ē . xv . car̄ . In dn̄io ſunt . v . car̄ . 7 xl . uiłłi cū

xxviii . borđ hn̄t . xi . car̄ . Ibi æccła 7 ix . ſerui . 7 uñ molin̄ de

xii . ſoł . 7 xl . ac̄ p̄ti . Silua . v . porc̄ . T . R . E . 7 poſt ualeb̄ . viii.

lib̄ . 7 m̄ . xxv . lib̄ . Qđ Ricard ten̄ in ſua Leuua ꞉ ual . x . ſoł.

Iſdē eps ten̄ _BORCHETELLE_ . _IN HVND DE ROVECESTRE._.

T . R . E . ꝓ . ii . ſolins ſe deſđ . 7 m̄ ꝓ uno ſolin 7 dimiđ . Tra . ē . iiii.

car̄ . In dn̄io ſunt . ii . car̄ . 7 vi . uiłłi cū . iii . car̄ . Ibi . l . ac̄ p̄ti.

7 ii . molini de . xx . ſoliđ . T . R . E . 7 poſt ꞉ ualeb̄ . vi . lib̄ . 7 modo

x . lib̄.

4

9   SNODLAND. Before 1066 it answered for 6 sulungs; now for 3.
Land for 6 ploughs. In lordship 2 ploughs.
   10 villagers with 6 smallholders have 6 ploughs.
   A church; 5 slaves; 3 mills at 40s; meadow, 30 acres;
      woodland, 4 pigs.
Value before 1066 and later £6; now £9.

5 d

in SHAMWELL Hundred
10   CUXTON. Before 1066 it answered for 2½ sulungs; now for only 2.
Land for 6 ploughs. In lordship 2.
   15 villagers with 9 smallholders have 5 ploughs.
   A church; 2 slaves; 1 mill at 30d; meadow, 20 acres.
Value before 1066 and later £4 10s; now £10 10s.

11   DENTON. Before 1066 it answered for 2 sulungs; now for ½ sulung.
Land for 2 ploughs. In lordship 1.
   6 villagers have 1 plough.
   A church; 4 slaves; meadow, 4 acres; woodland, 15 pigs.
Value before 1066 and later 100s; now £7 15s.

12   HALLING. Before 1066 it answered for 6 sulungs; now for 2½.
Land for 7 ploughs. In lordship 3 ploughs.
   15 villagers with 9 smallholders have 6 ploughs.
   A church; 2 slaves; meadow, 30 acres; woodland, 5 pigs.
Value before 1066 and later £7; now £16. Value of what Richard
holds in his territory 7s.

13   FRINDSBURY. Before 1066 it answered for 10 sulungs; now 7.
Land for 15 ploughs. In lordship 5 ploughs.
   40 villagers with 28 smallholders have 11 ploughs.
   A church; 9 slaves; a mill at 12s; meadow, 40 acres;
      woodland, 5 pigs.
Value before 1066 and later £8; now £25. Value of what Richard
holds in his territory 10s.

in the Hundred of ROCHESTER
14   BORSTALL. Before 1066 it answered for 2 sulungs; now for 1½
sulungs. Land for 4 ploughs. In lordship 2 ploughs;
   6 villagers with 3 ploughs.
   Meadow, 50 acres; 2 mills at 20s.
Value before 1066 and later £6; now £10.

I_N ROVECESTRE habuit eps 7 hr̄ adhuc q̃t xx . mãſuras
trǣ quǣ ptiñ ad Frandeſberie 7 Borcſtele ꝓpa ej̄ maneria.
T.R.E. 7 poſt.ualebãȵ . III . lib̄ . m̄ ualeȵ . VIII . lib̄ . 7 tam̃
ꝑ annũ reddunt . XI . lib̄ 7 XIII . ſol 7 IIII . denar̄.

Iſdē eps ten̄ EſTOCHES . T.R.E. ſe defđ I_N HOW HVND.
ꝑ v . ſolins . 7 m̄ ꝓ trib̄ . Tra . ē . v . car̄ . In dn̄io ſunt . II . car̄.
7 x . uilti cũ . v . borđ hn̄t . IIII . car̄ . Ibi ǣccła 7 IIII . ſerui.
7 IIII . ac̄ p̃ti . T.R.E. 7 poſt 7 modo uał . VIII . lib̄ 7 xx . den̄.
7 tam̃ reddit qui tenet . XIII . lib̄ 7 xx . denar̄.

Hoc m̄ fuit 7 eſt de epiſcopatu rofenſi . ſed Goduin̄
comes T.R.E. emit illud de duob̄ hōib̄ȝ qui eũ teneb̄
de epo . 7 eo ignorante facta . ē hǣc uenditio.

Poſtmodũ ũ regnante W . rege . diratiocinauit
illud Lanfranc̄ archieps c̄tra baiocenſē epm . et
inde eſt m̄ ſaiſita rofenſis ǣccła.

TERRA EP̄I BAIOCENSIS.

I_N LEſT DE SVDTONE. I_N ACHEſTAN HVND.
.V. De epo Baiocenſi ten̄ Hugo de porth HAGELEI.
ꝓ dimidio ſolin ſe defđ . Tra . ē .   In dn̄io ſunt . II.
car̄ . 7 XIIII . uilti cũ . III . borđ hn̄t . IIII . car̄ . Ibi . III . ſerui . 7 XII.
ac̄ p̃ti . 7 uñ molđ de . xx . ſol . 7 una dena ſiluǣ de . v . porc̄.
Tot̄ m̄ uał m̄ . xv . lib̄ . de . xx . in ora.
In hoc m̄ ten̄ uñ hō . xx . ac̄s trǣ . ualentes ꝑ annũ . v . ſol . Vluret
uocat . nec ptiñ ad illud m̄ . neqᷓ potuit habe dn̄m p̃t regē.
Helto ten̄ SVINESCAMP de epo . ꝓ x . ſolins ſe defđ.
Tra . ē . XIIII . car̄ . In dn̄io ſunt . III . 7 XXXIII . uilti cũ . III . borđ
hn̄t XIII . car̄ . Ibi uñ miles 7 x . ſerui . 7 XL . ac̄ p̃ti . Silua
III . porc̄ . 7 v . piſcariǣ de . xxx . den̄ . 7 vī . que ſeruit ad hallā.
7 una heda de . v . ſoliđ . 7 IIII . den̄ . De Silua huj̄ m̄ tenet
Ricarđ in ſua leuua qđ . uał . IIII . ſoliđ.
Totũ m̄ ualeb̄ xx . lib̄.   7 m̄ uał XXXII . lib̄.

15　In ROCHESTER the Bishop had and still has 80 dwellings of the land which belongs to Frindsbury and Borstall, his own manors. Value before 1066 and later £3; value now £8; however, they pay £11 13s 4d a year.

In HOO Hundred

16　The Bishop also holds STOKE. Before 1066 it answered for 5 sulungs; now for 3. Land for 5 ploughs. In lordship 2 ploughs.
　10 villagers with 5 smallholders have 4 ploughs.
　A church; 4 slaves; meadow, 4 acres.
Value before 1066, later and now £8 0s 20d; however, it's holder pays £13 0s 20d.
　This manor was and is the Bishopric of Rochester's, but Earl Godwin bought it before 1066 from two men who held it from the Bishop. This sale was made without his knowledge, but afterwards, in the reign of King William, Archbishop Lanfranc proved (his claim to) it against the Bishop of Bayeux; and so the Church of Rochester is in possession.

5　　LAND OF THE BISHOP OF BAYEUX　　6 a

In the [Half-]lathe of SUTTON
In AXTON Hundred

1　Hugh of Port holds HAWLEY from the Bishop of Bayeux. It answers for ½ sulung. Land for ... In lordship 2 ploughs.
　14 villagers with 3 smallholders have 4 ploughs.
　3 slaves; meadow, 12 acres; a mill at 20s; 1 pig pasture of woodland at 5 pigs.
Value of the whole manor now £15 at 20 (pence) to the *ora*.
　In this manor one man holds 20 acres of land which are valued at 5s a year. He is called Wilfred and he does not belong to that manor nor could he have any lord except the King.

From the Bishop

2　Helto holds SWANSCOMBE. It answers for 10 sulungs.
Land for 14 ploughs. In lordship 3.
　33 villagers with 3 smallholders have 13 ploughs. 1 man-at-arms; 10 slaves.
　Meadow, 40 acres; woodland, 3 pigs; 5 fisheries at 30d; a sixth which serves the hall; 1 landing place at 5s 4d.
　Of the woodland of this manor Richard holds in his territory what is valued at 4s.
Value of the whole manor £20; value now £32.

Radulf̕ fili̕ Turaldi ten̕ de ep̄o ERCLEI . ꝑ uno folin fe

defd . Tra̕.ē   In dn̄io funt . ii . car̕ . 7 ix.uil̃li cū.vi.

cot̕ hn̄t.iii.car̕.Ibi.iii.ſerui. 7 ſilua.x.porc̕.

Tot̕ ꝏ ualeƀ.iii.liƀ.   7 m̄.c.ſot.Quædā mulier tenuit.

Radulf̕ ten̕ de ep̄o EDDINTONE .ꝑ dimid̕ folin.

Tra.ē.i.car̕. 7 ibi.ē cū.iiii.bord̕ 7 ii.ſeruis. 7 ibi.i.molin

de.xxiii.ſot.Totū ꝏ appc̄iat̕.iiii.liƀ.T.R.E.parū ualeƀ.

Leſtan tenuit de rege E. 7 poſt mortē ej̕ uertit ſe ad

Alnod.7 m̄ eſt in calūpnia.

Anſgot̕ de Roueceſtre ten̕ de ep̄o MAPLEDESCAM . ꝑ di

midio folin.Tra̕.ē   In dn̄io.ē.i.car̕.cū uno uil̃lo 7 iiii.

bord̕.7 iiii.ſeruis.Ibi una ac̄ p̄ti. 7 ſilua viii.porc̕. 7 xvi.

denar̕ plus.Valuit.iiii.liƀ.   7 m̄.cx.ſot.

Euſtan tenuit de rege.E.

Adā filius Huƀti ten̕ de ep̄o REDLEGE .ꝑ uno folin fe

defd . Tra̕.ē   In dn̄io funt . ii . car̕ . 7 vi . uil̃li cū . v . bord̕.

hn̄t.ii.car̕.Ibi.v.ſerui.7 dim̄ ac̄ p̄ti.7 una dena ſiluæ

quā ten̕ Ricard̕ de Tonebrige.Valuit|iii.liƀ.7 m̄.iiii.liƀ

7 x.ſot.Siuuard tenuit de rege.E.

Hugo de port ten̕ de ep̄o EISSE .ꝑ triƀȝ folins ſe defd̕.

Tra̕.ē   In dn̄io.ē una car̕. 7 xii.uil̃li cū.viii.bord̕

hn̄t.iii.car̕.Ibi q̄da miles hn̄s.viii.int̕ ſeruos 7 ancillas.

7 tra̕ ad unā car̕.Præter hoc h̄t Hugo.ii.hōes tenentes

dimid̕ folin.qui potera[n].T.R.E.ire quolibet ſine licentia.

Vna tra̕ uocat̕ Didele. 7 alia Soninges.Tra̕.ē ibi.ad unā car̕.

7 appc̄iat̕.xx.ſot.Tot̕ ꝏ appc̄iabat̕.vii.liƀ. 7 m̄ ſimilit̕.

Qd̕ Ricard̕ ten̕ de Tonebrige: xl.ſot.appc̄iat̕.Rex h̄t

inde.ii.denas.quæ appc̄iant̕.vii.ſot.Godric tenuit

de rege.E.

3   Ralph son of Thorold holds HARTLEY.   It answers for 1 sulung.
Land for ...   In lordship 2 ploughs.
   9 villagers with 6 cottagers have 3 ploughs.
   3 slaves; woodland, 10 pigs.
Value of the whole manor £3; now 100s.
   A woman held it.

4   Ralph holds EDDINTONE. It answers for ½ sulung.
Land for 1 plough; it is there, with
   4 smallholders and 2 slaves.
   1 mill at 23s.
The whole manor is assessed at £4; value before 1066 a little more.
   Leofstan held it from King Edward; after his death it went to
Young Alnoth; now it is in dispute.

5   Ansgot of Rochester holds MAPLESCOMBE for ½ sulung.
Land for ...   In lordship 1 plough, with
   1 villager, 4 smallholders and 4 slaves.
   Meadow, 1 acre; woodland, 8 pigs and 16d too.
The value was £4; now 110s.
   Alstan held it from King Edward.

6   Adam son of Hubert holds RIDLEY.   It answers for 1 sulung.
Land for ...   In lordship 2 ploughs.
   6 villagers with 5 smallholders have 2 ploughs.
   5 slaves; meadow, ½ acre; 1 pig pasture of woodland which
      Richard of Tonbridge holds.
The value of the manor was £3; now £4 10s.
   Siward held it from King Edward.

7   Hugh of Port holds ASH.   It answers for 3 sulungs.
Land for ...   In lordship 1 plough.
   12 villagers with 8 smallholders have 3 ploughs. A man-at-arms
      who has 8 male and female slaves; land for 1 plough.
   In addition to this Hugh has 2 men who hold ½ sulung, who
could go where ever they would before 1066 without permission.
   One piece of land is called Idleigh, another 'Sonnings'.
Land for 1 plough. It is assessed at 20s.
The whole manor was assessed at £7; now the same; what
Richard of Tonbridge holds is assessed at 40s.
   From it the King has 2 pig pastures which are assessed
at 7s. Godric held it from King Edward.

Goisfrid de Ros ten̄ *LOLINGESTONE* . p̄ uno folin fe defđ.

T̄ra . ē   In dn̄io . ē una car̄ . 7 IIII . uiłłi cū uno cot hn̄t

II . car̄ . Ibi . VII . ſerui . 7 VI . āc paſturæ . Silua . xx . porc̄.

Q̄do receP.ᷓ ualeƀ . LX . ſoł . 7 m̄ . c . ſoł . Rex hŧ in manu ſua

qđ uał . x . ſoliđ . Brixe cilt tenuit de rege . E.

De eP̄o ten̄ Malger̄i *LÒLINĠESTÒNE* . p̄ dim̄ folin.

fe defđ . T̄ra ; ē .   In dn̄io . ē una car̄ . 7 III . uiłłi

cū . VI . borđ hn̄t . I . car̄ . Ibi . v . āc p̄ti;

Totū m̄ ualeƀ . LX . ſoł ; modo . LXX ; ſoł . De iſto m̄ hŧ

Rex qđ uał . x . ſoliđ . Bruning tenuit de rege . E.

Iſdē Malger̄i ten̄ in *FERLINGEHÁ* ; dimiđ jugū træ.

T̄ra . ē . III . boū . Ibi funt . II . boues ; cū uno borđ . 7 II . āc p̄ti.

Valuit 7 uał . xv . ſoł ; Brunefune tenuit . 7 potuit

cū t̄ra fua uertere fe quo uoluit ; De hoc m̄ ten̄ rex

qđ uał . VIII . ſoł.

Iſdē Malger̄i ten̄ in Pinnedene . dimiđ folin de eP̄o.

T̄ra . ē . VII . boū . Ibi . ē una car̄ cū . VI . uiłłis . 7 VI . āc p̄ti;

Valuit 7 uał . XVI . ſoł ; Aluret tenuit T . R . E . 7 potuit

fe uertere quo uoluit.

Oſƀnus paſtforeire ten̄ in Lolingeſton̄ dimiđ folin

de eP̄o . T̄ra . ē   In dn̄io . ē . I . car̄ . 7 III . uiłłi cū . I . borđ

7 . I . ſeruo hn̄t . I . car̄ . Ibi . v . āc p̄ti . Silua . v . porc̄ . 7 un̄

molin̄ de . xv . ſoliđ . 7 CL . anguiłł . Rex hŧ filuā p̄ nouo

dono epi . 7 uał . III . ſoł . Totū m̄ ualeƀ . LX . ſoł . Modo

LXXVII . ſoł . Seuuart fot tenuit . T . R . E . 7 potuit fe

uertere cū t̄ra fua quo uoluit.

Wadarđ ten̄ de eP̄o dimiđ folin in Ferningehā;

T̄ra . ē . III . car̄ . In dn̄io funt . II . car̄ . cū uno uiłło 7 II . cot.

7 v . feruis . Ibi dimiđ molđ de . v . folins . 7 IIII . āc p̄ti . Silua

v . porc̄ . Excepto iſto dim̄ folin . ten̄ Wadarđ dimiđ jugū

in eađ uilla . qđ nunq̄ fe quietauit apud regē . Int̄

5

8   Geoffrey of Rots holds LULLINGSTONE. It answers for 1 sulung.
Land for ... In lordship 1 plough.
     4 villagers with 1 cottager have 2 ploughs.
     7 slaves; pasture, 6 acres; woodland, 20 pigs.
Value when acquired 60s; now 100s; the King has in his hand
what is valued at 10s.
     Young Brictsi held it from King Edward.

9   Mauger holds LULLINGSTONE from the Bishop. It answers for ½   6 b
sulung. Land for ... In lordship 1 plough.
     3 villagers with 6 smallholders have 1 plough.
     Meadow, 5 acres.
The value of the whole manor was 60s; now 70s; of that manor
the King has what is valued at 10s.
     Browning held it from King Edward.

10   Mauger also holds ½ yoke of land in FARNINGHAM. Land
for 3 oxen. 2 oxen, with
     1 smallholder.
     Meadow, 2 acres.
The value was and is 15s.
     Brown's son held it and could go where he would with his land.
Of this manor the King holds what is valued at 8s.

11   Mauger also holds ½ sulung in PINDEN from the Bishop.
Land for 7 oxen. 1 plough, with
     6 villagers.
     Meadow, 6 acres.
The value was and is 16s.
     Alfred held it before 1066 and could go where he would.

12   Osbern Paisforiere holds ½ sulung in LULLINGSTONE from the Bishop.
Land for ... In lordship 1 plough.
     3 villagers with 1 smallholder and 1 slave have 1 plough.
     Meadow, 5 acres; woodland, 5 pigs; a mill at 15s and 150 eels.
     The King has a wood as a new gift of the Bishop; value 3s.
The value of the whole manor was 60s; now 77s.
     Siward Sot held it before 1066 and could go where he would
with his land.

13   Wadard holds ½ sulung in FARNINGHAM from the Bishop.
Land for 3 ploughs. In lordship 2 ploughs, with
     1 villager, 2 cottagers and 5 slaves.
     ½ mill at 5s; meadow, 4 acres; woodland, 5 pigs.
     Apart from that ½ sulung Wadard holds ½ yoke in the same
village which never was exempt (from tax) to the King.

totū ualuit IIII . liɓ . 7 m̅ . VI . liɓ . Eſtan tenuit . T . R . E ⁊
7 potuit ſe uertere quo uoluit.

Iſd̄ Wadard ten de epo MALPLESCAP . ꝑ dim̕ ſolin ſe
defđ . Tra . e̅ . II . car̕ . Ibi ſunt cū . I . uilło 7 IIII . borđ 7 v ⁊
ſeruis . 7 una ac̕ 7 dim̕ p̃ti . Silua . VIII . porc̕ 7 XVI . denar̕⁊
Valuit . III . liɓ . 7 m̅ . VI . liɓ . Vltan̕ tenuit ſub Heraldo⁊

Ernulf̕ de Heſding ten FERNINGEHA̅ . ꝑ ⸳ III . jugis
ſe defđ . Tra . e̅ . II . car̕ . Ibi ſunt m̅ . VI . boues cū . II ⸳ uilłis
7 III . borđ . Ibi uñ molđ de . X . ſoł . 7 VIII . ac̅ p̃ti . Paſtura
c . ouiɓ̕ . Silua . X . porc̕ 7 XIIII . deñ . Rex h̅ de ſilua
huj̕ m̅ . qđ uał . VIII . ſoł . Totū m̅ ualuit . III ⸳ liɓ ⸳ 7 m̅
XL . ſoliđ . Dering tenuit . 7 potuit ſe uertere quo uoluit⸳

Anſchitillus de ros ten̕ TARENT de epo . ꝑ dim̕ ſolin
ſe defđ . Tra . e̅ . I . car̕ 7 dim̕ . In dñio . e̅ una ⸳ 7 IIII . uilłi
cū . IIII . borđ hñt . I . car̕ . Ibi . III . ac̕ p̃ti . 7 II ⸳ molini de . XVIII ⸳
ſoł . Silua . III . porc̕ . Rex h̅ de iſto m̅ ꝑ nouo dono epi
qđ uał . X . denar̕ . Totū m̅ ualuit 7 uał . c . ſoł . Aluric
tenuit de rege . E.

In ead̕ uilla h̅ iſd̄ . A . I . maneriū de epo . ꝑ dim̕
ſolin ſe defđ . Tra . e̅ . I . car̕ 7 dimiđ . Ibi . V . uilłi 7 V . borđ
7 uñ molđ de . XX . ſoliđ . Ibi . III . ac̕ p̃ti . 7 I . ſeru̕ .
Totū m̅ ualuit . LX . ſoł . 7 modo . LXX . ſoliđ . Oſiert
tenuit de rege . E.

Iſd̄ Anſchitill̕ ten̕ de epo HORTVNE . ꝑ uno ſolin ſe
ⷡ defđ⸳

Tra . e̅ . III . car̕ . 7 ibi ſunt . IIII . borđ 7 uñ molđ de . V . ſoł .
7 VI . ac̕ p̃ti . Ibi æccła . e̅ . 7 ſilua . III . porc̕ . Rex h̅ ꝑ nouo
dono epi tant̕ ſiluæ de iſto m̅ . qđ uał . V . ſoł . Totū m̅
ualuit . IIII . liɓ . 7 m̅ . VI . liɓ . Godel de Brixi tenuit.
7 potuit ſe uertere cū hac tra quo uoluit.

Iſd̄ Anſchitill̕ ten̕ de epo in eod̕ m̅ dimiđ ſolin . Tra . e̅
uñ car̕ . 7 ibi . e̅ in dñio . 7 VIII . uilłi cū . VI . borđ hñt . I . car̕ .

In total the value was £4, now £6.
Alstan held it before 1066 and could go where he would.

14   Wadard also holds MAPLESCOMBE from the Bishop. It answers
for ½ sulung. Land for 2 ploughs. They are there, with
     1 villager, 4 smallholders and 5 slaves.
     Meadow, 1½ acres; woodland, 8 pigs and 16d.
The value was £3; now £6.
     Wulfstan held it under Harold.

15   Arnulf of Hesdin holds FARNINGHAM. It answers for 3 yokes.
Land for 2 ploughs. Now 6 oxen, with
     2 villagers and 3 smallholders.
     A mill at 10s; meadow, 8 acres; pasture, 100 sheep; woodland
       10 pigs and 14d.
Of the woodland of this manor the King has what is valued at 8s.
The value of the whole manor was £3; now 40s.
     Dering held it and could go where he would.

16   Ansketel of Rots holds DARENTH from the Bishop. It answers for
½ sulung. Land for 1½ ploughs. In lordship 1.
     4 villagers with 4 smallholders have 1 plough.
     Meadow, 3 acres; 2 mills at 18s; woodland, 3 pigs.
     Of that manor the King has what is valued at 10d as a new
gift of the Bishop.
The value of the whole manor was and is 100s.
     Aelfric held it from King Edward.

17   In the same village Ansketel also has 1 manor from the Bishop. It
answers for ½ sulung. Land for 1½ ploughs.
     5 villagers and 5 smallholders.
     A mill at 20s; meadow, 3 acres; 1 slave.
The value of the whole manor was 60s; now 70s.
     Osgeard held it from King Edward.

18   Ansketel also holds HORTON (Kirby) from the bishop. It answers
for 1 sulung. Land for 3 ploughs.   6 c
     4 smallholders.
     A mill at 5s; meadow, 6 acres. A church; woodland, 3 pigs.
     The King has as a new gift of the Bishop as much woodland
       of that manor as is valued at 5s.
The value of the whole manor was £4; now £6.
     Godel held it from Brictsi and could go where he would
with this land.
Ansketel also holds ½ sulung in the same manor from the Bishop.
Land for 1 plough. It is there in lordship.
     8 villagers with 6 smallholders have 1 plough.

Ibi . 1 . moliñ de xv . fot . 7 ix . ac p̃ti . Silua . v . porc̄.

Totū ⊕ ualuit . xl . fot . 7 m̃ . lx . Ording tenuit de rege.

Iſdē Anſchitill' teñ de ẽpo in eod̃ ⊕ unū ſolin . Tra . ē

iii . car̄ . In dñio eſt una car̄ . 7 viii . uitti cū . ii . car̄ . Ibi

uñ ſeruus . 7 viii . ac p̃ti . dim̃ mold de . v . ſolid . Silua

xv . porc̄ . Totū ⊕ ualuit . iiii . lib̄ . 7 m̃ . c . ſolid.

Aluuard' tenuit de Heraldo . H̃ . iiii . Maneria.

ſunt m̃ ꝓ uno ⊕   IN LITELAI HVND.

R̃obt' Latiñ teñ de ẽpo LOISNES . Tra . ē . xvii.

car̄ . In dñio . ē una . 7 lx . uitti cū . iii . bord hñt . xv.

car̄ . Ibi . ii . ſerui . 7 iii . cot̄ . 7 iii . piſcariæ de . iiii . ſol.

7 xxx . ac p̃ti . Silua . xx . porc̄ . T.R.E. ual . xx . lib̄.

Q̃do eṕs recep̃ xviii . lib̄ . 7 m̃ xxii . lib̄ . 7 tam̃

qui teñ redd̄ . xxx . lib̄ . Hoc ⊕ ſe defd̄ T.R.E.

ꝓ . x . ſolins . 7 m̃ ꝓ . iiii . ſolins . Azor tenuit.

Anſgot teñ de ẽpo HOV . qd̄ ſe defd̄ ꝓ uno ſolin.

Tra . ē   In dñio . ē una car̄ . 7 v . uitti cū . i . car̄

7 dimid̄ . 7 uñ mold de . x . fot . Ibi . ii . cot̄ 7 uñ ſeruus.

7 xii . ac p̃ti . Silua . iii . porc̄ . T.R.E. ualeb̄ lx . fot . Q̃do

recep̃ tñtd̄ . 7 m̃ . iiii . lib̄ . Anſchil de rege E . tenuit.

Ab̄b̄ S Auguſtini teñ de ẽpo baiocenſi PLVMESTEDE.

ꝓ . ii . ſolins 7 uno jugo ſe defd̄ . Tra . v . car̄ . In dñio . ē

una car̄ . 7 xvii . uitti cū . iii . bord hñt . iiii . car̄ . Ibi

ſilua . v . porc̄ . T.R.E. ualeb̄ . x . lib̄ . Q̃do recep̃ viii . lib̄.

7 m̃ tñtd̄ . 7 tam̃ qui teñ redd̄ . xii . lib̄ . Brixi cilt

tenuit de rege . E.   IN HELMESTREI HVND.

Malgeri' teñ de ẽpo ROCHELEI . ꝓ uno ſolin ſe defd̄.

Tra . ē   In dñio . ē una car̄ 7 dimid̄ . 7 x . uitti

cū . x . bord hñt . ii . car̄ 7 dim̃ . Ibi . i . moliñ de . xii.

ſolid . Silua . iii . porc̄ . T.R.E. ualeb̄ . iiii . lib̄ Q̃do recep̃

iii . lib̄ . 7 m̃ . c . ſolid . Aluuard' tenuit de rege . E.

1 mill at 15s; meadow, 9 acres; woodland, 5 pigs.
The value of the whole manor was 40s; now 60s.
  Ording held it from the King.
Ansketel also holds 1 sulung in the same manor from the Bishop.
Land for 3 ploughs. In lordship 1 plough;
    8 villagers with 2 ploughs. 1 slave.
    Meadow, 8 acres; ½ mill at 5s; woodland, 15 pigs.
The value of the whole manor was £4; now 100s.
    Alfward held it from Harold.
Now there are 4 manors in place of 1 manor.

In LITTLE Hundred
19 Robert Latimer holds LESSNESS from the Bishop. Land for 17
ploughs. In lordship 1.
    60 villagers with 3 smallholders have 15 ploughs. 2 slaves.
      3 cottagers.
    3 fisheries at 4s; meadow, 30 acres; woodland, 20 pigs.
Value before 1066 £20; when the Bishop acquired it £18; now
£22; however, its holder pays £30.
    This manor answered for 10 sulungs before 1066; now 4 sulungs.
Azor held it.

20 Ansgot holds HOWBURY from the Bishop which answers for 1 sulung.
Land for ... In lordship 1 plough,
    5 villagers with 1½ ploughs.
    A mill at 10s.
    2 cottagers and 1 slave.
    Meadow, 12 acres; woodland, 3 pigs.
Value before 1066, 60s; when acquired as much; now £4.
    Askell held it from King Edward.

21 The Abbot of St. Augustine's holds PLUMSTEAD from the Bishop of
Bayeux. It answers for 2 sulungs and 1 yoke. Land for 5 ploughs.
In lordship 1 plough.
    17 villagers with 3 smallholders have 4 ploughs.
    Woodland, 5 pigs.
Value before 1066 £10; when acquired £8; now as much;
however, its holder pays £12.
    Young Brictsi held it from King Edward.

In RUXLEY Hundred
From the Bishop
22 Mauger holds RUXLEY. It answers for 1 sulung. Land for ...
In lordship 1½ ploughs.
    10 villagers with 10 smallholders have 2½ ploughs.
    1 mill at 12s; woodland, 3 pigs.
Value before 1066 £4; when acquired £3; now 100s.
    Alfward held it from King Edward.

Ernulf' de hefding ten̄ de ep̄o CIRESFEL.

p̄ . ii . folins fe defd̄ . Tra . ē   In dn̄io funt . ii . car̄.

7 xx . uiłłi cū . iiii . bord hn̄t . viii . car̄ . Ibi . iiii . ferui.

7 un̄ molin̄ de . x . fot . 7 x . ac̄ p̄ti . 7 filua . x . porc̄.

T.R.E. ualeb xvi . lib̄ . 7 poft. xii . lib̄ . 7 m̄ xxv . lib̄.

7 tam̄ qui ten̄ redd̄ . xxx.v . lib̄ . Tochi tenuit de rege . E.

Ad̄a fili' Hub̄ti ten̄ de ep̄o SVDCRAI . p̄ uno folin fe

defd̄ . Tra . ē .   In dn̄io funt . ii . car̄ . 7 xiiii . uiłłi

cū . i . bord hn̄t . iiii . car̄ . Ibi . vi : ferui . 7 x . ac̄ p̄ti.

Silua . x . porc̄ . T.R.E. ualeb . vi . lib̄ . 7 poft. iiii . lib̄.

7 modo . x . lib̄ . Toli tenuit de rege . E.

Ifd̄e Ad̄a ten̄ de ep̄o WICHEILA . p̄ uno folin fe defd̄.

6 d

Tra . ē   In dn̄io funt . ii . car̄ . 7 xxiiii . uiłłi hn̄t . iiii . car̄.

Ibi . xiii . ferui . 7 una æccła . 7 un̄ molin̄ de . xx . den̄ . 7 una filua

de . x . porc̄ . T.R.E. ualeb . viii . lib̄ . 7 poft. vi . lib̄ . 7 m̄ . xiii . lib̄.

fit carte
Godric tenuit de rege . E.

Goisfrid de ros ten̄ de ep̄o LASELA . p̄ . vii . folins fe defd̄.

Tra . ē   In dn̄io funt . iii . car̄ . 7 xxxi . uiłłs cū . xiiii . bord

hn̄t xvi . car̄ . Ibi . x . ferui . 7 una pifcar̄ de q̄t xx . anguiłł . 7 x.

Silua . lxxv . porc̄ . Totū m̄ ualeb . T.R.E. xxx . lib̄ . Q̄do recēp.

xvi . lib̄ . 7 m̄ . xxiiii . lib̄ qd̄ Goisfrid ten̄ . Ricard̄ de Tone

brige qd̄ ten̄ in Leuua fua. appciat . vi . lib̄ . Qd̄ rex tenet

de hoc manerio. xxii . fot . Brixi cilt tenuit de rege . E.

Anfchitil de ros ten̄ de ep̄o CRAIE . p̄ dim̄ folin fe defd̄.

Tra . ē .   In dn̄io . ē . i . car̄ . 7 vii . uiłłi cū . vi . bord hn̄t

unā car̄ . Ibi æccła . 7 una ac̄ p̄ti . 7 iii . ac̄ pafturæ.

T.R.E. 7 poft. ualeb . iiii . lib̄ . 7 m̄ . iii . lib̄ . Leuric tenuit de rege . E.

Ifd̄e Anfchitill' ten̄ de ep̄o alia CRAIE . p̄ dim̄ folin fe defd̄.

Tra . ē   In dn̄io . ē una car̄ . 7 vii . uiłłi cū . v . bord

hn̄t . i . car̄ . Ibi . i . molin̄ de . xlii . den̄ . 7 v . ferui . Silua . vii . porc̄.

T.R.E. 7 poft. ualuit . iiii . lib̄ . 7 m̄. iii . lib̄ .   de Alnod cilt.

Hæ duæ træ fuer̄ . ii . m̄ T.R.E. 7 m̄ funt in uno . m̄ . Aluuin̄ tenuit

23   Arnulf of Hesdin holds CHELSFIELD. It answers for 2 sulungs.
Land for ... In lordship 2 ploughs.
    20 villagers with 4 smallholders have 8 ploughs.
    4 slaves; a mill at 10s; meadow, 10 acres; woodland, 10 pigs.
Value before 1066 £16; later £12; now £25; however, its holder
pays £35.
    Toki held it from King Edward.

24   Adam son of Hubert holds (St Mary) CRAY. It answers for 1 sulung.
Land for ... In lordship 2 ploughs.
    14 villagers with 1 smallholder have 4 ploughs.
    6 slaves; meadow, 10 acres; woodland, 10 pigs.
Value before 1066 £6; later £4; now £10.
    Toli held it from King Edward.

25   Adam also holds (West) WICKHAM. It answers for 1 sulung.   6 d
Land for ... In lordship 2 ploughs.
    24 villagers have 4 ploughs.
    13 slaves; a church; a mill at 20d; a wood at 10 pigs.
Value before 1066 £8; later £6; now £13.
    Godric son of Karl held it from King Edward.

26   Geoffrey of Rots holds SEAL. It answers for 7 sulungs.
Land for ... In lordship 3 ploughs.
    31 villagers with 14 smallholders have 16 ploughs.
    10 slaves; a fishery at 90 eels; woodland, 75 pigs.
Value of the whole manor before 1066 £30; when acquired £16;
now what Geoffrey holds £24. What Richard of Tonbridge holds
in his territory is assessed at £6; what the King holds from this
manor 22s.
    Young Brictsi held it from King Edward.

27   Ansketel of Rots holds (NORTH) CRAY. It answers for ½ sulung.
Land for ... In lordship 1 plough.
    7 villagers with 6 smallholders have 1 plough.
    A church; meadow, 1 acre; pasture, 3 acres.
Value before 1066 and later £4; now £3.
    Leofric held it from King Edward.

28   Ansketel also holds another (St Paul's) CRAY. It answers for ½ sulung.
Land for ... In lordship 1 plough.
    7 villagers with 5 smallholders have 1 plough.
    1 mill at 42d; 5 slaves; woodland, 7 pigs.
Value before 1066 and later £4; now £3.
    These two lands were 2 manors before 1066; now they are in
1 manor.
    Alwin held them from Young Alnoth.

Eps Lisiacensis ten de epo baiocsi GRENVIZ . p . II . solins
se desd . Tra . e̅   In dn̅io sunt . II . car̅ . 7 XXIIII . uitti hn̅t
IIII . car̅ . 7 IIII . bord 7 I . cot . 7 v . serui . Ibi . IIII . mold de . LXX . sot .
7 XXI . ac p̅ti . 7 XL . ac pasturæ . 7 Silua . x . porc .
Hi . II . solins T.R.E . fuer̅ . II . M̅ . Vnu̅ tenuit Herold . 7 aliu̅
Brixi . 7 m̅ sunt in uno . T.R.E 7 post . | ualebã . VIII . lib .
7 modo appciant . XII . lib .

Haimo ten de epo ALTEHA . p uno solin 7 dim se desd . Tra
e̅ XII . car̅ . In dn̅io sunt . II . car̅ . 7 XL . II . uitti cu̅ . XII . bord
hn̅t . XI . car̅ . Ibi . IX . serui . 7 XXII . ac p̅ti . Silua . L . porc
T.R.E . ualeb . XVI . lib . Qdo recep̅ . XII . lib . 7 m̅ . XX . lib .
Aluuold tenuit de rege .

Filius Turaldi de Roucest ten de epo WITENEMERS . p uno
solin se desd . Tra . e̅ . IIII . car̅ . In dn̅io sunt . II . car̅ . 7 XI . uitti
cu̅ . II . cot hn̅t . II . car̅ . Ibi . IIII . ac p̅ti . Silua . XV . porc .
T.R.E . ualeb . c . sot . Qdo recep̅ . IIII . lib . 7 m̅ . c . sot . Anschil
tenuit de rege . E .

Walteri de douuai ten de epo LEE . p dim solin se desd .
Tra . e̅ . IIII . car̅ . In dn̅io sunt . II . car̅ . 7 XI . uitti cu̅ . II . cot
hn̅t . II . car̅ . Ibi . II . serui . 7 v . ac p̅ti . Silua . x . porc . Ӻ de rege .
T.R.E . 7 qdo eps recep̅ . ual . III . lib . Modo . c . sot . Aluuin tenuit

Witts filius Ogerii ten de epo CERLETONE . p uno solin
se desd . Tra . e̅ . v . car̅ . In dn̅io e̅ . I . car̅ . 7 XIII . uitti hn̅t . III .
car̅ . Ibi . II . serui . 7 VIII . ac p̅ti . Silua . v . porc .
T.R.E . 7 post . 7 modo . ual . VII . lib . Hanc tra̅ tenuer̅
de rege . II . frs p . II . maneriis . Goduin 7 Aluuard .

Isd Witts ten de epo CRAI .   IN HELMESTREI HVND .
p dimid solin se desd . Tra . e̅   In dn̅io . e̅ una car̅ .
7 VIII . uitti cu̅ . I . car̅ 7 dimid . 7 IIII . cot . 7 I . moli̅ de . x . solid .

In the Half-Lathe of SUTTON

In GREENWICH Hundred

29   The Bishop of Lisieux holds GREENWICH from the Bishop
of Bayeux. It answers for 2 sulungs. Land for ... In lordship 2
ploughs.
>   24 villagers have 4 ploughs; 4 smallholders, 1 cottager
>   and 5 slaves.
>   4 mills at 70s; meadow, 22 acres; pasture, 40 acres;
>   woodland, 10 pigs.

These 2 sulungs were two manors before 1066. Earl Harold
held one, Brictsi the other; now they are in one.
Value together before 1066 and later £8; now they are
assessed at £12.

30   Hamo the Sheriff holds ELTHAM from the Bishop. It answers
for 1½ sulungs. Land for 12 ploughs. In lordship 2 ploughs.
>   42 villagers with 12 smallholders have 11 ploughs.
>   9 slaves; meadow, 22 acres; woodland, 50 pigs.

Value before 1066 £16; when acquired £12; now £20.
Alfwold held it from the King.

31   Thorold of Rochester's son holds WRICKLESMARSH from the Bishop.
It answers for 1 sulung. Land for 4 ploughs. In lordship 2 ploughs.
>   11 villagers with 2 cottagers have 2 ploughs.
>   Meadow, 4 acres; woodland, 15 pigs.

Value before 1066, 100s; when acquired £4; now 100s.
Askell held it from King Edward.

32   Walter of Douai holds LEE from the Bishop. It answers for
½ sulung. Land for 4 ploughs. In lordship 2 ploughs.
>   11 villagers with 2 cottagers have 2 ploughs.
>   2 slaves; meadow, 5 acres; woodland, 10 pigs.

Value before 1066 and when the Bishop acquired it £3; now 100s.
Alwin held it from the King.

33   William son of Odger holds CHARLTON from the Bishop.
It answers for 1 sulung. Land for 5 ploughs. In lordship 1 plough.
>   13 villagers have 3 ploughs.
>   2 slaves; meadow, 8 acres; woodland, 5 pigs.

Value before 1066, later and now £7.
>   Two brothers, Godwin and Alfward, held this land as two

manors from the King.

In RUXLEY Hundred

34   William also holds (Foots) CRAY from the Bishop. It answers
for ½ sulung. Land for ... In lordship 1 plough;
>   8 villagers with 1½ ploughs and 4 cottagers.

Ibi . uñ ſerů . 7 ſilua . vi . porc . T.R.E. ualeb . iiii . lib . 7 poſt:/
iii . lib . Modo:/ iiii . lib . Goduin tenuit de rege . E.

Anſchitill ten de epo CROCTVNE . p uno ſolin 7 uno jugo
ſe defđ . Tra . ē   In dñio nichil . ē . ſed . iii . uilli 7 iiii . borđ
ibi ſunt.

T.R.E. 7 poſt ualebat . c . ſolid 7 m̃ . vi . lib . Aluuin tenuit
hanc tr̃a de rege . E . p duobʒ c̃o).

Giſlebt maminot ten de epo CODEHA . p . iiii . ſolins ſe defđ.
Tra . ē . x . car̃ . In dñio ſunt . iiii . 7 xv . uilli cũ . vi . borđ hñt
vi . car̃ . Ibi æccła . 7 xi . ſerui . 7 ii . molini de . xiiii . ſolid . 7 ii .
denar̃ . Silua . xl . porc . T.R.E. ualeb . xx . lib . 7 poſt:/ xvi .
lib . Modo:/ xxiiii . lib.

Iſđe Giſlebt ten de epo CHESTAN . p dimiđ ſolin ſe defđ.
Tra . ē   In dñio . ē . i . car̃ . 7 iiii . uilli cũ . i . car̃ . Ibi ſilua
. v . porc . T.R.E. 7 poſt:/ ualeb . lx . ſol . Modo:/ xl . ſolid.
Sberne biga tenuit de rege . E.

Hugo nepos herbti ten de epo SENTLINGE . p uno ſolin
7 dim ſe defđ . Tra . ē   In dñio ſunt . ii . car̃ . 7 xx . uilli
cũ . ii . car̃ . Ibi æccła 7 ix . ſerui . 7 vi . ãc p̃ti . 7 xx . ãc paſturæ.
Silua . viii . porc . T.R.E. ualeb . viii . lib . 7 poſt:/ vi . lib.
Modo:/ viii . lib . Bonde tenuit de Archiepo.

Anſgot de Rouec ten de epo BACHEHA . IN BRVNLEI HD.
p . ii . ſolins ſe defđ . Tra . ē . viii . car̃ . In dñio ſunt . ii . 7 xxii.
uilli cũ . viii . borđ hñt . viii . car̃ 7 dimiđ . Ibi . xii . ãc p̃ti.
7 iiii . ſerui . 7 uñ molđ . 7 ſilua . lx . porc .   ſ de rege . E.
T.R.E. 7 poſt:/ ualeb . ix . lib . Modo:/ xiii . lib . Anſchil tenuit

1 mill at 10s. 1 slave; woodland, 6 pigs.
Value before 1066 £4; later £3; now £4.
   Godwin Foot held it from King Edward.

35   Ansketel holds CROFTON from the Bishop. It answers for 1
sulung and 1 yoke. Land for ... In lordship nothing but
   3 villagers and 4 smallholders are there.
Value before 1066 and later 100s; now £6.
   Alwin held this land from King Edward as two manors.

36   Gilbert Maminot holds CUDHAM from the Bishop. It answers
for 4 sulungs. Land for 10 ploughs. In lordship 4.
   15 villagers with 6 smallholders have 6 ploughs.
   A church; 11 slaves; 2 mills at 14s 2d; woodland, 40 pigs.
Value before 1066 £20; later £16; now £24.

37   Gilbert also holds KESTON from the Bishop. It answers
for ½ sulung. Land for ... In lordship 1 plough;
   4 villagers with 1 plough.
   Woodland, 5 pigs.
Value before 1066 and later 60s; now 40s.
   Esbern Big held it from King Edward.

38   Hugh nephew of Herbert holds SANDLINGS from the Bishop.
It answers for 1½ sulungs. Land for ... In lordship 2 ploughs;
   20 villagers with 2 ploughs.
   A church; 9 slaves; meadow, 6 acres; pasture, 20 acres;
     woodland, 8 pigs.
Value before 1066 £8; later £6; now £8.
   Bondi held it from the Archbishop.

In BROMLEY Hundred
39   Ansgot of Rochester holds BECKENHAM from the Bishop.
It answers for 2 sulungs. Land for 8 ploughs. In lordship 2.
   22 villagers with 8 smallholders have 8½ ploughs
   Meadow, 12 acres; 4 slaves; a mill; woodland, 60 pigs.
Value before 1066 and later £9; now £13.
   Askell held it from King Edward.

Adā teñ de epo *Leleburne* . p̄ . ii . ſolins ſe defd̄ . Tra . ē

In dñio ſunt . iii . car . 7 xvi . uiłłi cū . ii . borđ

hñt . vii . car . Ibi æccła 7 x . ſerui . 7 uñ moliñ de . vii . ſolid̄ .

7 xii . ac p̄ti . Silua . l . porc . T.R.E. ualeb . viii . łib .

Q̄do recep̄. vii . lib . Modo. viii . lib . Ricard de Tonebrige

teñ in ſua Leuua . q̄d̄ uał . xxiiii . ſoł . Rex teñ p̄ ñouo

dono epi q̄d̄ uał . xxiiii . ſolid̄ 7 ii . deñ . Hoc ℳ tenuit

Turgis de Goduino comite.

Anſchitil teñ de epo *Elentun* . p̄ uno ſolin ſe defd̄ .

Tra . ē . iii . car . In dñio ſunt . ii . 7 xv . uiłłi cū. ii . borđ hñt

. i . car 7 dimid̄ . Ibi æccła 7 ii . ſerui . 7 dimid̄ moliñ 7 una

dena de . xv . ſoł . Silua . viii . porc . 7 una ac p̄ti .

T.R.E. ualeb . c . ſoł . Q̄do recep̄. lx . ſoł . Modo. c . ſolid̄ .

Vluric tenuit de Alnod cilt.

Haimo teñ de epo *Dictune* . p̄ uno ſolin ſe defd̄ . Tra . ē

iiii . car . In dñio ſunt . ii . 7 xx . uiłłi cū . v . borđ hñt . iii . car .

Ibi æccła 7 vi . ſerui . 7 uñ moliñ de . x . ſolid̄ . 7 viii . ac p̄ti .

7 xxx.v . ac paſturæ . Silua . vi . porc . T.R.E. ualeb . viii .

łib . Q̄do recep̄. c . ſoł . Modo. viii . lib . Sbern tenuit

de rege . E.

Uttalis teñ de epo *Sifletone* . p̄ . iii . jugis ſe defd̄ .

Tra . ē . i . car . In dñio . i . car 7 dimid̄ . 7 vi . uiłłi cū uno

borđ hñt dim car .   Ibi . vi . ſerui . 7 i . moliñ de . x .

ſolid̄.

Ibi . x . ac p̄ti . 7 xxx . ac paſturæ .

T.R.E. ualeb . xl . ſoł . Q̄do recep̄. iiii . lib . Modo.

c . ſolid̄ . Hanc tenuer T.R.E. duo hoēs in para

gio . Leuuiñ 7 Vluuiñ . 7 potuer cū tra ſua

ſe uertere quo uoluer.

In the Lathe of AYLESFORD

In LARKFIELD HUNDRED

40 Adam holds LEYBOURNE from the Bishop. It answers for 2 sulungs. Land for ... In lordship 3 ploughs.

16 villagers with 2 smallholders have 7 ploughs.

A church; 10 slaves; a mill at 7s; meadow, 12 acres; woodland, 50 pigs.

Value before 1066 £8; when acquired £7; now £8. Richard of Tonbridge holds in his territory what is valued at 24s. The King holds as a new gift from the Bishop what is valued at 24s 2d.

Thorgils held this manor from Earl Godwin.

41 Ansketel holds ALLINGTON from the Bishop. It answers for 1 sulung. Land for 3 ploughs. In lordship 2.

15 villagers with 2 smallholders have 1½ ploughs.

A church; 2 slaves; ½ mill; 1 pig pasture at 15s; woodland, 8 pigs; meadow, 1 acre.

Value before 1066, 100s; when acquired 60s; now 100s.

Wulfric held it from Young Alnoth.

42 Hamo the Sheriff holds DITTON from the Bishop. It answers for 1 sulung. Land for 4 ploughs. In lordship 2.

20 villagers with 5 smallholders have 3 ploughs.

A church; 6 slaves; a mill at 10s; meadow, 8 acres; pasture, 35 acres; woodland, 6 pigs.

Value before 1066 £8; when acquired 100s; now £8.

Esbern held it from King Edward.

43 Vitalis holds SIFFLETON from the Bishop. It answers for 3 yokes. Land for 1 plough. In lordship 1½ ploughs.

6 villagers with 1 smallholder have ½ plough.

6 slaves; 1 mill at 10s. Meadow, 10 acres; pasture, 30 acres. 7 b

Value before 1066, 40s; when acquired £4; now 100s.

Before 1066 two men, Leofwin and Wulfwin, held this land jointly and could go where they would with their land.

Radulf fili Turoldi ten de epo *AIGLESSA* . p . III . jugis
se defd . Tra . e̅   In dn̅io . e̅ . I car . 7 VII . uilli cu̅ . XIIII .
bord hn̅t . I . car . Ibi . I . seru . 7 XI . ac p̅ti . Silua . x . porc .
T . R . E . 7 post. ualeb . III . lib . Modo . IIII . lib .
Ricard qd ten in sua Leuua. xv . den . Rex . VI . solid
7 v . den p nouo dono epi . 7 in Rouecest habuit eps
III . domos de xxxi . denar . q̅s cepit de isto M̅ in | manu.
Hoc M̅ tenuit Alnod cilt.

Hugo de port ten de epo *PELLESORDE* . p dimid
solin se defd . Tra . e̅   In dn̅io . e̅ . I . car . 7 un uills
cu̅ . IIII . bord hn̅t . III . boues . Ibi æccla 7 II . serui .
7 v . ac p̅ti . 7 una ac pasturæ . T . R . E . ualeb . xx . sol.
Q̅do recep. xxx . sol . Modo. xL . sol.
Godric tenuit de rege . E.

Isde̅ Hugo ten de epo *RIESCE* . p . II . solins 7 dim
se defd . Tra . e̅ . v . car . In dn̅io sunt . II . 7 x . uilli cu̅
II . bord hn̅t . III . car . Ibi æccla 7 x . serui . 7 I . molin
de . x . sol . 7 IX . ac p̅ti . Silua . v . porc . T . R . E . ualeb
VIII . lib . Q̅do recep. c . sol . Modo . vi . lib . Alurie
tenuit de rege . E.

Isde̅ Hugo ten de epo *OFEHA* . p uno solin se defd .
Tra . e̅ . III . car . In dn̅io nichil . Ibi . vi . uilli cu̅ . I . bord
hn̅t . II . car . Ibi . I . molin de . L . den . 7 III . serui . 7 IIII .
ac p̅ti . Silua . x . porc . T . R . E . ualeb . xL . sol . Q̅do
recep. xx . sol . Modo. xxx . sol . Godric tenuit de rege . E

Rannulf de Colu̅bels ten de epo *ESSEDENE* .
p uno solin se defd . Tra . e̅ .   In dn̅io . e̅ una car .
7 xix . uilli cu̅ . III . bord hn̅t . III . car . Ibi . III . serui .
7 VIII . ac p̅ti . T . R . E . ual . III . lib . Q̅do recep . IIII . lib .
Modo . v . lib . Leuuin tenuit.

7 b

44 Ralph son of Thorold holds ECCLES from the Bishop. It answers
for 3 yokes. Land for ... In lordship 1 plough.
   7 villagers with 14 smallholders have 1 plough.
   1 slave; meadow, 11 acres; woodland, 10 pigs.
Value before 1066 and later £3; now £4; what Richard holds
in his territory 15d; (what) the King (holds) 8s 5d as a new
gift from the Bishop.
   In Rochester the Bishop had 3 houses at 31d which he took
into his own hand from that manor.
   Young Alnoth held this manor.

45 Hugh of Port holds PADDLESWORTH from the Bishop. It answers
for ½ sulung. Land for ... In lordship 1 plough.
   1 villager with 4 smallholders have 3 oxen.
   A church; 2 slaves; meadow, 5 acres; pasture, 1 acre.
Value before 1066, 20s; when acquired, 30s; now 40s.
   Godric held it from King Edward.

46 Hugh also holds RYARSH from the Bishop. It answers for 2½
sulungs.Land for 5 ploughs. In lordship 2.
   10 villagers with 2 smallholders have 3 ploughs.
   A church; 10 slaves; 1 mill at 10s; meadow, 9 acres;
      woodland, 5 pigs.
Value before 1066 £8; when acquired, 100s; now £6.
   Aelfric held it from King Edward.

47 Hugh also holds OFFHAM from the Bishop. It answers for 1
sulung. Land for 3 ploughs. Nothing in lordship.
   6 villagers with 1 smallholder have 2 ploughs.
   1 mill at 50d; 3 slaves; meadow, 4 acres; woodland, 10 pigs.
Value before 1066, 40s; when acquired, 20s; now 30s.
   Godric held it from King Edward.

48 Ranulf of Colombières holds NASHENDEN from the Bishop.
It answers for 1 sulung. Land for ... In lordship 1 plough.
   19 villagers with 3 smallholders have 3 ploughs.
   3 slaves; meadow, 8 acres.
Value before 1066 £3; when acquired, £4; now £5.
   Earl Leofwin held it.

Rotbt Latin teñ ad firmã de Rege *TOTINTVNE*.

de nouo dono epi baioc . ᵽ dim folin fe defd . Tra . ē

uni car 7 dim . In dñio . ē una . 7 iii . uilti cũ . ix . bord

hñt dim car . Ibi . iiii . ferui . 7 v . ac ᵽti . Silua . ii . porc.

T . R . E . ualeb . xxx . fol . Qdo recep: xx . fol . Modo . xl . fol.

Vlnod tenuit de rege . E.

Ifdē Rotbt teñ In Totintune ad firmã de rege . i . jugũ.

7 iftud . ē de nouo dono epi baioc . 7 ibi nil . ē nifi . ii . ac

ᵽti . Val 7 ualuit fep . x . fol . Goduin tenuit de rege . E.

Radulf fili Turaldi teñ de epo *EDDINTVNE* . ᵽ . ii . folins

fe defd | Tra . ē . v . car . In dñio funt . ii . 7 vi . uilti cũ

. ix . bord hñt . i . car . Ibi æccla 7 x . ferui . 7 ii . molini

de . xi . folid 7 ii . den . 7 xii . ac ᵽti . Silua . x . porc.

T . R . E . ualeb . viii . lib . Qdo recep: c . fol . Modo: vi . lib.

Agelred tenuit de rege . E.

7 c

Radulf fili Turoldi . teñ de epo *IN TOLLENTREV HD*.

MELETVNE . ᵽ uno folin 7 iii . jugis fe defd . Tra . ē . iiii.

car . In dñio . ē una . 7 xxi . uilts cũ . ii . bord hñt . ii . car.

Ibi æccla . 7 i . moliñ de xlix . den . 7 Heda de xx . folid.

7 iii . ferui . T . R . E . ualeb . iiii . lib . 7 poft: iii . lib . Modo.

vi . lib . Ricard qd teñ in fua Leuua: v . fol in una filua.

Ifdē Radulf teñ de epo ⌐ Leuuin com tenuit.

LEDESDVNE . ᵽ ii . folins 7 dimidio . 7 dim jugo fe defd.

Tra . ē . vi . car . In dñio funt . ii . 7 xvii . uilti cũ . iiii . bord

hñt . v . car . Ibi æccla 7 i . feruus . 7 iii . ac ᵽti 7 dimid.

Silua . xx . porc . T . R . E . ualeb . vi . lib . 7 poft: c . folid.

Modo . viii . lib . Ricard qd ht in fua Leuua: xx . den.

Eps teñ in fua manu jnt ciuitatē Rouceft . iiii.

dom ad hoc ɔ̃ ptiñ . de quibɀ ht . ix . fol 7 x . deñ.

49 Robert Latimer holds TOTTINGTON at a revenue from the King by a new gift of the Bishop of Bayeux. It answers for ½ sulung. Land for 1½ ploughs. In lordship 1.
   3 villagers with 9 smallholders have ½ plough.
   4 slaves; meadow, 5 acres; woodland, 2 pigs.
   Value before 1066, 30s; when acquired, 20s; now 40s.
   Wulfnoth held it from King Edward.

50 Robert also holds 1 yoke in TOTTINGTON at a revenue from the King, that is by a new gift from the Bishop of Bayeux. There is nothing there except
   meadow, 2 acres.
   The value is and always was 10s.
   Godwin held it from King Edward.

51 Ralph son of Thorold holds ADDINGTON from the Bishop.
   It answers for 2½ sulungs. Land for 5 ploughs. In lordship 2.
   6 villagers with 9 smallholders have 1 plough.
   A church; 10 slaves; 2 mills at 11s 2d; meadow, 12 acres;
      woodland, 10 pigs.
   Value before 1066 £8; when acquired, 100s; now £6.
   Aethelred held it from King Edward.

In TOLTINGTROUGH Hundred   7 c
52 Ralph son of Thorold holds MILTON from the Bishop. It answers for 1 sulung and 3 yokes. Land for 4 ploughs. In lordship 1.
   21 villagers with 2 smallholders have 2 ploughs.
   A church; 1 mill at 49d; an enclosure at 20s; 3 slaves.
   Value before 1066 £4; later £3; now £6; what Richard holds in his territory in a wood, 5s.
   Earl Leofwin held it.

53 Ralph also holds LUDDESDOWN from the Bishop. It answers for 2½ sulungs and ½ yoke. Land for 6 ploughs. In lordship 2.
   17 villagers with 4 smallholders have 5 ploughs.
   A church; 1 slave; meadow, 3½ acres; woodland, 20 pigs.
   Value before 1066 £6; later 100s; now £8; what Richard has in his territory 20d.
   The Bishop holds 4 houses in his hand in the City of Rochester which belong to this manor, from which he has 9s 10d.
   Earl Leofwin held it.

Herbt̃ fili̾ Iuonis ten̄ de ep̃o GRAVESHAⁱ. ⌐ Leuuin̄ ten̄

ꝑ ıı . ſolins 7 uno jugo ſe defđ . Tra̅ . e̅ . ıııı . car̄ . In dñio

eſt una . 7 ıııı . uiłłi cū vııı . ſeruis hñt . ıı . boues . Ibi æccła

7 ı . heda . T . R . E . ualeb̃ . x . lib̃ . Q̨do recep̄ꞏ t̅ntđ . Modo .

xı . lib̃ . Hoc ꝳ fuer̄ ıı̅ı̅ . ꝳ T . R . E . Leuric 7 Vluuin̄

7 Goduin̄ tenuer̄ . Nc̄ eſt in unū.

W̅adarđ ten̄ de ep̃o NOTESTEDE . ꝑ ıı . ſolins ſe

defđ . Tra̅ . e̅ . ıı . car̄ . In dñio . e̅ una . 7 ibi . ıııı . borđ . 7 æccła .

7 ıııı . ſerui . Silua . ııı . porc̄ . T . R . E . ualeb̃ . ıııı . lib̃ .

Q̨do recep̄ꞏ ııı . lib̃ . Modo . v . lib̃ . Vlſtan tenuit de rege . E.

A̅nſchitil̄ ten̄ de ep̃o OFEHAⁱ IN LAVROCHESFEL HĐ.

ꝑ uno ſolin̄ ſe defđ Tra̅ . e̅   In dñio . e̅ . ı . car̄ . 7 vı .

uiłłi cū . ıı . borđ hñt . ı . car̄ . Ibi . ıııı . ſerui . 7 ı . molin̄

de . x . ſoł . 7 vıı . ac̄ p̃ti . Silua . x . porc̄ . 7 in ciuitate

Rouec̄ . ı . dom̄ reddens . xxx . den̄ . T . R . E . ualeb̃ ꝳ

c . ſoł . Q̨do recep̄ꞏ ıııı . lib̃ . Modo . ıııı . lib̃ 7 ıx . ſolid̄ .

Ricarđ de Tonebrige qđ ten̄ꞏ xı . ſoł ual . Vluric

tenuit de Alnod cilt.

R̅adulf̄ de Curbeſpine ten̄ de ep̃o BERLINGE.

ꝑ . vı . ſolins ſe defđ . Tra̅ . e̅ .   In dñio . e̅ una car̄ .

7 x . uiłłi cū xıııı . borđ hñt . vı . car̄ . Ibi æccła . 7 vı .

ſerui . 7 ı . molin̄ de . x . ſoł . 7 ccc . 7 xxx . anguiłł . 7 piſcaria

de . ʟx . anguiłł . Ibi . xıı . ac̄ p̃ti . 7 paſtura . ʟ . animalib̃ .

Silua . xʟ . porc̄ . T . R . E . ualeb̃ . xıı . lib̃ . Q̨do recep̄ꞏ

vı . lib̃ . Modoꞏ xıı . lib̃ . Sbern biga tenuit de rege . E.

I̅ſđe̅ Radulf̄ ten̄ de ep̃o BORHAM . ꝑ . vı . ſolins ſe

defđ . Tra̅ . e̅ . vııı . car̄ . In dñio ſunt . ıı . 7 xv . uiłłi cū

xx . borđ hñt . vı . car̄ . Ibi æccła 7 vıı . ſerui . 7 ı . molin̄

de . vı . ſoł . 7 x . ac̄ p̃ti . Silua . xx . porc̄ .

T . R . E . ualeb̃ . x . lib̃ . 7 qdo recep̄ꞏ t̅ntđ . Modoꞏ xıı . lib̃ .

54 Herbert son of Ivo holds GRAVESEND from the Bishop. It answers
for 2 sulungs and 1 yoke. Land for 4 ploughs. In lordship 1.
  4 villagers with 8 slaves have 2 oxen.
  A church; 1 enclosure.
Value before 1066 £10; when acquired as much; now £11.
  Before 1066 this manor was three manors. Leofric, Wulfwin
and Godwin held them. Now it is in one.

55 Wadard holds NURSTEAD from the Bishop. It answers for 2
sulungs. Land for 2 ploughs. In lordship 1.
  4 smallholders.
  A church; 4 slaves; woodland, 3 pigs.
Value before 1066 £4; when acquired £3; now £5.
  Wulfstan held it from King Edward.

In LARKFIELD Hundred

56 Ansketel holds OFFHAM from the Bishop; It answers for 1
sulung. Land for ... In lordship 1 plough.
  6 villagers with 2 smallholders have 1 plough.
  4 slaves; 1 mill at 10s; meadow, 7 acres; woodland, 10 pigs.
  In the City of Rochester 1 house which pays 30d.
Value of the manor before 1066, 100s; when acquired £4;
now £4 9s. Value of what Richard of Tonbridge holds 11s.
  Wulfric held it from Young Alnoth.

57 Ralph of Courbépine holds BIRLING from the Bishop. It
answers for 6 sulungs. Land for ... In lordship 1 plough.
  10 villagers with 14 smallholders have 6 ploughs.
  A church; 6 slaves; 1 mill at 10s and 330 eels; a fishery
    at 60 eels. Meadow, 12 acres; pasture for 50 cattle;
    woodland, 40 pigs.
Value before 1066 £12; when acquired £6; now £12.
  Esbern Big held it from King Edward.

58 Ralph also holds BURHAM from the Bishop. It answers
for 6 sulungs. Land for 8 ploughs. In lordship 2.
  15 villagers with 20 smallholders have 6 ploughs.
  A church; 7 slaves; 1 mill at 6s; meadow, 10 acres;
    woodland, 20 pigs.
Value before 1066 £10; when acquired as much; now £12.

Eps de Roueceſt ht domos de h· ꟽ. 7 ual . vii . ſolid.

Hoc ꟽ tenuit Leuuin   *IN LITEFELLE HVND.*

Corbin ten de epo *PECHEHÃ* . ꝑ . ii . ſolins ſe defd.

Tra . e . vi . car . In dnio . e una . 7 xii . uiłłi hnt . v . car.

7 viii . bord 7 v . ſerui . 7 iii . ãc ꝑti . Silua . x . porc . T.R.E.

7 poſt: ualeb xii . lib . Modo: viii . lib . Rex ht de h· ꟽ

|7 taɱ redd . xii . lib. |

tres denas . ubi maneꝗ . iiii . uiłłi . 7 ual . xl . ſol . Leuuin tenuit.

Ricard de Tonebrige ten de epo *HASLOW* . ꝑ . vi . ſolins ſe defd.

Tra . e . xii . car . In dnio ſunt . iii . 7 xlvii . uiłłi cu . xv . bord

hnt . xv . car . Ibi æccła 7 . x . ſerui . 7 ii . molini de . xi . ſolid.

7 xii . piſcariæ de . vii . ſolid 7 vi . den . 7 xii . ãc ꝑti . Silua . lx.

porc . T.R.E. 7 poſt . 7 modo . ual . xxx . lib . Eddeuã tenuit de rege.

Radulf fili Turoldi ten de epo dimid ſolin In *ESTOCHINGE*

BERGE . T.R.E. tenuer . ii . libi hoes 7 ɱ ſimilit . 7 ual . xx . ſol.

IN LEST DE ELESFORD .   *IN WACHELESTAN HVND.*

Ricard de Tonebrige ten de epo *TIVEDELE* . ꝑ uno jugo ſe.

defd . Tra . e . i . car . 7 ibi . e in dnio . 7 æccła . 7 Silua . ii . porc.

Val 7 ualuit ſep . xv . ſol . Eddeua tenuit de rege.

Hugo nepos Herbti ten de epo   *IN AIHORDE HVND.*

HARIARDESHAM . ꝑ . ii . ſolins ſe defd . Tra . e . vi . car . In dnio

xviii . uiłłi cu . x . bord hnt . iiii . car . Ibi æccła

7 xi . ſerui . 7 ii . molini de xi . ſolid 7 vi . den . 7 vii . ãc ꝑti.

Silua . xv . porc . T.R.E: ualeb . x . lib . Qdo recep: viii . lib.

Modo: x . lib . Oſuuard tenuit de rege . E.

Iſdẽ Hugo ten de epo *FEREBVRNE* . ꝑ uno ſolin ſe defd.

Tra . e . ii . car . In dnio   iiii . uiłłi cu . i . car 7 dimid.

7 ii . molini de . xl . den . T.R.E. ualeb . iiii . lib . Poſt 7 ɱ: iii . lib.

Aluuin tenuit de Goduino.

The Bishop of Rochester has houses from this manor; value 7s.
Earl Leofwin held this manor.

In LITTLEFIELD Hundred

59   Corbin holds (West) PECKHAM from the Bishop. It answers for 2
sulungs. Land for 6 ploughs. In lordship 1.
    12 villagers have 5 ploughs; 8 smallholders and 5 slaves.
    Meadow, 3 acres; woodland, 10 pigs.
Value before 1066 and later £12; now £8; however, it pays £12.
    From this manor the King has 3 pig pastures where 4 villagers
live; value 40s. Earl Leofwin held this manor.   7 d

60   Richard of Tonbridge holds HADLOW from the Bishop. It answers
for 6 sulungs. Land for 12 ploughs. In lordship 3.
    47 villagers with 15 smallholders have 15 ploughs.
    A church; 10 slaves; 2 mills at 11s; 12 fisheries at 7s 6d;
        meadow, 12 acres; woodland, 60 pigs.
Value before 1066, later and now £30.
    Edeva held it from King Edward.

61   Ralph son of Thorold holds ½ sulung in 'STOKENBURY' from the
Bishop. Before 1066 2 free men held it; now likewise.
Value 20s.

In the Lathe of AYLESFORD

In WASHLINGSTONE Hundred

62   Richard of Tonbridge holds TUDELEY from the Bishop. It answers
for 1 yoke. Land for 1 plough. It is there, in lordship.
    A church; woodland, 2 pigs.
The value is and always was 15s.
    Edeva held it from the King.

In EYEHORNE Hundred

63   Hugh nephew of Herbert holds HARRIETSHAM from the Bishop.
It answers for 2 sulungs. Land for 6 ploughs. In lordship ...
    18 villagers with 10 smallholders have 4 ploughs.
    A church; 11 slaves; 2 mills at 11s 6d; meadow, 7 acres;
        woodland, 15 pigs.
Value before 1066 £10; when acquired £8; now £10.
    Osward held it from King Edward.

64   Hugh also holds FAIRBOURNE from the Bishop. It answers for
1 sulung. Land for 2 ploughs. In lordship ...;
    4 villagers with 1½ ploughs.
    2 mills at 40d.
Value before 1066 £4; later and now £3.
    Alwin held it from Earl Godwin.

Iſdē Hugo teñ de epo . I . jugū liberæ træ in SELESBVRNE.

7 ibi h̄ dimid caȓ cū . I . bord 7 v . ſeruis . 7 una aȓ p̄ti 7 dim.

Val 7 ualuit ſep . xx . ſol . Aluuin tenuit de Goduino comite.

Iſdē Hugo 7 Adelold camerari teñ de epo FREDENESTEDE.

p̄ uno ſolin ſe defd . Tra . ē . III . caȓ . In dñio   III . uiłłi

hñt . VII . boues . Ibi æccła 7 II . aȓ p̄ti 7 dimid . 7 ſiłua . II . porc.

Val 7 ualuit ſep . xx . ſol . Leuuin tenuit de rege . E.

Adelold teñ epo ESLEDES . p̄ . III . ſolins ſe defd . Tra . ē

XII . caȓ . In dñio ſunt . II . caȓ . 7 xxviii . uiłłi cū . viii . bord

hñt . VII . caȓ . Ibi æccła 7 xviii . ſerui . Ibi . II . Arpendi uineæ

7 viii . aȓ p̄ti . Silua . xx . porc . 7 v . molini uillanoȝ.

T.R.E . uałeƀ . xvi . liƀ . Similit qdo recep̄ʼ Modo . xx . liƀ.

7 tam̄ reddit . xxv . liƀ.   Leuuin tenuit.

De hoc M̄ hȓ abƀ S̄ Auguſtini dimid ſolin . qd ual . x . ſol.

p̄ excābio parchi epi ƀaioc . Comes de Ow hȓ . IIII . denas.

de iſto M̄ . quæ ual . xx . ſolid.

Anſgot de Roueceſt teñ de epo AVDINTONE . p̄ . II . ſolins

ſe defd . Tra . ē . III . caȓ 7 dimid . In dñio ſunt . II . 7 VII . uiłłi cū . v.

bord hñt . I . caȓ 7 dim̄ . Ibi æccła 7 IIII . ſerui . 7 vi . aȓ p̄ti . 7 I . moliñ

de . IIII . ſol 7 II . den . Silua . x . porc . T.R.E . 7 poſtʼ ualuit . IIII . liƀ.

Modo . vii . liƀ . Goduin 7 Aluuin tenueȓ de rege E . p̄ . II . M̄.

Iſdē Anſgot teñ de epo STOCHINGEBERGE . p̄ . II . ſolins ſe defd.

Tra . ē   In dñio . ē . I . caȓ . 7 v . uiłłi cū ix . bord hñt . II.

caȓ . Ibi æccła 7 II . ſerui . 7 I . moliñ de . LXIIII . deñ . Silua . xv . porc.

T.R.E . 7 poſt . ualuit . IIII . liƀ . Modo . vi . liƀ . Elueua tenuit de rege . E.

Hugo de Port teñ de ALNOITONE . p̄ . III . ſolins ſe defd . Tra . ē

viii . caȓ . In dñio ſunt . II . caȓ . 7 xviii . uiłłi cū . vi . bord hñt

vi . caȓ . Ibi æccła . 7 viii . ſerui .   7 II . molini 7 dim̄ de . xvii.

                                                     ſolid.

Ibi . v . aȓ p̄ti . Silua . xl . porc . T.R.E . uałeƀ . ix . liƀ . 7 tn̄td

qdo recep̄ . Modo . x . liƀ . 7 tam̄ reddit . xii . liƀ.

65 Hugh also holds 1 yoke of free land in SHELBOROUGH from the
Bishop. He has ½ plough, with
   1 smallholder and 5 slaves.
   Meadow, 1½ acres.
The value is and always was 20s.
   Alwin held it from Earl Godwin.

66 Hugh and Aethelwold the Chamberlain also hold FRINSTED from
the Bishop. It answers for 1 sulung. Land for 3 ploughs.
In lordship ...
   3 villagers have 7 oxen.
   A church; meadow, 2½ acres; woodland, 2 pigs.
The value is and always was 20s.
   Leofwin held it from King Edward.

67 Aethelwold holds LEEDS from the Bishop. It answers for 3
sulungs. Land for 12 ploughs. In lordship 2 ploughs.
   28 villagers with 8 smallholders have 7 ploughs.
   A church; 18 slaves. 2 arpents of vines; meadow, 8 acres;
     woodland, 20 pigs, 5 villagers' mills.
Value before 1066 £16; the same when acquired; now £20;
however, it pays £25.
   Earl Leofwin held it.
From this manor the Abbot of St. Augustine's has ½ sulung,
in exchange for the Bishop of Bayeux's park, value 10s. The
Count of Eu has 4 pig pastures of this manor, value 20s.

68 Ansgot of Rochester holds ALDINGTON from the Bishop. It
answers for 2 sulungs. Land for 3½ ploughs. In lordship 2.
   7 villagers with 5 smallholders have 1½ ploughs.
   A church; 4 slaves; meadow, 6 acres; 1 mill at 4s 2d;
     woodland, 10 pigs.
Value before 1066 and later £4; now £7.
   Godwin and Alwin held it from King Edward as two manors.

69 Ansgot also holds STOCKBURY from the Bishop. It answers
for 2 sulungs. Land for ... In lordship 1 plough.
   5 villagers with 9 smallholders have 2 ploughs.
   A church; 2 slaves; 1 mill at 64d; woodland, 15 pigs.
Value before 1066 and later £4; now £6.
   Aelfeva held it from King Edward.

70 Hugh of Port holds ALLINGTON. It answers for 3 sulungs. Land
for 3 sulungs. Land for 8 ploughs. In lordship 2 ploughs.
   18 villagers with 6 smallholders have 6 ploughs.
   A church; 8 slaves; 2½ mills at 17s. Meadow, 5 acres;
     woodland, 40 pigs.
Value before 1066 £9; as much when acquired; now £10;
however, it pays £12.

8 a

Huic ꝯ adjaceꝫ . iii . manſiones t̃ræ in Rouceſtre.

⁊ reddt̃ . v . ſol ꝑ annū . Oſuuard tenuit de rege . E.

Adã fili Hubti teñ de eꝓ SVDTONE . ꝓ . iiii . ſolins ſe defd̃.

T̃ra . ẽ . vii . caɼ . In dñio ſunt . ii . ⁊ xviii . uilti cū v . bord

hñt . iiii . caɼ . Ibi æccła ⁊ iiii . ac p̃ti . ⁊ i . moliñ

Silua . l . porc̃ . T . R . E . ualeƀ . xii . liƀ . Q̃do recep̃. x . liƀ.

Modo. xiiii . liƀ . ⁊ tam̃ reddit . xviii . liƀ . Leuuin tenuit.

Iſdẽ Adã teñ de eꝓ CERTH . ꝓ . iii . ſolins ſe defd̃ . T̃ra . ẽ

viii . caɼ . In dñio . ẽ una . ⁊ xx . uilti cū . v . bord hñt

. vi caɼ . Ibi æccła ⁊ viii . ſerui . ⁊ vi . ac p̃ti . Silua . l . porc̃.

Ibi . iii . arpend uineæ . ⁊ parc ſiluatic beſtiarū.

T . R . E . ⁊ poſt . ⁊ modo. ual . xii . liƀ . Alnod tenuit.

Iſdẽ Adã teñ de eꝓ SVDTONE . ꝓ uno ſolin ⁊ dimid

ſe defd̃ . T̃ra . ẽ . viii . caɼ . In dñio ſunt . ii . ⁊ xv . uilti

cū . ix . bord . hñt . iiii . caɼ . Ibi æccła ⁊ x . ſerui . ⁊ viii . ac

p̃ti . Silua . l . porc̃ . T . R . E . ⁊ poſt. ualeƀ . x . liƀ.

Modo . xii . liƀ . ⁊ tam̃ redd xviii . liƀ . Leuenot tenuit de rege . E.

Iſdẽ Adã teñ de eꝓ BOGELEI . ꝓ . ii . ſolins ſe defd̃.

T̃ra . ẽ . ii . caɼ ⁊ dim̃ . In dñio . ẽ una caɼ . ⁊ ii . uilti cū

ii . bord hñt dimid caɼ . Ibi æccła ⁊ iiii . ſerui . ⁊ i . moliñ

de . v . ſolid . ⁊ vi . ac p̃ti . Silua . xx . porc.

De iſto ꝯ ht̃ uñ hõ Adã uñ ſolin ⁊ uocat Merlea.

⁊ ibi ht̃ . i . caɼ . ⁊ iiii . uiltos cū . i . caɼ . ⁊ ecclam . ⁊ ii.

ſeruos . ⁊ ſiluā . iiii . porc̃ . Turgis tenuit de rege . E.

Totū ꝯ T . R . E . ualeƀ . vi . liƀ . ⁊ poſt. tntd . Modo vii . liƀ.

Iſdẽ Adã teñ de eꝓ LANGVELEI . ꝓ uno ſolin ⁊ dim̃

ſe defd̃ . T̃ra . ẽ . iiii . caɼ . In dñio ſunt . ii . ⁊ vii . uilti cū

v . bord hñt . iii . caɼ . Ibi æccła ⁊ vii . ſerui . ⁊ iii . ac p̃ti.

Silua . xx . v . porc̃ . T . R . E . ualeƀ . lx . ſol . Q̃do recep̃.

l . ſol . Modo. lx . ſolid . Turgis tenuit de rege . E.

To this manor are attached 3 measures of land in Rochester; they pay 5s a year.

Osward held it from King Edward.

71   Adam son of Hubert holds SUTTON (Valence) from the Bishop. It answers for 4 sulungs. Land for 7 ploughs. In lordship 2.

     18 villagers with 5 smallholders have 4 ploughs.

A church; meadow, 4 acres; 1 mill; woodland, 50 pigs.

Value before 1066 £12; when acquired, £10; now £14; however, it pays £18.

Earl Leofwin held it.

Adam also holds from the Bishop

72   CHART (Sutton). It answers for 3 sulungs. Land for 8 ploughs. In lordship 1.

     20 villagers with 5 smallholders have 6 ploughs.

A church; 8 slaves; meadow, 6 acres; woodland, 50 pigs.

     3 *arpents* of vines; a park of wild beasts.

Value before 1066, later and now £12.

Young Alnoth held it.

73   (East) SUTTON. It answers for 1½ sulungs. Land for 8 ploughs. In lordship 2.

     15 villagers with 9 smallholders have 4 ploughs.

A church; 10 slaves; meadow, 8 acres; woodland, 50 pigs.

Value before 1066 and later £10; now £12; however, it pays £18.

Leofnoth held it from King Edward.

74   BOWLEY. It answers for 2 sulungs. Land for 2½ ploughs. In lordship 1 plough.

     2 villagers with 2 smallholders have ½ plough.

A church; 4 slaves; 1 mill at 5s; meadow, 6 acres;

     woodland, 20 pigs.

One man, Adam, has 1 sulung of this manor; it is called Marley. He has 1 plough, and

     4 villagers with1 plough.

A church; 2 slaves; woodland, 4 pigs.

Thorgils held it from King Edward.

Value of the whole manor before 1066 £6; later as much; now £7.

75   LANGLEY. It answers for 1½ sulungs. Land for 4 ploughs. In lordship 2.

     7 villagers with 5 smallholders have 3 ploughs.

A church; 7 slaves; meadow, 3 acres; woodland, 25 pigs.

Value before 1066, 60s; when acquired, 50s; now 60s.

Thorgils held it from King Edward.

Iſdē Adā ten de epo *OTRINGEDENE* . ꝑ dimiđ ſolin

ſe defđ . Tra . ē . ıı . caꝛ . In dñio . ē una . 7 ıı . uiłłi cū . ıııı.

borđ hñt dim caꝛ . Ibi . ıı . ſerui . 7 una ač ꝑti . Silua.

v . porč . T . R . E . 7 poſt . ualuit . x . ſoł . Modo . xxx . ſoł.

Huic ꝳ ꝑtiñ . ıı . manſure trǣ in Cantuaria . de . xıı.

denaꝛ . Aluuarđ tenuit de rege . E . hoc ꝳ .

Iſdē Adā ten de epo *EſſELVE* . ꝑ dimiđ ſolin ſe

defđ . Tra . ē . ı . caꝛ . 7 ibi . ē in dñio . cū uno uiłło 7 uno

borđ . 7 v . ſeruis . Ibi . ıııı . ač ꝑti . Silua . ıııı . porč .

T . R . E . 7 poſt . 7 modo : uał . xx . ſoliđ . Godric tenuit

Wiłłs fili Roḃti ten de epo　　　ꝼ de rege . E .

WEſTſELVE . ꝑ uno ſolin ſe defđ . Tra . ē . ııı . caꝛ

7 dimiđ . In dñio ſunt . ıı . 7 q̃đā francig cū . x . uiłłis

7 ı . borđ . hñt . ı . caꝛ 7 dim . Ibi . v . ſerui . 7 ı . ač ꝑti .

7 uñ moliñ de . xv . den . Silua xv . porč .

T . R . E . 7 poſt . 7 modo : uał . ıııı . liḃ . Eddiđ tenuıt

de rege . E . Huic ꝳ ꝑtineḃ in cantuaria . T . R . E .

una dom . reddeꝭ . xxv . denaꝛ .

8 b

Hugo nepos Herḃti ten de epo *BOLTONE* . ꝑ uno ſoliñ

ſe defđ . Tra . ē . ıı . caꝛ . In dñio nichil . ſed . v . uiłłi

hñt . ı . caꝛ . ibi . 7 ıı . ač ꝑti . Silua . xx . porč . Ibi ǣccła.

T . R . E . 7 poſt : ualeḃ . vııı . liḃ . Modo : vı . liḃ.

Aluuiñ tenuit de Goduino.

Iſdē Hugo ten de epo *GODEſELLE* . ꝑ uno ſolin ſe

defđ . Tra . ē . ıı . caꝛ . In dñio . ē una . 7 v . uiłłi hñt . ı . caꝛ

7 dim . Ibi eccła . 7 ıı . ſerui . 7 ıı . ač ꝑti . 7 ſilua . x . porč.

T . R . E . 7 poſt . 7 modo : uał . ıııı . liḃ . Eduuiñ tenuit

de rege . E . 7 potuit ire cū tra ſua quo uoluit.

Iſdē Hugo ten de epo *WINCHELEſMERE* .

ꝑ dimiđ ſolin ſe defđ . Tra . ē . ı . caꝛ . 7 ibi . ē in dñio

cū . ııı . ſeruıs . 7 ǣccła . 7 ſilua . v . porč . 7 T . R . E . in can

tuaria . ııı . dom ꝑtineḃ huic ꝳ reddĩes . xL . deñ.

76   OTTERDEN. It answers for ½ sulung. Land for 2 ploughs. In lordship 1.
    2 villagers with 4 smallholders have ½ plough.
    2 slaves; meadow, 1 acre; woodland, 5 pigs.
  Value before 2066 and later 10s; now 30s.
    To this manor belong 2 measures of land in Canterbury at 12d.
    Alfward held this manor from King Edward.

77   (Old) SHELVE. It answers for ½ sulung. Land for 1 plough. It is
there in lordship, with
    1 villager, 1 smallholder and 5 slaves.
    Meadow, 4 acres; woodland, 4 pigs.
  Value before 1066, later and now 20s.
    Godric held it from King Edward.

78   William son of Robert holds (New) SHELVE from the Bishop.
It answers for 1 sulung. Land for 3½ ploughs. In lordship 2.
    A Frenchman with 10 villagers and 1 smallholder have 1½ ploughs.
    5 slaves; meadow, 1 acre; a mill at 15d; woodland, 15 pigs.
  Value before 1066, later and now £4.
    Edith held it from King Edward.
    Before 1066 one house in Canterbury which pays 25d belonged
to this manor.

79   Hugh nephew of Herbert holds BOUGHTON (Malherbe) from the   8 b
Bishop It answers for 1 sulung. Land for 2 ploughs. In lordship
nothing, but
    5 villagers have 1 plough there.
    Meadow, 2 acres; woodland, 20 pigs. A church.
  Value before 1066 and later £8; now £6.
    Alwin held it from Earl Godwin.

  Hugh also holds from the Bishop
80   WORMSHILL. It answers for 1 sulung. Land for 2 ploughs.
In lordship 1.
    5 villagers have 1½ ploughs.
    A church; 2 slaves, meadow, 2 acres; woodland, 10 pigs.
  Value before 1066, later and now £4.
    Edwin held it from King Edward and could go with his land
where he would.

81   WICHLING. It answers for ½ sulung. Land for 1 plough. It is there,
in lordship, with
    3 slaves.
    A church; woodland, 5 pigs.
    Before 1066 3 houses in Canterbury which pay 40d belonged
to this manor.

Tot̃ T.R.E. ualeb̃ . c . fot . 7 poſt . 7 modo:ˊ xL . fot.

Vluiet tenuit de rege.E. 7 potuit ire quo libuit.

Iſd̃e Hugo ten̓ de eṗo ESTSELVE . ꝓ dimiđ ſolin

ſe defđ . T̓ra . ē . i . caꝛ̃ . 7 ibi . ē in dñio . cũ . i . uiłto 7 unó

borđ . 7 ii . ſeruis . Ibi . iiii . ać p̓ti . 7 ſilua . iiii . porc̃.

T.R.E. 7 poſt . 7 m̃:ˊ uał xL . fot . Vluiet tenuit de rege . E.

Goisfriđ de Ros ten̓ de eṗo OTEHÃ . ꝓ uno ſolin 7 uño jugo ſe

defđ . T̓ra . ē . ii . caꝛ̃ 7 dimiđ . In dñio . ē una . 7 ix . uiłłi cũ . iii .

borđ hñt . i . caꝛ̃ . Ibi eccła . 7 ii . ſerui . 7 i . molin̄ de . v . ſoliđ.

7 iii . ác p̓ti . Silua . viii . porc̃ . T.R.E. ualeb̃ . iiii . lib̃ . Q̇do

receṗ:ˊ iii . lib̃ . Modo:ˊ iiii . lib̃ . Aluuin̓ tenuit de rege . E.

Rotb̃t Latin̓ ten̓ ad firmã HERBRETITOV . Adeloldus

tenuit de eṗo . ꝓ uno ſolin ſe defđ . T̃ra . ē   In dñio

ē una caꝛ̃ . 7 ii . uiłłi cũ . i . borđ hñt . ii . Aalia . 7 ibi . iiii . aćc

p̓ti . T.R.E. 7 poſt. uał modo:ˊ . Lx . fot . 7 tam̃ eſt ad firmã . ꝓ . iiii . lib̃.

Aluric̃ tenuit de Goduino.

Iſd̃e Rotb̃t ten̓ ad firmã BRVNFELLE . Adelolđ tenuit de eṗo.

ꝓ uno ſolin ſe defđ . T̓ra . ē   In dñio ſunt . ii . caꝛ̃ . 7 v . uiłłi

cũ . x . borđ hñt . i . caꝛ̃ 7 dim̃ . Ibi . i . molin̄ de . vi . ſoliđ

7 viii . den̄ . 7 paſtura de xv . fot . Ibi . xii . ſerui . 7 viii . aćc

p̓ti . Silua . xx . porc̃ . T.R.E. 7 poſt . uał . iiii . lib̃ . M̊ . c . ſoliđ.

Aluuin̓ tenuit de Goduino . Huic cõm̃ p̓tin̓ quædã libera

tra ad . iii . boues . 7 uał . v . fot.

Radulf̓ curbeſpine ten̓ de eṗo TVRNEHÃ . ꝓ iii . folins

ſe defđ . Tra . ē . viii . caꝛ̃ . In dñio . ē una . 7 xvi . uiłłi cũ xviii.

borđ hñt . iiii . caꝛ̃ . Ibi æccła 7 vi . ſerui . 7 i . molin̄ de . vi.

ſoliđ . 7 iiii . aćc p̓ti . Silua . xL . porc̃ .

T.R.E. 7 poſt . ualeb̃ . x . lib̃ . Modo xii . lib̃ . 7 tam̃ redđ . xiiii.

Sbern biga tenuit de rege . E.

Value of the whole before 1066, 100s; later and now 40s.
Wulfgeat held it from King Edward and could go where he would.

82 (Old) SHELVE. It answers for ½ sulung. Land for 1 plough.
It is there, in lordship, with
   1 villager, 1 smallholder and 2 slaves.
   Meadow, 4 acres; woodland, 4 pigs.
Value before 1066, later and now 40s.
   Wulfgeat held it from King Edward.

83 Geoffrey of Rots holds OTHAM from the Bishop. It answers for
1 sulung and 1 yoke. Land for 2½ ploughs. In lordship 1.
   9 villagers with 3 smallholders have 1 plough.
   A church; 2 slaves; 1 mill at 5s; meadow, 3 acres;
      woodland, 8 pigs.
Value before 1066 £4; when acquired, £3; now £4.
   Alwin held it from King Edward.

84 Robert Latimer holds HARBILTON at a revenue. Aethelwold
held it from the Bishop. It answers for 1 sulung. Land for ...
In lordship 1 plough.
   2 villagers with 1 smallholder have 2 cattle.
   Meadow, 4 acres.
Value before 1066, later and now 60s; however, it is at a
revenue for £4.
   Aelfric held it from Earl Godwin.

85 Robert also holds BROOMFIELD at a revenue. Aethelwold held it
from the Bishop. It answers for 1 sulung. Land for ...
In lordship 2 ploughs.
   5 villagers with 10 smallholders have 1½ ploughs.
   1 mill at 6s 8d; pasture at 15s. 12 slaves; meadow, 8 acres;
      woodland, 20 pigs.
Value before 1066 and later £4; now 100s.
   Alwin held it from Earl Godwin.
To this manor belongs free land for 3 oxen, value 5s.

86 Ralph (of) Courbépine holds THURNHAM from the Bishop.
It answers for 3 sulungs. Land for 8 ploughs. In lordship 1.
   16 villagers with 18 smallholders have 4 ploughs.
   A church; 6 slaves; 1 mill at 6s; meadow, 4 acres;
      woodland, 40 pigs.
Value before 1066 and later £10; now £12; however, it pays [£] 14.
   Esbern Big held it from King Edward.

Iſđ Radulf⁹ ten de epo *FEREBVRNE* . p uno ſolin ſe defđ.

Tra . ē   In dñio . ē una car . 7 ii . uiłłi cũ . i . borđ . 7 ii.

ſerui . 7 una ãc p̃ti 7 dimiđ . Silua . vi . porc . T . R . E . 7 poſt.

7 modo:ʹ uał . xxx . ſoliđ . Sbern biga tenuit de rege . E.

Odo ten de epo *GELINGEHÃ* . p dimiđ ſolin ſe defđ.

Tra . ē . i . car . In dñio ſunt . ii . 7 vi . borđ hñt dim car.

Ibi . i . moliñ de . xvi . ſoł 7 vii . deñ . 7 xiii . ãc p̃ti . 7 viii . ãc

                                              ℩ paſturæ.

T . R . E . ualeƀ . xl . ſoł . Qđo recep:ʹ xxx . ſoł . Modo . lx . ſoł.

Rotƀt⁹ Latin ten ad firmã de epo *IN CETEHÃ HVND.*

CETEHAM . p vi . ſolins ſe defđ . Tra . ē . xvi . car . In dñio

ſunt . iii . 7 xxx . iii . uiłłi cũ . iiii . borđ hñt . x . car , Ibi

æccła 7 xv . ſerui . 7 i . moliñ de . xxx . ii . deñ . 7 xx . ãc p̃ti.

7 piſcariæ vi . de . xii . deñ . Silua . i . porc.

T . R . E . 7 poſt:ʹ ualuit . xii . liƀ . Modo . xv . liƀ . 7 tam redđ

xxxv . liƀ . Goduiñ tenuit.

IN LEST DE EILESFORD.   IN ROVECESTRE HVND.

Filius Wiłłi tahũ ten de epo *DELCE* . p uno ſolin

7 uno jugo ſe defđ . Tra . ē   In dñio . ē . una car.

7 v . uiłłi hñt . ii . car . Ibi . xii . ãc p̃ti . Silua . i . porc.

T . R . E . 7 poſt . ualuit . iii . liƀ . 7 m̃ lxx . ſoł.

Godric tenuit de rege . E.

Anſgot⁹ de Rouceſtre ten de epo *DELCE* . p uno ſolin

ſe defđ . Tra . ē . ii . car . 7 ibi ſunt in dñio . 7 cũ uno uiłło

7 v . borđ . 7 vi . ſeruis . Ibi . xii . ãc p̃ti . 7 lx . ãc paſturæ.

T . R . E . 7 poſt . 7 modo:ʹ uał . c . ſoliđ . Oſuuarđ tenuit de rege . E.

Iſdem Anſgot⁹ ten de epo *STOCHES* . *IN HOV HVND.*

p . ii . ſolins ſe defđ . Tra . ē . ii . car . 7 ibi ſunt in dñio cũ

vii . borđ . Ibi una piſcaria de . ii . ſoliđ . T . R . E . 7 poſt:ʹ

ualuit . c . ſoliđ . Modo . cx . ſoliđ . Anſchil tenuit de rege . E.

87   Ralph also holds FAIRBOURNE from the Bishop. It answers for 1 sulung. Land for ... In lordship 1 plough;
> 2 villagers with 1 smallholder and 2 slaves.
> Meadow, 1½ acres; woodland, 6 pigs.
Value before 1066, later and now 30s.
> Esbern Big held it from King Edward.

88   Odo holds GILLINGHAM from the Bishop. It answers for ½ sulung. Land for 1 plough. In lordship 2.
> 6 smallholders have ½ plough.
> 1 mill at 16s 7d; meadow, 13 acres; pasture, 8 acres.
Value before 1066, 40s; when acquired, 30s; now 60s.   8 c

In CHATHAM Hundred

89   Robert Latimer holds CHATHAM from the Bishop at a revenue. It answers for 6 sulungs. Land for 16 ploughs. In lordship 3.
> 33 villagers with 4 smallholders have 10 ploughs.
> A church; 15 slaves; 1 mill at 32d; meadow, 20 acres;
> > 6 fisheries at 12d; woodland, 1 pig.
Value before 1066 and later £12; now £15; however, it pays £35.
> Earl Godwin held it.

In the Lathe of AYLESFORD

In ROCHESTER Hundred

90   The son of William Thaon holds (Little) DELCE from the Bishop. It answers for 1 sulung and 1 yoke. Land for ... In lordship 1 plough.
> 5 villagers have 2 ploughs.
> Meadow, 12 acres; woodland, 1 pig.
Value before 1066 and later £3; now 70s.
> Godric held it from King Edward.

91   Ansgot of Rochester holds (Great) DELCE from the Bishop. It answers for 1 sulung. Land for 2 ploughs. They are there, in lordship, with
> 1 villager, 5 smallholders and 6 slaves.
> Meadow, 12 acres; pasture, 60 acres.
Value before 1066, later and now 100s.
> Osward held it from King Edward.

In HOO Hundred

92   Ansgot also holds STOKE from the Bishop. It answers for 2 sulungs. Land for 2 ploughs. They are there, in lordship, with
> 7 smallholders,
> A fishery at 2s.
Value before 1066 and later 100s; now 110s.
> Askell held it from King Edward.

Ipſe eps Baioc̄ſis ten̄ in dn̄io *Hov*.

p̄ . L . ſolins ſe defđ T.R.E. 7 m̄ p̄ xxx.iii᷎. Tra . ē . L . car̄.

In dn̄io ſunt . iiii . 7 c . uiłłi . iii . min cū . LXI . cot h̄nt

xL.iii . car̄ . Ibi . vi . æcclæ . 7 xii . ſerui . 7 xxx.ii . ac̄ p̄ti.

Silua . xxx . porc̄.

Totū m̄ T.R.E. . ualeb̄ . Lx . liƀ . Q̇do eps recep̄ ſimilit̄.

7 modo tntđ . 7 tam̄ qui eū ten̄ reddit . c 7 xiii . liƀ.

Huic m̄ p̄tineƀ . ix . dom̄ in Rouecest̄ ciuitate . 7 vi . ſoliđ

reddeƀ . nc̄ ablatæ ſunt . Hoc m̄ tenuit Goduin̄ comes.

De hoc m̄ ten̄ Ricard̄ de Tonebrige dimiđ ſolin.

7 ſiluā . xx . porc̄ . T.R.E. 7 poſt . 7 modo᷎ uał . xL . ſoliđ.

Adā filius Huƀti ten̄ de eod̄ m̄ un̄ ſolin . 7 un̄ jugū de epo.

7 ibi h̄t un̄ hō ej in dn̄io dimiđ car̄ . 7 iiii . uiłłos cū dim̄ car̄.

7 uno cot̄ . Vał 7 ualuit . xxx . ſoliđ.

Anſchitil de Ros ten̄ de ipſo m̄ . iii . ſolins . 7 ibi h̄t in dn̄io

. i . car̄ . 7 v . uiłłi cū . xii . cot h̄nt . i . car̄ 7 dim̄ . Ibi . v . ſerui.

7 un̄ molin̄ de . x . ſoliđ . 7 xii . ac̄ p̄ti . 7 ii . piſcar̄ . de . v . ſoł.

T.R.E. 7 poſt . ualeb̄ . vi . liƀ . Modo . vi . liƀ . 7 v . ſoliđ.

Adā ten̄ de epo . i . jugū in *PINPA* . IN TVIFERDE HVNĐ.

Tra . ē   Ibi h̄t dim̄ car̄ cū . ii . ſeruis . 7 iiii . ac̄s p̄ti.

7 dimiđ piſcariā ſine cenſu . Silua᷎ vi . porc̄ .   ⎰ xv . ſoł.

T.R.E. ualeb̄ . vi . ſoł . 7 poſt᷎ v . ſoł . Modo᷎ x . ſoł . 7 tam̄ redđ

Godric tenuit de rege . E.

Rannulf̄ de Colūbels ten̄ de epo *FERLAGA* . p̄ uno ſolin

ſe defđ . Tra . ē . iiii . car̄ . Rann̄ n̄ ten̄ niſi . iii . juga . 7 ibi

h̄t in dn̄io . i . car̄ . 7 x . uiłłos cū . iiii . cot h̄nt . iii . car̄.

Ibi æccła . 7 vii . ſerui . 7 i . molin̄ de . v . ſoł . 7 x . ac̄ p̄ti . Silua.

xv . porc̄ . T.R.E. 7 poſt . 7 modo . uał . vii . liƀ . Alnod tenuit

De iſto ſolin ten̄ Rayner . i . jugū de epo in m̄ *PINPE*.

8 d

7 ibi h̄t . i . car̄ ; cū . ix . ſeruis . 7 iii . ac̄s p̄ti . Silua . iiii . porc᷎̄

T.R.E. 7 poſt ualeb̄ . xx . ſoł . Modo᷎ xL . ſoliđ . Alnod tenuit de rege . E.

93   The Bishop of Bayeux himself holds HOO in lordship.
Before 1066 it answered for 50 sulungs; now for 33.
Land for 50 ploughs. In lordship 4.

     100 villagers less 3 with 61 cottagers have 43 ploughs.

     6 churches; 12 slaves; meadow, 32 acres; woodland, 30 pigs.
Value of the whole manor before 1066 £60; when the Bishop
acquired it, the same; now as much; however, its holder pays
£113.

     9 houses in the City of Rochester belonged to this manor;
they paid 6s; now they have been taken away.

     Earl Godwin held this manor.

     Richard of Tonbridge holds ½ sulung of this manor.

       Woodland, 20 pigs.
Value before 1066, later and now, 40s.

     Adam son of Hubert holds 1 sulung and 1 yoke of the same
manor from the Bishop. One of his men has ½ plough in
lordship, and

     4 villagers with ½ plough and 1 cottager.
The value is and was 30s.

     Ansketel of Rots holds 3 sulungs of this manor. He has 1
plough in lordship.

     5 villagers with 12 cottagers have 1½ ploughs.

     5 slaves; a mill at 10s; meadow, 12 acres; 2 fisheries at 5s.
Value before 1066 and later £6; now £6 5s.

In TWYFORD Hundred

94   Adam holds 1 yoke in PIMP'S (Court) from the Bishop. Land for ...
He has ½ plough, with

     2 slaves.

     Meadow, 4 acres; ½ fishery without dues; woodland, 6 pigs.
Value before 1066, 6s; later 5s; now 10s; however, it pays 15s.

     Godric held it from King Edward.

95   Ranulf of Colombières holds (West) FARLEIGH from the Bishop.
It answers for 1 sulung. Land for 4 ploughs. Ranulf holds only
3 yokes. He has 1 plough in lordship.

     10 villagers with 4 cottagers have 3 ploughs.

     A church; 7 slaves; 1 mill at 5s; meadow, 10 acres;
       woodland, 15 pigs.
Value before 1066, later and now £7.

     Alnoth held it from the King.

     Rainer holds 1 yoke of this sulung in the manor of Pimp's (Court)
from the Bishop. He has 1 plough, with   8 d

     9 slaves.

     Meadow, 3 acres; woodland, 4 pigs.
Value before 1066 and later 20s; now 40s.

     Young Alnoth held it from King Edward

Haimo ten de epo NEDESTEDE .p .III. solins se defd. Tra. e
VI . car . In dnio. e una . 7 XIIII . uitti hnt . v . car . Ibi æccta.
7 XIIII . serui . 7 II . molini de XIIII . solid . 7 piscaria de . II . sot.
7 VII . ac pti . Silua . XXX.v . porc . T.R.E. ualeb . VIII . lib.
7 post. VI . lib . Modo. VIII . lib 7 v . sot . Norman tenuit de rege . E.
De isto cõ ht eps . XXX . sot . p . II . hagas.
Radulf fili Turaldi ten de epo OTRINGEBERGE . p . II.
solins se defd . Tra . e . v . car . In dnio sunt . II . 7 VI . uitti
cũ . VIII . bord hnt . III . car . Ibi æccta . 7 II . molini de . III . solid.
7 II . ac pti . 7 piscaria de . XXX . anguitt . Silua . II . porc.
T.R.E. 7 post ualuit . XL . solid . Modo. VI . lib . Leueua tenuit
de rege . E . Huic cõ adjacen . IIII . hagæ in ciuitate . redd . III . sct.
Hugo de braiboue ten de epo OTRINBERGE . p . II . solins
se defd . Tra . e . IIII . car . In dnio . e una . 7 IX . uitti cũ . IIII.
bord hnt . II . car . Ibi . III . serui . 7 I . molin de . XVI . denar.
7 III . ac pti . Silua . II . porc . T.R.E. 7 post. ualuit . IIII . lib.
Modo. c . solid . Godil tenuit de rege . E.
Adelold tenuit de epo TESTAN . 7 Robt m ten ad firmã.
p uno solin se defd . Tra e   In dnio sunt . II . car 7 dimid.
7 VII . uitti cũ . III . bord hnt . I . car . Ibi . XII . serui . 7 I . molin
de . III . sot . 7 VIII . ac pti . Silua . XX . porc.
T.R.E. ualeb . c . sot . 7 post. LX . sot . Modo. c . solid . Eduuard de rege . E. ten
Hanc trã tenuer . III . frs T.R.E. p tribʒ Manerijs . Nc . e in unũ.
Isdẽ Adelold tenuit de epo BENEDESTEDE . 7 Robt ten ad firmã.
p uno jugo se defd . Tra . e   In dnio . e . I . car . cũ . v . seruis.
7 una ac pti . Silua . VI . porc . T.R.E. 7 post. ualuit . XX . solid.
Modo. XL . sot . Godric tenuit de Alnodo cilt . IN MEDESTAN HD.
Rannulf de Colũbels ten de epo BERMELIE . p uno jugo
se defd . Tra . e   In dnio . e una car . cũ . v . seruis . 7 IIII . ac
pti . Silua . III . porc . T.R.E. ualeb . XV . sot . Qdo recep. XX . sot.
Modo. XL . sot.

8 d

96   Hamo holds NETTLESTEAD from the Bishop. It answers for 3
      sulungs. Land for 6 ploughs. In lordship 1.
        14 villagers have 5 ploughs.
        A church; 14 slaves; 2 mills at 14s; a fishery at 2s;
            meadow, 7 acres; woodland, 35 pigs.
      Value before 1066 £8; later £6; now £8 5s.
        Norman held it from King Edward.
      Of this manor the Bishop has 30s for 2 sites.

97   Ralph son of Thorold holds WATERINGBURY from the Bishop.
      It answers for 2 sulungs. Land for 5 ploughs. In lordship 2.
        6 villagers with 8 smallholders have 3 ploughs.
        A church; 2 mills at 3s; meadow, 2 acres; a fishery at 30 eels;
            woodland, 2 pigs.
      Value before 1066 and later 40s; now £6.
        Leofeva held it from King Edward.
      3 sites in the city are attached to this manor; they pay 3s.

98   Hugh of Bréboeuf holds WATERINGBURY from the Bishop.
      It answers for 2 sulungs. Land for 4 ploughs. In lordship 1.
        9 villagers with 4 smallholders have 2 ploughs.
        3 slaves; 1 mill at 16d; meadow, 3 acres; woodland, 2 pigs.
      Value before 1066 and later £4; now 100s.
        Godil held it from King Edward.

99   Aethelwold held TESTON from the Bishop; now Robert holds
      it at a revenue. It answers for 1 sulung. Land for ...
      In lordship 2½ ploughs.
        7 villagers with 3 smallholders have 1 plough.
        12 slaves; 1 mill at 3s; meadow, 8 acres; woodland, 20 pigs.
      Value before 1066, 100s; later 60s; now 100s.
        Edward held it from King Edward.
      Before 1066, 3 brothers held this land as three manors, now
      it is in one.

100   Aethelwold also held BENSTED from the Bishop; Robert holds
      it at a revenue. It answers for 1 yoke. Land for ... In lordship
      1 plough, with 5 slaves.
        Meadow, 1 acre; woodland, 6 pigs.
      Value before 1066 and later 20s; now 40s.
        Godric held it from Young Alnoth.

      In MAIDSTONE Hundred
101   Ranulf of Colombières holds (West) BARMING from the Bishop.
      It answers for 1 yoke. Land for ... In lordship 1 plough,
      with 5 slaves.
        Meadow, 4 acres; woodland, 3 pigs.
      Value before 1066, 15s; when acquired, 20s; now 40s.

Rotbt Latin ten ad firmā *BOSELEV*. Tra.ē.xx.car.in

dñio funt.III.car. 7 XLVII.uiłłi cū.XI.bord hñt.XVI.car.

Ibi.III.molini de XXXVI.foł 7 VIII.den. 7 XVI.ferui. 7 XX.

ac pti. Silua.L.porc. T.R.E. 7 poſt.ualuit.XXV.lib.

Modo.XXX.lib. 7 tam Rotbt reddit.LV.lib. Alnod tenuit.

De hoc m̃ ten Helto dim folin. 7 ibi hŧ.I.car.cū uno

bord. 7 I.franc 7 II.ac̃s pti. 7 filuā: VI.porc. 7 Vał.XL.foł.

Radulf fili Turaldi ten de epo

LITELBROTEHA.p uno folin 7 dim fe defd. Tra.ē

In dñio.ē.I.car. 7 IIII.uiłłi cū.IIII.bord hñt.II.car. Ibi

II.ferui. 7 II.molini de.IIII.folid. 7 II.ac pti. Silua.v.porc.

T.R.E. 7 poſt.ualuit.XL.foł. Modo.LX.foł 7 LIIII.den.

Ricard de Tonebrige hŧ in fua Leuua qd uał.XIII.foł.

7 Siluā.L.porc. 7 Rex hŧ de eod m̃ qd uał.XVI.den.

Hanc trā T.R.E.tenuer Goduin 7 Eduun p.II.Maner.

Adā ten de epo *CELCA* p.III.folins fe defd. Tra.ē

VII.car. In dñio funt.II. 7 XIIII.uiłłi cū.VI.bord hñt

v.car. Ibi æcclā. 7 IIII.ferui. 7 uñ molin de.v.folid.

7 XVI.ac pti. T.R.E.uałeb.VII.lib. 7 poſt.

ʃ c.folid.

Modo.x.lib. 7 tam qui|redd.XIIII.lib.

De hoc m̃ eſt in manu regis qd uał.VII.foł. de nouo

dono epi.

In manu fua retinuit eps in Ciuitate Roueceſtre.III.

hagas.quæ ualent.L.denar.

In Exeſſe.ē una hida que juſte ad hoc m̃ ptinet.

Goduin fili dudeman tenuit. Modo ten Rannulf peurel.

Iſdē Adā ten de epo *HEHAM*. p.v.folins fe defd.

Tra.ē.XII.car. In dñio funt.III.car. 7 XXIIII.uiłłi cū

XII.bord.hñt.VI.car 7 dimid. Ibi.XX.ferui. 7 XXX.ac

pti. Ibi æcclā 7 I.molin de.x.foł. 7 pifcaria de.III.folid.

102   Robert Latimer holds BOXLEY at a revenue. Before 1066 it
answered for 7 sulungs; now for 5 sulungs. Land for 20 ploughs.
In lordship 3 ploughs.
>   47 villagers with 11 smallholders have 16 ploughs.
>   3 mills at 36s 8d; 16 slaves; meadow, 20 acres; woodland,
>   50 pigs.

Value before 1066 and later £25; now £30; however, Robert
pays £55.
>   Young Alnoth held it.

Helto holds ½ sulung of this manor. He has 1 plough, with
>   1 smallholder and 1 Frenchman.
>   Meadow, 2 acres; woodland, 6 pigs.

Value 40s.

103   Ralph son of Thorold holds WROTHAM (Heath) from the Bishop.
It answers for 1½ sulungs. Land for ... In lordship 1 plough.
>   4 villagers with 4 smallholders have 2 ploughs.
>   2 slaves; 2 mills at 4s; meadow, 2 acres; woodland, 5 pigs.

Value before 1066 and later 40s; now 60s 54d.
>   Richard of Tonbridge has in his territory what is valued at 13s.
>   Woodland, 50 pigs.
>   The King has what is valued at 16d from this manor.
>   Before 1066 Godwin and Edwin held this land as two manors.

104   Adam holds CHALK from the Bishop. It answers for 3 sulungs.
Land for 7 ploughs. In lordship 2.
>   14 villagers with 6 smallholders have 5 ploughs.
>   A church; 4 slaves; a mill at 5s; meadow, 16 acres.

Value before 1066 £7; later 100s; now £10; however, its   9 a
holder pays £14.
>   Of this manor there is in the King's hands what is valued at
>   7s from a new gift of the Bishop. The Bishop kept in his hands
>   3 sites in the City of Rochester, value 50d.
>   In Essex there is 1 hide which rightly belongs to this manor.
>   Godwin son of Dudeman held it; now Ranulf Peverel holds it.

105   Adam also holds HIGHAM from the Bishop. It answers for 5
sulungs. Land for 12 ploughs. In lordship 3 ploughs.
>   24 villagers with 12 smallholders have 6½ ploughs.
>   20 slaves; meadow, 30 acres. A church; 1 mill at 10s;
>   a fishery at 3s;

7 in Exeſſe paſtura . cc . ouibȝ . T . R . E . ualeƀ . xii . liƀ.

7 poſt . vi . liƀ . Modo꞉ xv . liƀ.

Hanc trã tenuer̄ . T . R . E . Goduin fili⁹ carli . 7 Toli . ꝑ . ii . Man.

Iſdē Adã ten de epo |COLINGE . i . ſolin 7 dimiđ . Tra . ē

. i . car̄ 7 dim . In dñio ſunt . ii . car̄ . 7 v . uilli h̄nt

dimiđ car̄ . Ibi . iiii . ſerui . 7 vii . ac ꝑti . Silua . x . porc̄.

T . R . E . 7 poſt꞉ ualuit . xl . ſol . Modo꞉ iiii . liƀ.

Ricard⁹ de Tonebrige qđ h̄ in ſua Leuua꞉ ual . vii . ſol.

Vluuin⁹ tenuit de Leuuino comite.

Iſdē Adã ten de epo BICHELEI . ꝑ dimiđ ſolin ſe defđ.

Tra . ē dim car̄ . In dñio . ē dim car̄ . 7 un uills cū dim car̄.

7 ii . borđ . Ibi . i . moliñ de . v . ſol.　　　Vluuin⁹ tenuit de Leuuino com̄.

T . R . E . 7 poſt꞉ ualuit . x . ſol . Modo . xv . ſoliđ . IN ESSĀLE HĐ.

Radulf⁹ fili⁹ Turaldi ten de epo ARCLEI . ꝑ uno ſolin ſe

defđ . Tra . ē dim car̄ . 7 ibiđ ſuꝑ adhuc . xxx . ac træ

In dñio . ē una car̄ . 7 vi . uilli h̄nt dimiđ car̄ . Ibi . xii.

ac ꝑti . T . R . E . 7 poſt꞉ ualuit . xl . ſol . Modo꞉ iiii . liƀ.

Hvnef tenuit de Heraldo com̄.

Anſgot⁹ de Roueceſt ten HANEHEST . ꝑ dim ſolin

ſe defđ . Tra . ē . i . car̄ . In dñio . ē una car̄ . 7 ii . uilli cū . iiii.

ſeruis . T . R . E . ualeƀ . xx . ſol . Q̓do recep꞉ xxx . ſol . Modo꞉

xl . ſoliđ . Goduin⁹ tenuit de Goduino com'.

Ernulf⁹ de Heſding ten de epo CLIVE . ꝑ dim ſolin

ſe defđ . Tra . ē　　　In dñio dimiđ car̄ . 7 ii . uilli . 7 x.

ac ꝑti . 7 Paſtura . c . ouiũ . T . R . E . 7 poſt꞉ ual xxx . ſol.

Duo fr̄s tenuer̄ de rege . E . Aluric 7 Ordric.

Iſdē Ernulf⁹ ten de epo HADONE . ꝑ . iii . jugis ſe

defđ . Tra . ē . i . car̄ . 7 ibi . ē in dñio . 7 vi . uilli cū . i . borđ

h̄nt . i . car̄ . Ibi . vi . ac ꝑti . T . R . E . 7 poſt꞉ ual . l . ſoliđ.

Modo꞉ lx . ſol . Oſuuard⁹ tenuit de rege . E.

in Essex pasture for 200 sheep.
Value before 1066 £12; later £6; now £15.
Before 1066 Godwin son of Karl and Toli held this land
as two manors.

106   Adam also holds 1½ sulungs in COOLING from the Bishop.
Land for 1½ ploughs. In lordship 2 ploughs.
    5 villagers have ½ plough.
    4 slaves; meadow, 7 acres; woodland, 10 pigs.
Value before 1066 and later 40s; now £4; value of what
Richard of Tonbridge has in his territory, 7s.
    Wulfwin held it from Earl Leofwin.

107   Adam also holds BECKLEY from the Bishop. It answers for ½
sulung. Land for ½ plough. In lordship ½ plough;
    1 villager with ½ plough and 2 smallholders.
    1 mill at 5s.
Value before 1066 and later 10s; now 15s.
    Wulfwin held it from Earl Leofwin.

In SHAMWELL Hundred

108   Ralph son of Thorold holds OAKLEIGH from the Bishop. It
answers for 1 sulung. Land for ½ plough. There are a further
30 acres of land. In lordship 1 plough.
    6 villagers have ½ plough.
    Meadow, 12 acres.
Value before 1066 and later 40s; now £4.
    Hunef held it from Earl Harold.

109   Ansgot of Rochester holds HENHURST. It answers for ½
sulung. Land for 1 plough. In lordship 1 plough.
    2 villagers with 4 slaves.
Value before 1066, 20s; when acquired, 30s; now 40s.
    Godwin held it from Earl Godwin.

110   Arnulf of Hesdin holds CLIFFE from the Bishop. It answers
for ½ sulung. Land for ... In lordship ½ plough.
    2 villagers.
    Meadow, 10 acres; pasture, 100 sheep.
Value before 1066 and later 30s.
    Two brothers, Aelfric and Ordric, held it from King Edward.

111   Arnulf also holds HAVEN from the Bishop. It answers for 3 yokes.
Land for 1 plough. It is there, in lordship.
    6 villagers with 1 smallholder have 1 plough.
    Meadow, 6 acres.
Value before 1066 and later 50s; now 60s.
    Osward held it from King Edward.

Odo teñ de epo in ead Hadone . i . jugũ . Tra . ē dim̃
car̃ . In dñio nichil . ē . T . R . E . 7 poſt . 7 m̃ ual . xx . ſolid.

Iſdē Odo teñ de epo COLINGES . ꝑ dim̃ ſolin ſe deſd.
Tra . ē dimid car̃ . Ibi . ē cũ uno bord . 7 iiii . ac̃ p̃ti.
T . R . E . 7 poſt . ualuit . xx . ſolid . Modo . xxx . ſolid . God

Helto teñ de epo MELESTVN . ꝑ dimid ſolin ⌐ tenuit de rege.
ſe deſd . Tra . ē . i . car̃ . 7 ibi . ē cũ . v . uiłłis . 7 i . ac̃ p̃ti.
T . R . E . 7 poſt. ualuit . x . ſolid . Modo . xxx . ſolid.
Vluuard tenuit de rege . E.

IN DIMIDIO LEST DE MIDDELTONE . IN MILDETONE . HVND.

9 b

Hugo de port teñ de epo TYNESTELLE . ꝑ . iii . ſolins
. . . . . . 7 dim̃ ſe deſd . Tra . ē . iiii . car̃ . In dñio ſunt . ii . car̃.
7 ix . uiłłi cũ . i . car̃ . 7 ix . ſerui . Silua . x . porc̃ . 7 ſalina de . xii.
denar̃ . T . R . E . 7 poſt . ualeb . vii . lib . Modo . viii . lib.
Oſuuard tenuit de rege . E.

Iſdē Hugo teñ de epo CERCE . ꝑ . ii . ſolins ſe deſd . Tra . ē . ii.
car̃ . In dñio . ē una . 7 cũ v . bord 7 uno ſeruo . 7 uñ molin de
vi . ſolid 7 viii . deñ . Val ~~xxx . ſolid~~ . Oſuuard tenuit.

Iſdē Hugo teñ de epo TANGAS . ꝑ . ii . ſolins ſe deſd . Tra . ē
iii . car̃ . In dñio ſunt . ii . 7 v . uiłłi cũ . i . car̃ . Ibi æccła 7 iiii . ſerui.
7 uñ molin de . viii . ſolid . Silua . iiii . porc̃.
T . R . E . 7 poſt . ualuit . vii . lib . Modo . x . lib 7 x . ſolid . Oſuuard
De iſtis ſolins quos hugo de port h̃ . tenuit Oſuuard . v.
ad gablũ . 7 iii . ſolins 7 uñ jugũ 7 dimid . quos abſtulit
uillanis regis .

Iꝺ . H . teñ' de epo
STEPEDONE . Oſuuard
teneb T . R . E . 7 t̃ ſe deſdb
.ꝑ . i . ſolin dimidio jugo m̃
Tra . ē . ii . car̃ . In dñio . ē
cũ . i . ſeruo 7 v . bord.
Val . xxx . ſolid.

112　Odo holds 1 yoke from the Bishop, also in HAVEN.　Land for
½ plough. In lordship nothing.
Value before 1066, later and now 20s.

113　Odo also holds COOLING from the Bishop. It answers for ½
sulung. Land for ½ plough. It is there, with
　1 smallholder.
　Meadow, 4 acres.
Value before 1066 and later 20s; now 30s.
　Godwin held it from King Edward.

114　Helto holds MERSTON from the Bishop. It answers for ½
sulung. Land for 1 plough. It is there, with
　5 villagers.
　Meadow, 1 acre.
Value before 1066 and later 10s; now 30s.
　Wulfward White held it from King Edward.

In the Half-Lathe of MILTON
In MILTON Hundred

115　Hugh of Port holds TUNSTALL from the Bishop. It answers　　9 b
for 3 sulungs .... and ½. Land for 4 ploughs. In lordship 2 ploughs;
　9 villagers with 1 plough and 9 slaves.
　Woodland, 10 pigs; a salt-house at 12d.
Value before 1066 and later £7; now £8.
　Osward held it from King Edward.

116　Hugh also holds UPCHURCH from the Bishop. It answers for 2
sulungs. Land for 2 ploughs. In lordship 1, with
　5 smallholders and 1 slave.
　A mill at 6s 8d.
Value £6.
　Osward held it.

117　Hugh also holds STUPPINGTON from the Bishop. Osward held it before
1066. Then it answered for 1 sulung less ½ yoke. Land for 2 ploughs.
In lordship ... with 1 slave and 5 smallholders.
Value 30s.

118　Hugh also holds TONGE from the Bishop. It answers for 2 sulungs.
Land for 3 ploughs. In lordship 2;
　5 villagers with 1 plough.
　A church; 4 slaves; a mill at 8s; woodland, 4 pigs.
Value before 1066 and later £7; now £10 10s.
　Osward held it.
　Of these sulungs which Hugh of Port has, Osward held 5 for
tribute, and 3 sulungs and 1½ yokes which he took from the
King's villagers.

Ricard fili'Witti ten de epo *Borne* . p . vi . folins fe
defd . Tra . e . viii . car . In dnio funt . iii . car . 7 xliiii . uitti
cu . iii . bord hnt . x . car . Ibi æccta . 7 un feru . 7 iiii . mo
lini de . xvi . folid 7 viii . den . Pifcaria de . vi . den . Paftura
unde arauer extnei hoes . vi . ac̃s terræ . Silua . iiii . porc.
T . R . E . ualeb . xviii . lib . Qdo recep: x . lib . Modo . xix . lib.

Ipfe eps Baioc ten in dnio *Hardes* . p ii . folins fe defd.
Tra . e . iiii . car . In dnio . e una . 7 ix . uitti cu . ii . car . Ibi
æccta 7 v . ferui . Silua . xx . porc . T . R . E . ualeb . vii . lib.
7 poft: c . fol . Modo: vii . lib . 7 tam reddit . x . lib . Eduin tenuit

Ifde eps ten in dnio *Stellinges* . p uno jugo ⌐ de rege . E.
fe defd . Tra . i . car 7 dimid . In dnio nichil . e nifi . i . bord
Ibi æccta . Silua . ii . porc.

T . R . E . ualeb . lx . fol . 7 poft 7 modo: xl . folid . Alret tenuit de rege . E.

Ifde eps ten | dnio *Bvrnes* . p . ii . folins fe defd . Tra . e . vi . car.
In dnio funt . ii . 7 xxv . uitti cu . iiii . bord hnt . vii . car.
Ibi æccta . 7 vi . ferui . 7 un molin de . xxxviii . denar . 7 una
falina de . xxx . den . 7 dimid pifcaria . iiii . den . De paftura
xl . den . Silua . vi . porc 7 dimid . ⌐ Leuinc tenuit de rege . E.
T . R . E . ualeb . xii . lib . 7 poft: vii . lib . Modo: xii . lib . 7 tam
redd xviii . lib . Qd Hugo de monfort ten: ual . v . fol.

H iii . Maneria epi Baioc . tenet Rannulf' ad firma.

Rannulf' de colubels ten de epo *Hardes* . p uno folin
fe defd . Tra . e . iiii . car . In dnio . e dimid car . 7 ix . uitti
hnt . ii . car . Ibi æccta 7 viii . ferui . 7 xiii . ac pti . Silua
iiii . porc . T . R . E . ualeb . vi . lib . 7 poft: iiii . lib . Modo:
c . folid . Azor tenuit de rege . E. *In Donamesford hvnd.*

Ipfe eps ten in dnio *Wicheha* . p iiii . folins fe defd.
Tra . e . xi . car . In dnio funt . ii . car . 7 xxxvi . uitti cu xxx.ii.
cot hnt . ix . car . Ibi æccta 7 un pbr qui dat . xl . fol p ann.

In BOROUGH Lathe
In BRIDGE Hundred

119   Richard son of William holds PATRIXBOURNE from the Bishop.
It answers for 6 sulungs. Land for 8 ploughs. In lordship 3 ploughs.
   44 villagers with 3 smallholders have 10 ploughs.
   A church; 1 slave; 4 mills at 16s 8d; a fishery at 6d; pasture,
     from which outsiders have ploughed 6 acres of land;
     woodland, 4 pigs.
Value before 1066 £18; when acquired, £10; now £19.

120   The Bishop of Bayeux himself holds (Upper) HARDRES in lordship.
It answers for 2 sulungs. Land for 4 ploughs. In lordship 1;
   9 villagers with 2 ploughs.
   A church; 5 slaves; woodland, 20 pigs.
Value before 1066 £7; later 100s; now £7; however, it pays £10.
Edwin held it from King Edward.

121   The Bishop also holds STELLING in lordship. It answers for 1 yoke.
Land for 1½ ploughs. In lordship nothing except
   1 smallholder.
   A church; woodland, 2 pigs.
Value before 1066, 60s; later and now 40s.
Aelred held it from King Edward.

122   The Bishop also holds BEKESBOURNE in lordship. It answers
for 2 sulungs. Land for 6 ploughs. In lordship 2.
   25 villagers with 4 smallholders have 7 ploughs.
   A church; 6 slaves; a mill at 38d; a salt-house at 30d;
     ½ fishery at 4d; from pasture 40d; woodland, 6½ pigs.
   Leofwin held it from King Edward.
Value before 1066 £12; later £7; now £12; however, it pays £18.
Value of what Hugh de Montfort holds 5s.

   Ranulf holds these three manors from the Bishop of Bayeux
at a revenue.

123   Ranulf of Colombières holds (Lower) HARDRES from the Bishop.
It answers for 1 sulung. Land for 4 ploughs. In lordship ½ plough.
   9 villagers have 2 ploughs.
   A church; 8 slaves; meadow, 13 acres; woodland, 4 pigs.
Value before 1066 £6; later £4; now 100s.
Azor held it from King Edward.

In DOWNHAMFORD Hundred
124   The Bishop himself holds WICKHAMBREUX in lordship. It answers
for 4 sulungs. Land for 11 ploughs. In lordship 2 ploughs.
   36 villagers with 32 cottagers have 9 ploughs.
   A church; a priest who gives 40s a year.

Ibi un̄ parcus . 7 ɪɪ . molini de . ʟ . foliđ . 7 ɪɪ . falinæ de

xxxɪɪ . denar̄ . 7 ɪɪɪ . pifcariæ de . ɪɪɪɪ . foliđ . 7 xxx.ɪɪ . aͨc

p̄ti . Paſtura . ad . ccc . oues . 7 ad xxxɪ . anim̄ . Silua . qͨt xx .

porc̄ . T.R.E. ualeƀ xx.v . liƀ . Q̇do recep̄: xx . liƀ . Modo:

xxx . liƀ . Huic m̄ p̄tin in cantuaria . ɪɪɪ . mafuræ . reddtͤes

vɪ . foliđ 7 vɪɪɪ . denar̄ . Hoc m̄ tenuit Alured de rege . E.

Adhuc jacet ad hunͨ m̄ dimidiū folin liberæ terræ

9 c

quā Sired tenuit de Alured biga . 7 m̄ ten̄ Goisfrid

fili᷎ malæ træ de epo baioc̄ . 7 uaɫ 7 ſep̄ ualuit . ʟx . foliđ.

In HVNDRET 7 in Ciuitate cantuarienſi h̄t Adā

filius Huƀti de epo . ɪɪɪɪ . domos . 7 ɪɪ as . foris ciuitatē .

quæ reddunt . vɪɪɪ . foliđ .   *In Eoᴅ HVNᴅ.*

Haimo uicecom̄ ten̄ de epo *LATINTONE* . p̄ dim̄ folin

fe defđ . Tra . ē . ɪ . car̄ 7 dim̄ . In dn̄io . ē una . cū . ɪɪ . borđ .

Ibi paruū nem̄ de . xɪɪ . acris paſturæ . T.R.E. 7 poſt . 7 m̄

uaɫ . ɪɪɪ . liƀ.

Iſđe Haimo ten̄ de epo dimidiū folin . 7 ē tra . ɪɪɪɪ . car̄ .

In dn̄io funt . ɪɪ æ . car̄ . 7 xɪ . borđ cū . ɪɪɪ . car̄ . 7 xvɪ . ac̄ filuæ

minutæ . T.R.E. ualeƀ . c̄ . foɫ . 7 poſt . vɪ . liƀ . 7 m̄ . ɪx . liƀ.

Has t̄ras . T.R.E. tenuer̄ burgenfes cantuariæ . 7 ufq̖ ad ep̄m

baioc̄ qui ab eis cepit.

In LIMOWART LEST .   *In FVLCHESTAN HVNᴅ.*

Willelm᷎ de arcis ten̄ *FVLCHESTAN.*

T.R.E. fe defđ p̄ . xʟ . folins . 7 m̄ p̄ xxxɪx.

Tra . ē . c 7 xx . car̄ . In dn̄io funt . xɪɪɪɪ . car̄ . 7 cc ti . 7 ɪx .

uiɫɫi 7 q̇ter xx 7 ɪɪɪ . borđ . Int om̄s h̄nt . xʟ.v . car̄ .

Ibi . v . æcclæ . de qƀƶ h̄t Archiep̄s . ʟv . foliđ . Ibi . ɪɪɪ .

ferui . 7 vɪɪ . molini de . ɪx . liƀ . 7 xɪɪ . foɫ . Ibi . c . ac̄

p̄ti . Silua . xʟ . porc̄ . Hoc m̄ tenuit Goduin comes.

De hoc m̄ ten̄ Hugo fili᷎ Wiɫɫi . ɪx . folins de t̄ra

uillanoƶ . 7 ibi h̄t in dn̄io . ɪɪɪɪ . car̄ 7 dim̄ . 7 xxx

vɪɪɪ . uiɫɫos cū . xvɪɪ . borđ qui h̄nt . xvɪ . car̄ . Ibi

A park; 2 mills at 50s; 2 salt-houses at 32d; 3 fisheries at 4s;
meadow, 32 acres; pasture for 300 sheep and for 31 cattle;
woodland, 80 pigs.
Value before 1066 £25; when acquired £20; now £30.
To this manor belong 3 dwellings in Canterbury which pay
6s 8d. Alfred Big held this manor from King Edward. Further,
in (the lands of) this manor lies ½ sulung of free land which Sired
held from Alfred Big, and which Geoffrey son of Malleterre now
holds from the Bishop of Bayeux.
The value is and always was 60s.

125 In the Hundred and in the City of CANTERBURY Adam son of Hubert
has 4 houses, and 2 outside the City, from the Bishop which pay 8s.

In the same Hundred
126 Hamo the Sheriff holds NACKINGTON from the Bishop. It answers
for ½ sulung. Land for 1½ ploughs. In lordship 1, with
2 smallholders.
A small wood of 12 acres of pasture.
Value before 1066, later and now £3.

127 Hamo also holds ½ sulung from the Bishop. Land for 4 ploughs.
In lordship 2 ploughs;
11 smallholders with 3 ploughs.
Underwood, 16 acres.
Value before 1066, 100s; later £6; now £9.
The burgesses of Canterbury held these lands before 1066 and
until [the time of] the Bishop of Bayeux, who took them from
them.

In LYMPNE Lathe
In FOLKESTONE Hundred
128 William of Arques holds FOLKESTONE. Before 1066 it answered
for 40 sulungs; now for 39. Land for 120 ploughs. In lordship
14 ploughs;
209 villagers and 83 smallholders; between them all they
have 45 ploughs.
5 churches, from which the Archbishop has 55s. 3 slaves.
7 mills at £9 12s. Meadow, 100 acres; woodland, 40 pigs.
Earl Godwin held this manor.
Of this manor Hugh son of William holds 9 sulungs of the
villagers' land. He has 4½ ploughs there in lordship, and
8 villagers with 17 smallholders who have 16 ploughs.

III . æcclæ 7 uñ moliñ 7 dimid de . XVI . folid 7 v . den.

7 una falina de . XXX . den . Silua . VI . porc . Val . XX . lib.

FWalter de Appeuile ten de hoc M̃ . III . juga 7 XII . acs træ.

7 ibi ht . I . car in dñio . 7 III . uittos cũ . I . bord . Val . XXX . folid.

FAlured ten . I . foliñ . 7 XL . acs træ . 7 ibi ht in dñio . II . car.

cũ . VI . bord . 7 XII . acs p̃ti . Val . IIII . lib.

FWalter fili Engelbti ten dimid folin 7 XL . acs . 7 ibi ht

in dñio . I . car . cũ . VII . bord . 7 v . ac p̃ti . Val . XXX . folid.

FWefman ten . I . folin . 7 ibi ht in dñio . I . car . 7 II . uittos cũ

VII . bord hñtes . I . car 7 dim . Val . IIII . lib.

FAlured dapifer ten . I . folin 7 uñ jugũ . 7 VI . acs træ . 7 ibi ht

in dñio . I . car . cũ . XI . bord . Val . L . folid.

FEudo ten dimid folin . 7 ibi ht in dñio . I . car cũ . IIII.

bord . 7 III . ac p̃ti . Val . XX . folid.

FBernard de S̃ Audoeno . IIII . folins . 7 ibi ht in dñio . III.

car . 7 VI . uitti cũ . XI . bord hñt . II . car . Ibi . IIII . ferui.

7 II . molini de . XXIIII . folid . 7 XX . ac p̃ti . Silua . II . porc.

De una Dena 7 de tra quæ data . e ab his folins ad firmã

exeuñ . III . lib . Int totũ Val . IX . lib.

FBaldric ten dimid folin . 7 ibi ht . I . car . 7 II . uittós

cũ . VI . bord hñt . I . car . 7 uñ moliñ de . XXX . den . Val . XXX . fot.

FRicard ten . LVIII . acs træ . 7 ibi ht . I . car cũ . v . bord . Val . X . fot.

FTotũ Fulcheftan T . R . E . ualeb . c 7 x . lib . Q̃do recep . XL.

lib . Modo qd ht in dñio ꞏ uat . c . lib . Q̃d milites ten fup̃dict.

Ffimul uat . XL . v . lib.

7 X . fot.

3 churches; 1½ mills at 16s 5d; a salt-house at 30d;
  woodland, 6 pigs.
Value £20.
  Of this manor Walter of Abbeville holds 3 yokes and 12 acres
of land. He has 1 plough in lordship, and
  3 villagers with 1 smallholder.
Value 30s.
  Alfred holds 1 sulung and 40 acres of land. He has 2 ploughs
in lordship, with
  6 smallholders.
  Meadow, 12 acres.
Value £4.
  Walter son of Engelbert holds ½ sulung and 40 acres. He has
1 plough in lordship, with
  7 smallholders.
  Meadow, 5 acres.
Value 30s.
  Wesman holds 1 sulung. He has 1 plough in lordship, and
  2 villagers with 7 smallholders who have 1½ ploughs.
Value £4.
  Alfred the Steward holds 1 sulung, a yoke and 6 acres of land.
He has 1 plough in lordship, with
  11 smallholders.
Value 50s.
  Eudo holds ½ sulung. He has 1 plough in lordship, with
  4 smallholders.
  Meadow, 3 acres.
Value 20s.
  Bernard of St. Ouen (holds) 4 sulungs. He has 3 ploughs
in lordship.
  6 villagers with 11 smallholders have 2 ploughs.
  4 slaves; 2 mills at 24s; meadow, 20 acres; woodland, 2 pigs.
  From a pig pasture and from the land which has been given
  from these sulungs at a revenue comes £3.
In total, value £9.
  Baldric holds ½ sulung. He has 1 plough.
  2 villagers with 6 smallholders have 1 plough.
  A mill at 30d.
Value 30s.
  Richard holds 58 acres of land. He has 1 plough, with
  5 smallholders.
Value 10s.
Value of the whole of Folkestone before 1066 £110; when
acquired, £40; now value of what he has in lordship £100;
value of what the aforesaid men-at-arms hold together £45 10s.

Eps baiocſis ten in dñio *Alham* . p . vi . ſolins ſe defđ.

Tra . ē . xxiiii . car . In dñio ſunt . v . car . 7 xl.i . uiłłs

cū . viii . borđ hñt . xviii . car . Ibi æccła 7 viii . ſerui.

7 ii . molini de . vi . ſoliđ . 7 xxviii . ac p̃ti . Silua . c . porc.

T.R.E. 7 poſt. ualuit . xxx . liƀ | m̃ xl. 7 tam reddit . l . liƀ.

Hoc ꝏ tenuit Ederic de rege . E. *In Rovinden Hvnd.*

Adã fili hubti ten de epo . i . denā de dimiđ jugo . quæ

remanſit ext diuiſionē hugon de montfort . 7 jacuit in

Belice . Ibi hŧ . ii . uiłłos cū dim̃ car . Val 7 ualuit li ſep . x . ſoł.

Ansfrid ten de epo jn Bochelande *In Stotinges Hvnd.*

dimiđ ſolin . 7 ibi hŧ in dñio . i . car . cū uno uiłło . Tra . ē . ii . car.

T.R.E. ualeƀ . xx . ſoł . Q̃do recep̃. xxx . ſoliđ . Modo. xl . ſoł.

In Estrea Lest . In Estre Hvnd.

Radulf de curbeſpine ten de epo uñ jugū in Berfreſtone.

Ibi una paupcula mulier redđ . iii . den 7 uñ obolū.

Val 7 ualuit ſep . x . ſoł hoc jugū.

Rannulf de Colūbels ten ibł uñ jugū . qđ in hardes eſco

tauit . 7 nunc uſq̃ ſcotū regis ñ ſcotauit.

Adelold tenuit de epo *Eswalt* . p . iii . ſolins ſe defđ . Tra . ē

     In dñio . ē una car . 7 vi . uiłłi cū . ii . borđ hñt . iii.

car . Ibi . ii . ſerui . 7 ſiluula ad clauſurā . T.R.E. ual . ix . liƀ . m̃ . xv.

Alnod cit tenuit de rege . E.

Osƀn fili Letardi ten de epo . i . ſolin in *Selinge* . Ibi hŧ uñ

uiłłm reddentē . ii . ſoł . T.R.E. ualeƀ . lx . ſoł . 7 poſt 7 m̃. xxxx ſoliđ.

Aluuin tenuit T.R.E.

Iſdē Osƀn ten de epo *Popeselle* . p uno ſolin ſe defđ.

Tra . ē.   In dñio ſunt . ii . car . 7 uñ uiłłs cū . iiii . borđ . hñt

dimiđ car . Hanc trā tenuer̃ . ii . libi hões de rege . E.

Quidã miles ej ten dimiđ jugū . 7 ibi hŧ . i . car in dñio.

Totū T.R.E. ualuit . lx . ſoł . 7 poſt. xx . ſoł . Modo . c . ſoliđ.

In LONINGBOROUGH Hundred

129   The Bishop of Bayeux holds ELHAM in lordship. It answers
for 6 sulungs. Land for 24 ploughs. In lordship 5 ploughs.
   41 villagers with 8 smallholders have 18 ploughs.
   A church; 8 slaves; 2 mills at 6s; meadow, 28 acres;
      woodland, 100 pigs.
Value before 1066 and later £30; now £40; however, it pays £50.
Edric held this manor from King Edward.

In ROLVENDEN Hundred

130   Adam son of Hubert holds 1 pig pasture of ½ yoke which
remained outside Hugh de Montfort's territory from the
Bishop; it lay in *Belice*. He has
   2 villagers with ½ plough.
The value of this is and always was 10s.

In STOWTING Hundred

131   Ansfrid holds ½ sulung in BOCHELANDE from the Bishop.
He has 1 plough in lordship, with
   1 villager.
Land for 2 ploughs.
Value before 1066, 20s; when acquired, 30s; now 40s.

In EASTRY Lathe
In EASTRY Hundred

132   Ralph of Courbépine holds 1 yoke in BARFRESTON from the
Bishop. There a poor woman pays 3½d.
The value of this yoke is and always was 10s.

133   Ranulf of Colombières holds 1 yoke there which paid the levy
in Hardres; it has never yet paid the King's levy.

134   Aethelwold held EASOLE from the Bishop. It answers for 3
sulungs. Land for ... In lordship 1 plough.
   6 villagers with 2 smallholders have 3 ploughs.
   2 slaves; a little wood for fencing.
Value before 1066 £9; now £15.
Young Alnoth held it from King Edward.

135   Osbern son of Ledhard holds 1 sulung in SHELVING from the
Bishop. He has
   1 villager who pays 2s.
Value before 1066, 60s; later and now 40s.
Alwin held it before 1066.

136   Osbern also holds (North) PONSHALL from the Bishop. It answers
for 1 sulung. Land for ... In lordship 2 ploughs.
   1 villager with 4 smallholders have ½ plough.
   2 free men held this land from King Edward.
   A man-at-arms of his holds ½ yoke; he has 1 plough there
in lordship.
Value of the whole before 1066, 60s; later 20s; now 100s.

Radulf⁹ de Curbefpine ten̍   *In Bevsberge hvnd̄.*

dimid jugū in Popeſſale . 7 ibi hī . iii . boues.

T.R.E. 7 poſt:̍ ualuit , iiii . fot . m̄ . viii . folid . Vluric tenuit de rege . E.

Fulbt⁹ ten̍ de epo *Berham* . p̄ . vi.   *In Berhā hvnd̄.*

folins ſe defd̄ . T̄ra . ē . xxxii . car̄ . In dn̄io funt . iii . car̄.

7 lii . uitti cū . xx . cot hn̄t . xviii . car̄ . Ibi æccta . 7 unū

molin̄ de . xx . folid 7 iiii . den̄ . Ibi . xxv . piſcariæ de . xxxv.

folid . iiii . deū min̄⁹ . De Auera . ideſt ſeruitiū . lx . fot . De

herbagio . xxvi . fot . 7 . xx̄ . ac̄ p̄ti . De paſnagio . cl . porc̄.

De iſto M̄ dedit eps unā bereuuichā herbto filio Iuonis . quæ

uocat̄ *Hvhā* . 7 ibi hī . i . car̄ in dn̄io . 7 xii . uittos cū . ix . car̄.

7 xx . ac̄s p̄ti.

De eod̄ q̄q̄ M̄ dedit eps Osbno paisforere . i . folin . 7 ii . molin̄.

de l . fot . 7 ibi . ē in dn̄io . i . car̄ . 7 iiii . uitti cū . i . car̄.

Totū *Berhā* . T.R.E. ualeb . xl . lib . Qdo eps recep:̍ ſimilit.

7 tam̄ reddebat ei . c . lib.

Modo p ſe Berhā . uat . xl . lib . 7 Huchā . x . lib . 7 Hoc qd Osbn̄⁹

hī:̍ vi . lib . 7 tra cujdā Rannulfi militis . uat . xl . fot.

Hoc M̄ tenuit Stigand̄ Archieps . fed n̄ erat de archiep̄atu.

10 a   ſ s; fuit de dn̄ica firma regis . E.

Uitalis de epo ten̍ *Soaneclive* .   *In Witenestaple hd̄.*

p̄ dimid folin ſe defd̄ . T̄ra : ē . i . car̄ 7 dim . In dn̄io . ē . i . car̄ . cū.

vxii . cot . q̄ reddt . iiii : fot 7 vi : den̄ . Silua : xx . porc̄.

T.R.E. ualeb . xxi . folid : Qdo uitat recep:̍ xii . fot : Modo:̍ xxx . fot:

Snoch
Eduuard̄⁹ tenuit de rege . E.

Iſde̅ Vitat ten̍ de epo . i . jugū in eod̄ Hund̄ : 7 ibi hī dimid car̄

in dn̄io . cū . iiii . bord̄ . redd̄ . vi . folid . T̄ra . ē dimid car̄ . Silua . x . porc̄.

T.R.E. 7 poſt . ualuit . x . folid . Modo:̍ xx . folid : Vlſi tenuit de rege . E.

In BEWSBOROUGH Hundred

137   Ralph of Courbépine holds ½ yoke in (South) PONSHALL
he has 3 oxen there.
Value before 1066 and later 4s; now 8s.
   Wulfric held it from King Edward.

In BARHAM Hundred

138   Fulbert holds BARHAM from the Bishop. It answers for 6
sulungs. Land for 32 ploughs. In lordship 3 ploughs.
   52 villagers with 20 cottagers have 18 ploughs.
   A church; a mill at 20s 4d. 25 fisheries at 35s less 4d;
     from cartage, that is, a service, 60s; from grazing, 26s;
     meadow, 20 acres; from pasturage, 150 pigs.
The Bishop gave Herbert son of Ivo an outlier of this manor
which is called Hougham. He has 1 plough in lordship, and
   12 villagers with 9 ploughs.
   Meadow, 20 acres.
From the same manor the Bishop also gave 1 sulung to
Osbern Paisforiere.
   2 mills at 50s.
In lordship 1 plough, and
   4 villagers with 1 plough.
Value of the whole of Barham before 1066 £40; when the
Bishop acquired it, the same; however, it paid him £100.
Value of Barham by itself now £40; Hougham £10; what
Osbern has £6; value of the land of Ranulf, a man-at-arms, 40s.
   Archbishop Stigand held this manor, but it was not the
Archbishopric's, but was of King Edward's household revenue.

In WHITSTABLE Hundred   10 a

139   Vitalis holds SWALECLIFFE from the Bishop. It answers for ½
sulung. Land for 1½ ploughs. In lordship 1 plough, with
   8 cottagers who pay 4s 6d.
   Woodland, 20 pigs.
Value before 1066, 21s; when Vitalis acquired it, 12s; now 30s.
   Edward Snook held it from King Edward.

140   Vitalis also holds 1 yoke from the Bishop in this Hundred; he
has ½ plough in lordship, with
   4 smallholders who pay 6s.
Land for ½ plough. Woodland, 10 pigs.
Value before 1066 and later 10s; now 20s.
   Wulfsi held it from King Edward.

Adã ten de epo . *Ore* . p . ii . folins fe defd . Tra . e . iiii . car.
In dñio . e una . 7 x . uitti cũ . x . bord hñt . ii . car . Ibi dimid æccla
7 uñ moliñ de . xxii . fot . 7 ii . pifcariæ fine cenfu . 7 i . falina
de . xxviii . den . Silua . vi . porc . T . R . E . ualeb . iiii . lib . . 7 poft : lx.
fot . Modo : c . folid .   Turgis tenuit de rege . E.

Ifdẽ Adã ten de epo *Stanefelle* . p . ii . folins fe defd : Tra . e
. iiii . car . In dñio . e . i . car . 7 x . uitti hñt . ii . car . Ibi æccla.
7 vi . ferui . 7 ii . ac pti . Silua . lx . porc . T . R . E . ualeb . lx . fot.
7 poft . xl . fot . Modo : c . folid . Turgis tenuit de Goduino.

Hugo de porth ten de epo *Nortone* . p . iiii . folins fe dfd.
Tra . e . iiii . car . In dñio funt . iii . car . 7 xviii . uitti cũ . vi . bord
hñt . v . car . Ibi . iii . æcclæ . 7 iii . molini fine cenfu . 7 ii . pifcar
de . xii . den . Silua . xl . porc.
T . R . E . ualeb . . viii . lib . 7 poft : vi . lib . Modo : xii . lib.
Ofuuard tenuit de rege . E .   *In Feleberge* hvnd.

Fulbt ten de epo *Cilleham* . p . v . folins fe defd . Tra . e . xx.
car . In dñio funt . ii . car . 7 xxxviii . uitti cũ . xii . cot hñt . xii.
car . Ibi æccla 7 vi . molini de . vi . lib 7 viii . folid . 7 ii . pifca
riæ de xvii . den . 7 paftura de . xviii . fot 7 vii . den.
In cantuaria ciuitate . xiii . mafuræ ptin huic ⊙ . redd . xv.
folid . 7 ix . ac pti . Silua . qt xx . porc.
T . R . E . ualeb . xl . lib . 7 poft : xxx . lib . Modo : xxx . lib fimilit.
7 tam reddeb epo baiocfi qt xx . lib 7 xl . fot.
Sired tenuit de rege . E .   *In Favreshant* hvnd.

Hugo nepos Herbti ten de epo *Ospringes* . p vii . folins 7 dim
fe defd . Tra . e . xx . car . In dñio non funt car.
Ibi . xxix . uitti cũ . vi . bord . hñt . xi . car . Ibi æccla . 7 i . moliñ
de . xi . folid 7 viii . den . 7 pifcaria de . x . den . 7 falina de . iiii.
den . 7 xiii . ac pti . Silua de qt xx . porc.
De tra huj ⊙ ten Herbt dimid folin 7 iii . uirg . 7 ibi ht in
dñio . i . car . 7 i . uitlm cũ . x . bord hñtes . i . car.

In the Lathe of WYE

In FAVERSHAM Hundred

141 Adam holds OARE from the Bishop. It answers for 2 sulungs.
Land for 4 ploughs. In lordship 1.
10 villagers with 10 smallholders have 2 ploughs.
½ church; a mill at 22s; 2 fisheries without dues; 1 salt-house
at 28d; woodland, 6 pigs.
Value before 1066 £4; later 60s; now 100s.
Thorgils held it from King Edward.

142 Adam also holds STALISFIELD from the Bishop. It answers for 2
sulungs. Land for 4 ploughs. In lordship 1 plough.
10 villagers have 2 ploughs.
A church; 6 slaves; meadow, 2 acres; woodland, 60 pigs.
Value before 1066, 60s; later 40s; now 100s.
Thorgils held it from Earl Godwin.

143 Hugh of Port holds NORTON from the Bishop. It answers for 4
sulungs. Land for 4 ploughs. In lordship 3 ploughs.
18 villagers with 6 smallholders have 5 ploughs.
3 churches; 3 mills without dues; 2 fisheries at 12d;
woodland, 40 pigs.
Value before 1066 £8; later £6; now £12.
Osward held it from King Edward.

In FELBOROUGH Hundred

144 Fulbert holds CHILHAM from the Bishop. It answers for 5 sulungs.
Land for 20 ploughs. In lordship 2 ploughs.
38 villagers with 12 cottagers have 12 ploughs.
A church; 6½ mills at £6 8s; 2 fisheries at 17d; pasture at 18s 7d.
To this manor belong 13 dwellings in the City of Canterbury
which pay 15s.
Meadow, 9 acres; woodland, 80 pigs.
Value before 1066 £40; later £30; now likewise £30; however, it
paid the Bishop of Bayeux £80 and 40s.
Sired held it from King Edward.

In FAVERSHAM Hundred

145 Hugh nephew of Herbert holds OSPRINGE from the Bishop. It
answers for 7½ sulungs. Land for 20 ploughs. In lordship no
ploughs.
29 villagers with 6 smallholders have 11 ploughs.
A church; 1 mill at 11s 8d; a fishery at 10d; a salt-house at 4d;
meadow, 13 acres; woodland at 80 pigs.
Herbert holds ½ sulung and 3 virgates of the land of this manor.
He has 1 plough in lordship, and
1 villager with 10 smallholders who have 1 plough.

Ricard̃ de maris ten̄ dimid̃ ſolin de hoc m̄. 7 ibi ħ . vi . uiłłos

7 ɪ . bord̃ cū . ɪ . car̄ . 7 q̃d̃a Turſtin ten̄ . ɪ . jugū . q̃d̃ redd̃ . v . ſolid̃.

Totū m̄ T . R . E . ualeƀ . xx . liƀ . Q̃do herƀt recep̃ꞓ xv . liƀ.

Modo ꞓ xx . liƀ . Huic m̄ p̃tin̄ in cantuaria . ɪ . maſura

de . xxx . denar̄ . Hoc m̄ tenuit

Ansfrid̃ ten̄ de ep̃o *CILDRESHÃ* . ꝓ uno ſolin ſe defd̃ . T̃ra . ē

ɪɪɪ . car̄ . In dn̄io . ē una . 7 ɪɪɪɪ . uiłłi cū . ɪɪ . bord̃ hn̄t . ɪ . car̄

7 dimid̃ . Ibi . v . ſerui . 7 ɪɪ . ãc p̃ti . Silua . ē s; nil redd̃ .

De hoc m̄ ten̄ q̃d̃a miles tr̃a ad . ɪ . car̄ . In̄t tot̃ T . R . E .

ualeƀ . lx . ſol . 7 poſt ꞓ xl . ſol . Modo ꞓ ɪɪɪɪ . liƀ .

Iſdē Ansfrid̃ ten̄ de ep̃o *ERNOLTVN* . ꝓ uno ſolin ſe defd̃ .

T̃ra . ē . ɪɪɪ . car̄ . In dn̄io . ē una . 7 vɪɪɪ . uiłłi cū . ɪɪ . car̄

7 dimid̃ . Ibi . ɪɪ . ſalinæ .

7 in ciuitate cantuaria . ɪ . maſura de . xxɪ . den̄ .

T . R . E . ualeƀ . ɪɪɪɪ . liƀ . 7 poſt ꞓ xl . ſol . Modo ꞓ c . ſol . hoc m̄

Burnod de rege . E . tenuit ꞓ De iſto m̄ ten̄ Rannulf

x . acs . quæ jacen̄ juxta ciuitate . 7 reddeƀ . xl . ɪɪ . den̄ . T . R . E .

Iſdē Ansfrid̃ ten̄ de ep̃o *MACHEHEVET* . ꝓ uno jugo ſe

defd̃ . T̃ra . ē dimid̃ car̄ . Ibi ſunt . ɪɪ . uiłłi redd̃ . l . denar̄ .

T . R . E . ualeƀ . l . den̄ . m̄ ual . lx . den̄ . Seuuold̃ tenuit . T . R . E .

Iſdē Anfrid̃ ten̄ de ep̃o *BADELESMERE* . ꝓ uno ſolin

ſe defd̃ . T̃ra . ē . ɪɪ . car̄ 7 dim̄ . In dn̄io . ē una . 7 x . uiłłi

hn̄t . ɪ . car̄ 7 dim̄ . Ibi æccła . 7 ɪɪ . ſerui . 7 piſcaria de xɪɪ .

den̄ . Silua ꞓ ɪɪɪɪ . porc̄ . T . R . E . ualeƀ . lx . ſol . 7 poſt ꞓ lx . ſol .

Modo ꞓ ɪɪɪɪ . liƀ . Hoc m̄ reclamat abƀ S̃ Auguſtini ꞓ

qa habuit T . R . E . 7 hund̃ atteſtant ei . S; fili h̃ois dicit

patr̃e ſuū ſe poſſe uertere ubi uoluerit . 7 hoc n̄ annuṽ monachi .

Iſdē Ansfrid̃ ten̄ de ep̃o *PERIE* . ꝓ uno jugo ſe defendeƀ .

Ibi . ē un̄ bord̃ redd̃ . v . den̄ . T . R . E . 7 poſt ꞓ 7 m̄ ꞓ ual . xvɪ . ſolid̃ .

Wlui tenuit de rege . E .

Richard of Le Marais holds ½ sulung of this manor. He has 6 villagers and 1 smallholder with 1 plough.

Thurstan holds 1 yoke which pays 5s.

Value of the whole manor before 1066 £20; when Herbert acquired it, £15; now £20.

To this manor belongs 1 dwelling in Canterbury at 30d.

... held this manor.

146 Ansfrid holds CILDRESHAM from the Bishop. It answers for 1 sulung. Land for 3 ploughs. In lordship 1.

4 villagers with 2 smallholders have 1½ ploughs.

5 slaves; meadow, 2 acres; woodland, but it pays nothing.

Of this manor a man-at-arms holds land for 1 plough.

In total, value before 1066, 60s; later 40s; now £4.

Ansfrid also holds from the Bishop   10 b

147 ARNOLTON. It answers for 1 sulung. Land for 3 ploughs. In lordship 1.

8 villagers with 2½ ploughs.

2 salt-houses; in the City of Canterbury 1 dwelling at 21d.

Value before 1066 £4; later 40s; now 100s.

Burgnoth held this manor from King Edward.

Of this manor Ranulf holds 10 acres which lie near the city and paid 42d before 1066.

148 MACKNADE. It answers for 1 yoke. Land for ½ plough.

2 villagers who pay 50d.

Value before 1066, 50d; value now 60d.

Saewold held it before 1066.

149 BADLESMERE. It answers for 1 sulung. Land for 2½ ploughs. In lordship 1.

10 villagers have 1½ ploughs.

A church; 2 slaves; a fishery at 12d; woodland, 4 pigs.

Value before 1066, 60s; later 60s; now £4.

The Abbot of St. Augustine's claims this manor because he had it before 1066; the Hundred bear witness for him; but the man's son says that his father could turn where he would; the monks do not agree with this.

150 PERRY (Wood). It answered for 1 yoke.

1 smallholder who pays 5d.

Value before 1066, later and now 16s.

Wulfwy held it from King Edward.

Isdē Ansfrid ten de epo PERIE . p dimid solin se defd.

Tra . ē . ı . car . Ibi . ııı . bord . 7 una masura in ciuitate de . xvı .

denar . T . R . E . 7 post . 7 m̄ . ual . xxıııı . solid . Vlcua tenuit �🖊 de rege . E.

Osbñ ten de epo BOCHELAND . p . ııı . jugis se defd.

Tra . ē . ı . car . In dñio . ē una . 7 ıııı . uilli cū . ıı . bord hñt

dimid car . Ibi . vııı . serui .   �🖊 Seuuard tenuit de rege . E .

T . R . E . ualeb . ıııı . lib . 7 post . ııı . lib . 7 m̄ . Lxx . solid .

Isdē Osbñ ten uñ jugū de epo in eod m̄ . 7 p . ı . jugo

se defd . T . R . E . ualeb . xx . sol . 7 post 7 m̄ . ual . x . sol .

Leuuard tenuit de rege . E .

Hugo de porth ten de epo HERSTE . p . ıı͞ı . jugis

se defd . Tra . ē . ı . car . In dñio . ē . cū . ıı . bord 7 ıı . seruis .

T . R . E . 7 post . ualuit . x . solid . Modo . xxx . solid .

Osuuard tenuit de rege . E .

Adā ten de epo . unū jugū in ORE . 7 p . ı . jugo

se defd . Tra . ē . ı . car . Hanc ten . ııı . uilli m̄ ad

firmā . 7 reddt . xx . sol . 7 tantd sep ualuit . Ibi æccla . ē .

Leuuold tenuit de rege . E .

Herfrid ten TREVELAI . p . ııı . solins se defnd .

Tra . ē . vııı . car . In dñio . ē una . 7 xxıııı . uilli cū . v .

bord hñt . vı . car 7 dim . Ibi æccla . 7 v . serui .

Silua . xx . porc . 7 in ciuitate . ııı . hage . de . xxxıı .

denar . T . R . E . ualeb . vıı . lib . 7 post . vı . lib .

Modo . vııı . lib . Vlnod tenuit de rege . E .

Herbt tenuit de epo NORDESLINGE . Tra . ē

. ı . car . p dim solin se defd . Ibi . ıı . bord reddt

ıı . solid . T . R . E . 7 post . ualuit . xx . sol . Modo . xxv . sol .

Turgod tenuit T . R . E .

Hæc . ıı . m̄ tenuit Herbt fili Iuonis de epo Baioc .

151   PERRY (Court). It answers for ½ sulung. Land for 1 plough.
3 smallholders.
1 dwelling in the city at 16d.
Value before 1066, later and now 24s.
Wulfeva held it from King Edward.

152   Osbern holds BUCKLAND from the Bishop. It answers for 3 yokes.
Land for 1 plough. In lordship 1.
3 villagers with 2 smallholders have ½ plough.
8 slaves.
Value before 1066 £4; later £3; now 70s.
Saeward held it from King Edward.
Osbern also holds 1 yoke in this manor from the Bishop.
It answers for 1 yoke.
Value before 1066, 20s; value later and now 10s.
Leofward held it from King Edward.

153   Hugh of Port holds HURST from the Bishop. It answers for 3 yokes.
Land for 1 plough. It is in lordship, with
2 smallholders and 2 slaves.
Value before 1066 and later 10s; now 30s.
Osward held it from King Edward.

154   Adam holds 1 yoke in OARE from the Bishop. It answers for 1
yoke. Land for 1 plough.
3 villagers now hold it at a revenue.
It pays 20s; its value was always as much.
A church.
Leofwold held it from King Edward.

155   Herfrid holds THROWLEY. It answers for 3 sulungs. Land for 8
ploughs. In lordship 1.
24 villagers with 5 smallholders have 6½ ploughs.
A church; 5 slaves; woodland, 20 pigs; in the city 3 sites at 32d.
Value before 1066 £7; later £6; now £8.
Wulfnoth held it from King Edward.

156   Herbert held NORTH EASTLING from the Bishop. Land for 1 plough.
It answers for ½ sulung.
2 smallholders pay 2s.
Value before 1066 and later 20s; now 25s.
Thorgot held it before 1066.

Herbert son of Ivo held these 2 manors from the Bishop of Bayeux.

Turstin de girunde ten in Bochelande.i.jugū de epo.7 pro
.i.jugo se defd.Ibi.ē un uilłs reddens.vi.solid.Val 7 ualuit
semp.xii.solid.Turgot tenuit de rege.E.

Rogeri fili Anschitil ten de epo ESLINGES.ꝑ uno solin
se defd.Tra.ē.i.car.Ibi.ē in dnio.7 un bord hт dimid
car.Ibi æccła 7 i.molin de.x.solid.7 ii.ač pti.

T.R.E.ualeb lx.sol.7 post.'xx.sol.Modo.'xl.solid.

Vnlot tenuit de rege.E.7 potuit ire quo uoluit cū tra.

Fulbt ten de epo ESLINGES.ꝑ.v.solins se defd.T.R.E.
7 m̄.ꝑ.ii̅.7 sic fecit post�q eps dedit Ϻ Hugoni filio fulbti.
Tra.ē.vi.car.In dnio sunt.ii.car.7 xxx.uilli hnt.iii.
car.Ibi æccła 7 xxviii.serui.7 i.molin de.x.sol.Silua
.xxx.porc.T.R.E.ualeb.x.lib.7 qdo recep.'vi.lib.
Modo.iiii.lib.7 tam eps habuit.viii.lib.Sired tenuit de rege.E.

Isd Fulbt ten de epo DODEHA.ꝑ uno solin se defd.Tra
.ē   In dnio.ē una car.7 xvii.uilli cū.x.bord
hnt.ii.car.Ibi æccła 7 vi.serui.7 dimid piscar de.ccc.
allecib.7 in cantuaria ciuitate.v.hagæ de.vii.sol 7 x.den.
T.R.E.ualeb.x.lib.Eps misit ad firmā|x.lib.Qdo ful
btus recep.'vi.lib.7 m̄ similit.Sired tenuit de rege.E.

Ricard ten de epo RONGOSTONE.ꝑ uno solin se
defd.Tra.ē   Ibi.ii.uilli hnt.i.car.7 reddt.vi.sol.
T.R.E.7 post.7 m̄.ual.xl.solid.Vluiet tenuit rege.E.

IN FERLEBERGE HD.

Ansfrid ten de epo HORTONE.ꝑ dimid solin se defd.
Tra.ē.i.car.Ibi.ē in dnio.7 xiii.uilli hnt dimid car.
Ibi.i.seru.7 ii.molini de una marka arg.7 viii.ač pti.
7 c.ač siluæ minutæ. T.R.E.ualeb.xl......
xxx.sol.Modo.'c.solid.Godricus ten....ge.E.

157 Thurstan of Gironde holds 1 yoke in BUCKLAND from the Bishop. 10 c
It answers for 1 yoke.
  1 villager who pays 6s.
The value is and always was 12s.
  Thorgot held it from King Edward.

158 Roger son of Ansketel holds EASTLING from the Bishop. It answers
for 1 sulung. Land for 1 plough. It is there, in lordship.
  1 smallholder has ½ plough.
  A church; 1 mill at 10s; meadow, 2 acres.
Value before 1066, 60s; later 20s; now 40s.
  Wulfnoth held it from King Edward; he could go where he would
with his land.

159 Fulbert holds EASTLING from the Bishop. It answered for 5 sulungs
before 1066; now for 2; and did so after the Bishop gave the manor
to Hugh son of Fulbert. Land for 6 ploughs. In lordship 2 ploughs.
  30 villagers have 3 ploughs.
  A church; 28 slaves; 1 mill at 10s; woodland, 30 pigs.
Value before 1066 £10; when acquired £6; now £4; however, the
Bishop had £8.
  Sired held it from King Edward.

160 Fulbert also holds LUDDENHAM from the Bishop. It answers for 1
sulung. Land for ... In lordship 1 plough.
  17 villagers with 10 smallholders have 2 ploughs.
  A church; 6 slaves; ½ fishery at 300 herrings; in the City of
    Canterbury 5 sites at 7s 10d.
Value before 1066 £10; the Bishop put it at a revenue for £10;
when Fulbert acquired it, £6; now the same.
  Sired held it from King Edward.

161 Richard holds RINGLESTONE from the Bishop. It answers for 1
sulung. Land for ...
  2 villagers have 1 plough and pay 6s.
Value before 1066, later and now 40s.
  Wulfgeat held it from King Edward.

In FELBOROUGH Hundred
162 Ansfrid holds HORTON from the Bishop. It answers for ½ sulung.
Land for 1 plough. It is there, in lordship.
  13 villagers have ½ plough.
  1 slave; 2 mills at 1 silver mark; meadow, 8 acres;
    underwood, 100 acres.
Value before 1066, 40[s; later] 30s; now 100s.
  Godric held it from King Edward.

Adā ten de epō *FANNE* . p dim̄ ſolin *IN . . . . HVND*.

ſe defd . Tra . ē . I . car 7 dim . In dn̄io ſunt . II . car . 7 III . uilłi

7 III . ſerui . 7 æcla . 7 XIII . ac̄ p̄ti . Silua . x . porc̄.

. T . R . E . ualeb . IIII . lib . 7 poſt . xx . ſoł . Modo . IIII . lib.

Hugo de montfort ten inde q̄d uał . xx . ſolid.

Wadard ten de epō *BERCHVELLE* . p dim̄ ſolin

ſe defd . Tra . ē . I . car . Ibi . ē in dn̄io . 7 III . uilłi . 7 III.

ſerui . 7 un̄ molin̄ de XL . den̄ . 7 x . ac̄ p̄ti . 7 un̄ alnetū.

T . R . E . 7 poſt . ualuit . xx . ſoł . Modo . XL . ſolid.

Werelm tenuit de rege.

Iſdē Wadard ten de epō *CVMBE* . p uno ſolin ſe defd.

Tra . ē . II . car . In dn̄io . ē una . 7 IX . uilłi cū . v . bord

hn̄t . I . car 7 dimid . Ibi . XIIII . ac̄ p̄ti . Silua . v . porc̄.

T . R . E . ualeb . LX . ſoł . 7 poſt . L . ſoł . Modo . IIII . lib . 7 ſer

uitiū uni militis . Leuret de rochinge tenuit de rege . E.

Radulf de curbeſpine ten de epō *BETMONTESTVN*.

p uno ſolin ſe defd . Tra . ē . VI . car . In dn̄io ſunt . II.

7 XIII . uilłi cū . I . bord hn̄t . III . car . Ibi . XXX.III . ac̄ p̄ti.

7 ſilua . XL . porc̄ . De iſto m̄ ten Hugo de montfort

int ſiluā 7 paſturā q̄d ualeb T . R . E . VI . lib . 7 poſt

7 modo . tntd . Ailric tenuit de rege . E.

Adelold tenuit de epō *DENE* . p uno ſolin ſe defd . Tra . ē . II . car.

In dn̄io . ē una car . 7 IIII . bord . 7 II . ſerui . 7 una ac̄ p̄ti . 7 ſilua

VII . porc̄ . De iſto ſolino ten Radulf de curbeſpine . I . jugū

7 dimid . q̄d uał 7 ualuit ſep . x . ſolid . Adelold habuit dimid

ſolin 7 dimid jugū . 7 T . R . E . ualeb XL . ſolid . 7 poſt . xx . ſolid.

Modo . XL . ſoł . H̄ tra . ē in manu regis . Hanc trā tenuer̄

Vlnod 7 Wana 7 Aluuard 7 Vlueron de rege . E . 7 erat dis

ptita in tribʒ locis.

In [WYE] Hundred

163   Adam holds FANSCOMBE from the Bishop. It answers for ½ sulung.
Land for 1½ ploughs. In lordship 2 ploughs, and
    3 villagers and 3 slaves.
    A church; meadow, 13 acres; woodland, 10 pigs.
Value before 1066 £4; later 20s; now £4.
    Of this Hugh de Montfort holds what is valued at 20s.

164   Wadard holds BUCKWELL from the Bishop. It answers for ½
sulung. Land for 1 plough. It is there, in lordship.
    3 villagers and 3 slaves.
    A mill at 40d; meadow, 10 acres; an alder wood.
Value before 1066 and later 20s; now 40s.
    Warhelm held it from the King.

165   Wadard also holds COOMBE (Grove) from the Bishop. It answers
for 1 sulung. Land for 2 ploughs. In lordship 1.
    9 villagers with 5 smallholders have 1½ ploughs.
    Meadow, 14 acres; woodland, 5 pigs.
Value before 1066, 60s; later 50s; now £4 and the service of
1 man-at-arms.
    Leofred of Ruckinge held it from King Edward.

166   Ralph of Courbépine holds BEAMONSTON from the Bishop.
It answers for 1 sulung. Land for 6 ploughs. In lordship 2.
    13 villagers with 1 smallholder have 3 ploughs.
    Meadow, 33 acres; woodland, 40 pigs.
    Of this manor Hugh de Montfort holds both woodland
       and pasture, whose value before 1066 was £6; later and
       now as much.
    Aelfric held it from King Edward.

167   Aethelwold held DEAN (Court) from the Bishop. It answers   10 d
for 1 sulung. Land for 2 ploughs. In lordship 1 plough;
    4 smallholders and 2 slaves.
    Meadow, 1 acre; woodland, 7 pigs.
    Of this sulung Ralph of Courbépine holds 1½ yokes,
whose value is and always was 10s.
    Aethelwold had ½ sulung and ½ yoke; value before 1066,
40s; later 20s; now 40s.
    This land is in the King's hands.
    Wulfnoth, Waua, Alfward and Wulfrun held this land from
King Edward; it was divided out in three places.

Radulf de curbespine ten *PIVENTONE* de feudo epi . 7 Hugo
de eo . p uno solin se defđ . Tra . ē . v . car . In dnio . ē una 7 dimiđ .
7 vII . uilti cū . vII . borđ hnt . III . car 7 dim . Ibi æccła . 7 IX . serui .
7 un molin de LV . den . 7 xx . ac pti . Silua . LX . porc .
T.R.E. ualeb . vIII . lib . 7 post . c . sol . Modo . vI . lib . Sbern tenuit de rege . E .
Isđ Radulf ten . III . denas quæ remanser ext diuisione Hugon
de montfort . de pistinges M̃ . 7 ibi . ē un jugū træ . 7 una uirga .
7 ibi funt . II . uilti . Val 7 ualuit sep . xv . sol . *IN FERLIBERG HD̃.*

Herfrid ten de feudo epi *ESSAMELESFORD* . p dim solin
se defđ . Tra . ē . I . car . In dnio . ē . I . car . 7 III . uilti cū . I . borđ hnt
I . car . Ibi . III . serui . 7 vIII . ac pti . T.R.E . ual . LX . sol . 7 post .
XL . sol . Modo . LX . soliđ . Alret tenuit de rege . E .

Osbt ten de Witto filio tau *ALDELOSE* . *IN BILISSOLD HD̃.*
Ibi jacet dimiđ solin . Tra . ē . II . car . In dnio . ē una car . 7 III .
uilti hnt dimiđ car . T.R.E. ualeb xxx . sol . 7 post . xx . soliđ .
Modo . XL . sol . H̃ tra . ē de feudo epi baioc . 7 remansit foris
diuisione suā . Godric tenuit de rege . E . cū *BRADEBVRNE* M̃ .

IN LIMOWART LEST. *IN OXENAI HVND.*

Osbn paisfor ten de epo *PALESTREI* . p . III . jugis se defđ .
Tra . ē . II . car . In dnio . ē una . 7 IX . borđ hnt dim car . Ibi æccła
7 II . serui . 7 x . ac pti . 7 v . piscar de . xII . den . Silua . x . porc .
T.R.E. 7 post . ualuit . XL . sol . Modo . LX . soliđ . Eduui . tenuit de rege . E .

IN LEST DE ESTREI. *IN BEVSBERGE HVND.*

Isđe Osbn ten de epo xII . acs træ . quæ ual p annū . IIII . soliđ .

Hugo de porth ten de epo *PESINGES* 7 *PIHA* . p . II . solins
se defđ . Tra . ē   In dnio . II . car 7 dimiđ . 7 vI . uilti cū . xIIII .
borđ hnt . I . car .   T.R.E. ualeb . c . sol . 7 post . nichil . M̃ . vI . lib .
Lefstan 7 Leuuin 7 Eluret 7 Sired 7 alii . II . tenuer . T.R.E .
7 poterant ire qlibet cū tris suis .

In CALEHILL Hundred

168 Ralph of Courbépine holds PIVINGTON from the Bishop's Holding and Hugh from him. It answers for 1 sulung. Land for 5 ploughs. In lordship 1½.
7 villagers with 7 smallholders have 3½ ploughs.
A church; 9 slaves; a mill at 55d; meadow, 20 acres; woodland, 60 pigs.
Value before 1066 £8; later 100s; now £6.
Esbern Big held it from King Edward.

169 Ralph also holds 3 pig pastures of POSTLING manor, which remained outside Hugh de Montfort's territory. 1 yoke of land and 1 virgate.
2 villagers.
The value is and always was 15s.

In FELBOROUGH Hundred

170 Herfrid holds SHALMSFORD (Street) from the Bishop's Holding.
It answers for ½ sulung. Land for 1 plough. In lordship 1 plough.
3 villagers with 1 smallholder have 1 plough.
3 slaves; meadow, 8 acres.
Value before 1066, 60s; later 40s; now 60s.
Aelred held it from King Edward.

171 Osbert holds ALDGLOSE from William of Thaon's son. ½ sulung lies there. Land for 2 ploughs. In lordship 1 plough.
3 villagers have ½ plough.
Value before 1066, 30s; later 20s; now 40s.
This land is from the Bishop of Bayeux' Holding and remained outside his territory.
Godric held it from King Edward; it is with Brabourne manor.

In LYMPNE Lathe
In OXNEY Hundred

172 Osbern Paisforiere holds PALSTRE (Court) from the Bishop. It answers for 3 yokes. Land for 2 ploughs. In lordship 1.
9 smallholders have ½ plough.
A church; 2 slaves; meadow, 10 acres; 5 fisheries at 12d; woodland, 10 pigs.
Value before 1066 and later 40s; now 60s.
Edwy the priest held it from King Edward.

In the Lathe of EASTRY
In BEWSBOROUGH Hundred

173 Osbern also holds 12 acres of land from the Bishop, value 4s a year.

174 Hugh of Port holds PISING and PINEHAM from the Bishop. They answer for 2 sulungs. Land for ... In lordship 2½ ploughs.
6 villagers with 14 smallholders have 1 plough.
Value before 1066, 100s; later nothing; now £6.
Leofstan, Leofwin, Alfred, Sired and two others held them before 1066; they could go wherever they would with their lands.

Eps Baiocsis ten in dñio *Bilsvitone* . ᵽ iiii . solins

se defd . Tra . ē xv . car . In dñio sunt . v . 7 xlvii . uilli cũ

xxvii . bord hñt . xiiii . car . Ibi æccla 7 x . salinæ de . c . denar.

7 x . ac ᵱti . Silua . l . porc . 7 ii . piscar de . v . den.

T . R . E . ualeb . x . lib . 7 post.´ xxx . lib . Modo´ l . lib . 7 tam reddit

de firma . lxx . lib . Alnod tenuit . In hoc ⏁ misit eps . iii.

denas . quæ remanser ext diuisioñe comitis de Ow.

Rotbt de Romenel ten de eᵱo   *In Lantport Hvnd.*

Afettvne . ᵽ uno solin se defd . Tra . ē . iii . car . In dñio . ē una .

7 ix . uilli cũ . iii . bord hñt . iii . car 7 dimid . Ibi . ii . serui.

T . R . E .´ ualeb . c . sot . 7 post.´ l . solid . m . iiii . lib.

Isdē Rotbt ten de eᵱo in Maresc dim solin . 7 ᵽ tanto se defd.

Tra . ē . ii . car . Ibi . xi . uilli . cũ . ii . bord hñt . iii . car . 7 piscaria

Isd Robt hr . l . burgses in burgo de *Romenel* . 7 de eis ſ de . ii . solid.

hr rex omē seruitiũ . 7 st ḋeti ᵽ seruitio maris ab omi csuetudine ᵱt

tribȝ . Latrocin . pace infracta . 7 forstel.

<hr />

11 a

com.
de Goduino

T . R . E . 7 post ualuit . xl . sot . Modo´ l . sot . Alfi tenuit

Isdē Robtus ten de eᵱo dimid solin in Maresc . 7 ᵽ tanto se

defd . Tra . ē . ii . car . In dñio . ē dimid car . 7 xv . uilli cũ . ii . bord

hñt . iii . car 7 dimid . T . R . E . 7 post.´ ualeb . xxx . sot . m . xl . sot.

Sex sochi tenuer T . R . E .   *In Rovindene Hvnd.*

Isdē Rotbt ten de eᵱo *Benindene* . ᵽ dimid solin se defd.

Tra . ē . ii . car . In dñio . ē una car . 7 iiii . uilli cũ . ix . bord hñt . ii . car.

Ibi silua . v . porc . 7 una æccla . T . R . E . 7 post . ualuit . xl . sot.

Modo´ l . solid . Osier tenuit de rege . E . *In Adilovtesbrige*

Isdē Rotbt ten de eᵱo dimid jugũ . 7 ᵽ tanto se defd .   *Hvnd.*

In LYMPNE Lathe

In NEWCHURCH (Hundred)

175   The Bishop of Bayeux holds BILSINGTON in lordship. It answers for 4 sulungs. Land for 15 ploughs. In lordship 5.
     47 villagers with 27 smallholders have 14 ploughs.
     A church; 10 salt-houses at 100d; meadow, 10 acres; woodland, 50 pigs; 2 fisheries at 5d.
   Value before 1066 £10; later £30; now £50; however, it pays £70 in revenue.
     Young Alnoth held it.
     The Bishop put 3 pig pastures into this manor which remained outside the Count of Eu's territory.

In LANGPORT Hundred

176   Robert of Romney holds *AFETTUNE* from the Bishop. It answers for 1 sulung. Land for 3 ploughs. In lordship 1.
     9 villagers with 3 smallholders have 3½ ploughs. 2 slaves.
   Value before 1066, 100s; later 50s; now £4.

177   Robert also holds ½ sulung in (Denge) MARSH from the Bishop. It answers for as much. Land for 2 ploughs.
     11 villagers with 2 smallholders have 3 ploughs.
     A fishery at 2s.

178   Robert also has 50 burgesses in the Borough of ROMNEY. The King has all the service from them; they are exempt because of service at sea from all customary dues except three: theft, breach of the peace and highway robbery.
   Value before 1066 and later 40s; now 50s.   11 a
     Alfsi held it from Earl Godwin.

179   Robert also holds ½ sulung in (Denge) MARSH from the Bishop. It answers for as much. Land for 2 ploughs. In lordship ½ plough.
     15 villagers with 2 smallholders have 3½ ploughs.
   Value before 1066 and later 30s; now 40s.
     6 Freemen held it before 1066.

In ROLVENDEN Hundred

180   Robert also holds BENENDEN from the Bishop. It answers for ½ sulung. Land for 2 ploughs. In lordship 1 plough.
     4 villagers with 9 smallholders have 2 ploughs.
     Woodland, 5 pigs; a church.
   Value before 1066 and later 40s; now 50s.
     Osgeard held it from King Edward.

In ALOESBRIDGE Hundred

181   Robert also holds ½ yoke from the Bishop. It answers for as much.

Ibi unã uidua manet reddeɴs xīīī . denar p̄ annũ . Val̄ 7 ua

luit ſēp . x . ſolid . Duo ſochi tenuer̄ T.R.E. ſine aulis 7 dñiis.

Iſdē Rotb̄t̄ ten de ep̄o dimidiã denã de Ꝏ . *TITENTONE*.

qđ ten Hugo de montfort . 7 ibi h̄t̄ trã ad dimiđ car̄.

7 uñ uiłłm cũ . iii . borđ 7 dimiđ car̄ . 7 ī̅ī̅ . piſcar̄ de . v . ſolid.

Val̄ h̄· totũ 7 ualuit . xv . ſolid . H̄ trā . ē ext̄ diuiſionē hugon̄.

IN LEST DE ESTREI.   *IN ESTREI HVND.*

Herb̄t̄ ten ad firmã de rege *RINGETONE* . De feudo . ē ep̄i.

T̄ra . ē   In dñio ſunt . ī̅ī̅ . car̄ . 7 iiii . uiłłi cũ . vii . borđ

h̄nt . ii . car̄ 7 dimiđ . Ibi uñ moliñ de . xl . ſolid.

T.R.E. ualeb̄ . viii . lib̄ . Q̄do recep̄: c . ſol̄ . Modo . viii . lib̄ . 7 tam̄

reddit . xiir . lib̄ . Eduuard tenuit de rege . E.

Adã ten de feudo ep̄i in *HAMOLDE* dimiđ jugũ . Riculf̄

ten̄ de adã . 7 aliud dimiđ jugũ de *AIMOLDE* ten̄ Herb̄t̄ de

hugone nēpote Herbt̄i . Hoc utrunq̄ . ual̄ . xx . ſol̄.

Hugo ten̄ *EꝶELLE* de ep̄o . p̄ . iii . ſolins *IN BEVSBERG HVND.*

ſe defđ . T̄ra . ē   In dñio . ē . i . car̄ . 7 xv . uiłłi cũ . xii . borđ

h̄nt . ii . car̄ . Ibi . ii . molini de . xl.vi . ſolid . 7 iiii . ac̄ p̄ti . Silua

iiii . porc̄ . T.R.E. ualeb̄ xii . lib̄ . 7 poſt: c . ſol̄ . Modo: x . lib̄.

7 tam̄ redd xii . lib̄ 7 xii . ſolid . Edric de Alhã tenuit de rege . E.

De iſto Ꝏ ten̄ Hugo de Montfort . xvii . ac̄s tre . 7 unã denã.

7 dimiđ . qđ ap̄p̄ciat̄ . vii . ſolid.

Iſdē Hugo ten̄ de ep̄o *WESCLIVE* . p̄ ii . ſolins ſe defđ . T̄ra . ē

          In dñio . ē . i . car̄ . 7 xvii . uiłłi h̄nt . ii . car̄.

T.R.E. ualeb̄ . viii . lib̄ . Q̄do recep̄: vi . lib̄ . Modo: viii . lib̄.

De hoc Ꝏ ten̄ Hugo de montfort . ii . moliñ . de . xxviii . ſolid.

Edricus tenuit . de rege . E.

Iſdē ten̄ ^(Hugo) *SOLTONE* . de ep̄o . p̄ uno ſolin ſe defđ . T̄ra . ē

          In dñio . ē una car̄ . 7 iii . uiłłi cũ uno borđ

reddt̄ . iiii . ſolid 7 vii . den.

T.R.E. ualeb̄ . xv . lib̄ . 7 poſt . 7 modo: xxx . ſolid . In hoc Ꝏ

manſit Godric 7 ten̄ . xx . ac̄s de alodio ſuo.

A widow who pays 22d a year lives there.
The value is and always was 10s.
Before 1066, 2 Freemen held it without halls and lordships.

182   Robert also holds ½ pig pasture from TINTON manor from the
Bishop, which Hugh de Montfort holds. He has land for ½ plough;
1 villager with 3 smallholders and ½ plough.
2 fisheries at 5s.
The value of the whole of this is and was 15s.
This land is outside Hugh's territory.

In the Lathe of EASTRY

In EASTRY Hundred

183   Herbert holds RINGLETON at a revenue from the King. It is of
the Bishop's Holding. Land for ... In lordship 2 ploughs.
4 villagers with 7 smallholders have 2½ ploughs.
A mill at 40s.
Value before 1066 £8; when acquired 100s; now £8; however,
it pays £13.
Edward held it from King Edward.

184   Adam holds ½ yoke in HAMMIL from the Bishop's Holding. Riculf
holds from Adam. Herbert holds another ½ yoke of Hammil from
Hugh nephew of Herbert.
Value of both of these 20s.

In BEWSBOROUGH Hundred

185   Hugh holds (Temple) EWELL from the Bishop. It answers for 3 sulungs.
Land for ... In lordship 1 plough.
15 villagers with 12 smallholders have 2 ploughs.
2 mills at 46s; meadow, 4 acres; woodland, 4 pigs.
Value before 1066 £12; later 100s; now £10; however, it pays
£12 12s.
Edric of Elham held it from King Edward.
Of this manor Hugh de Montfort holds 17 acres of land and
1½ pig pastures which are assessed at 7s.

186   Hugh also holds WEST CLIFFE from the Bishop. It answers for 2
sulungs. Land for ... In lordship 1 plough.
17 villagers have 2 ploughs.
Value before 1066 £8; when acquired £6; now £8.
Of this manor Hugh de Montfort holds 2 mills at 28s.
Edric held it from King Edward.

187   Hugh also holds SOLTON from the Bishop. It answers for 1
sulung. Land for ... In lordship 1 plough.
3 villagers with 1 smallholder pay 4s 7d.
Value before 1066 £15; later and now 30s.
Godric lived in this manor; he held 20 acres as his freehold.

Idē Hugo ten̄ in *DOVERE* uñ moliñ . qui reddit . XLVIII.

ferlingels de frum̄to . 7 ñ p̄tiñ ulli Manerio.

Ansfrid ten̄ de feudo ep̄i in Leucberge dimid jugū . 7 ibi

hт̄ . I . uiltm 7 I . bord .   Val . V . solid . Leuuiñ tenuit de rege . E

Ibidē mansit q̄da Altet qui tenuit de rege . E . II . ac̄s

in alodiu . 7 tenuit eas de Ansfrido . 7 ap̄pciat̄ . VI . solid.

Radulf de curbespine ten̄ *COLRET* de ep̄o . Tra . ē

        In dñio . I . car̄ 7 dim̄ . 7 VI . uilti cū . VII . bord

hñt . II . car̄ . Ibi . II . serui . 7 IIII . ac̄ p̄ti . p . II . solins se defd.

T.R.E. ualeb̄ . VIII . lib̄ . 7 post ꞏ xx . solid . Modo ꞏ VI . lib̄.

Molleue tenuit de rege . E.

Isdē Radulf ten̄ *EWELLE* . p III . solins se defd̄ . Tra . ē

        In dñio . ē una car̄ . 7 V . uilti cū . IIII . bord

hñt . II . car̄ . Ibi silua . x . porc̄.

De hoc M̄ ten̄ q̄da miles . I . solin de Radulfo . 7 ibi hт̄ . I . car̄

                         cū . III . bord.

Totū M̄ . T.R.E. ualeb̄ . XII . lib̄ . 7 post ꞏ xx . sol̄ . Modo ꞏ XL . sol̄.

7 tam̄ qd̄ Radulf hт̄ . reddit . IIII . lib̄ .   Hugo de montfort

hт̄ cap̄ manerii . 7 ibi . V . molin̄ 7 dimid de . VI . lib̄.

Isdē Radulf ten̄ de ep̄o *SVANETONE* .   Molleue tenuit de rege . E.

p . II . solins se defd̄ . Tra . ē   In dñio . I . car̄ . 7 II . bord cū

dimid car̄.

De hac tra ten̄ Robt̄ de barbes . I . solin . 7 ibi hт̄ . III . uiltos

cū dimid car̄ . 7 q̄da Hugo ten̄ . I . solin 7 hт̄ ibi . I . car̄ in dñio.

7 uñ bord . T.R.E. ualeb̄ . x . lib̄ . Qdo recep̄ ꞏ xxx . solid.

Modo ꞏ XL . solid . 7 tam̄ redd̄ . IIII . lib̄ . Coloen tenuit de rege . E.

Isdē Radulf ten̄ de ep̄o *APLETONE* . p uno solin se defd̄.

Tra . ē   In dñio sunt . II . car̄ . cū . VI . bord.

T.R.E. ualeb̄ . C . sol̄ . 7 post ꞏ x . sol̄ . Modo ꞏ XL . solid.

Ascored tenuit de rege . E.

188   Hugh holds a mill in DOVER which pays 48 measures of corn; it does not belong to any manor.

189   Ansfrid holds ½ yoke in *LEUEBERGE* from the Bishop's Holding. He has
      1 villager and 1 smallholder.
Value 5s.
      Leofwin held it from King Edward.

190   There also lived a certain Altet who held 2 acres in freehold from King Edward and held them from Ansfrid. It is assessed at 6s.

191   Ralph of Courbépine holds COLDRED from the Bishop. Land for ... In lordship 1½ ploughs.
      6 villagers with 7 smallholders have 2 ploughs.
      2 slaves; meadow, 4 acres.
It answers for 2 sulungs.
Value before 1066 £8; later 20s; now £6.
      Molleva held it from King Edward.

192   Ralph also holds (Temple) EWELL. It answers for 3 sulungs. Land for ... In lordship 1 plough.
      5 villagers with 4 smallholders have 2 ploughs.
      Woodland, 10 pigs.
      A man-at-arms holds 1 sulung of this manor from Ralph.
He has 1 plough, with
      3 smallholders.
Value of the whole manor before 1066 £12; later 20s; now 40s;   11 b
however, what Ralph has pays £4.
      Hugh de Montfort has the head of the manor and 5½ mills at £6.
Molleva held it from King Edward.

193   Ralph also holds SWANTON from the Bishop. It answers for 2 sulungs. Land for ... In lordship 1 plough;
      2 smallholders with ½ plough.
      Robert of Barbes holds 1 sulung of this land. He has
        3 villagers with ½ plough.
      Hugh holds 1 sulung. He has 1 plough in lordship, and
        1 smallholder.
Value before 1066 £10; when acquired 30s; now 40s; however, it pays £4.
      Colswein held it from King Edward.

194   Ralph holds APPLETON from the Bishop. It answers for 1 sulung. Land for ... In lordship 2 ploughs, with
      6 smallholders.
Value before 1066, 100s; later 10s; now 40s.
      Ashred held it from King Edward.

Herfrid ten de Hugone BROCHESTELE . 7 ē de feudo epi.

.p uno folin fe defđ . Tra . ē   In dñio . ē . I . car . 7 II . ferui.

T.R.E. ualeb . LX . foł . 7 poft: LX . Modo: XL . Qdo herbt recep:

III . juga . Modo: II . juga . Vlnod tenuit de rege . E.

Turftin tinel 7 uxor ej ten ad firmā de rege . W . jn Leue

berge . I . jugū 7 V . acs . 7 ibi funt . II . uiłłi cū . II . borđ.

Vał 7 ualuit fēp . VIII . foliđ . Boche tenuit de rege . E.

In Lest de Estrei.   *In Estrei Hvnd.*

Ansfrid ten de epo GOLLESBERGE . .p . II . folins 7 III.

jugis fe defđ . Tra . ē   ·   In dñio funt . II . car . 7 XXIIII.

uiłłi

T.R.E. ualeb . XII . lib . 7 poft: XX . foł . Modo: IX . lib.

In Sanduuic ht Archiefs XXX.II . mafuras . ad hoc M̄

ptinent 7 redđ . XLII . foliđ 7 VIII . den . 7 Adeluuold

ht . I . jugū qđ uał . X . foliđ.

Hoc M̄ ten . . . : teigni de rege . E . 7 III . manebant

ibi affidu . . . . . tenebant inde . II . folins . in paragio.

fed non . . . . . nt ibi . Qdo Ansfrid recep: fecit uñ M̄.

Turftin ten de epo CHENOLTONE . .p uno folin fe defđ.

Tra . ē   In dñio funt . II . car . cū . II . borđ . T.R.E: 7 poft

.IIII . lib . Modo: VII . lib . 7 tam reddit . VIII . lib . Eduuard

Osbt fili Letardi ten de epo BEDESHAM .   ſ tenuit de rege . E.

.p uno jugo 7 dim fe defđ . Tra . ē   In dñio . ē una car.

cū uno uiłło 7 IIII . borđ . T.R.E: ualeb LX . foł . 7 poft XXX . foł.

Modo: L . foliđ . Godefa tenuit de rege . E.

In eođ M̄ ten de ipfo osbno . X . teigni . uñ folin 7 dim

jugū . 7 ibi hñt ipfi . IIII . car 7 dimiđ . T.R.E . ualeb . c . foliđ.

7 poft: XXX . foliđ . Modo . LX . foliđ.

195 Herfrid holds BOSWELL (Banks) from Hugh; it is from the Bishop's Holding. Before 1066 it answered for 1 sulung. Land for ...
In lordship 1 plough and 2 slaves.
Value before 1066, 60s; later 60[s]; now 40[s].
    When Herbert acquired it, 3 yokes; now 2 yokes.
        Wulfnoth held it from King Edward.

196 Thurstan Tinel and his wife hold 1 yoke and 5 acres in
LEUEBERGE at a revenue from King William.
    2 villagers with 2 smallholders.
The value is and always was 8s.
    Buck held it from King Edward.

In the Lathe of EASTRY
In EASTRY Hundred
197 Ansfrid holds WOODNESBOROUGH from the Bishop. It answers for 2 sulungs and 3 yokes. Land for ... In lordship 2 ploughs;
    24 villagers.
Value before 1066 £12; later 20s; now £9.

198 In SANDWICH the Archbishop has 32 dwellings which belong to this manor and pay 42s 8d; Aethelwold has 1 yoke, value 10s.
    ... of King Edward's thanes held this manor; 3 remained there permanently ... they held 2 sulungs of it jointly, but they do not [live] there.
    When Ansfrid acquired it he made one manor.

199 Thurstan holds KNOWLTON from the Bishop. It answers for 1 sulung. Land for ... In lordship 2 ploughs, with
    2 smallholders.
Value before 1066 and later £4; now £7; however, it pays £8.
    Edward held it from King Edward.

200 Osbern son of Ledhard holds BETTESHANGER from the Bishop. It answers for 1½ yokes. Land for ... In lordship 1 plough, with
    1 villager and 4 smallholders.
Value before 1066, 60s; later 30s; now 50s.
    Godesa held it from King Edward.
In the same manor 10 thanes hold 1 sulung and ½ yoke from Osbern himself. They themselves have 4½ ploughs.
Value before 1066, 100s; later 30s; now 60s.

Ansfrid ten de epo SOLES . p uno folin fe defd . Tra . e

In dnio funt . II . car . 7 VIII . uilli cu dimid car.

T.R.E. ualeb . c . fol . 7 poft: xx . fot . Modo . VI . lib . Elmer
tenuit de rege . E.

Radulf fili Robti ten de epo HERTANGE . p uno folin
fe defd . Tra . e   In dnio . e una car . 7 v . uilli cu . II . bord

hnt . II . car . T.R.E. ualeb . XL . folid . 7 poft: x . fot . Modo . LX . folid.

Eddid tenuit de Rege . E.

Osbn ten de epo . I . jug 7 dimid . In eod hund.

7 ibi ht . VII . bord.

T.R.E. ualuit . x . lib 7 poft: x . folid . Modo: xxx . folid.

Ernold tenuit de rege . E.

IN BEVSBERGE HVND.

Hugo de montfort ten de epo . I . folin uacuæ træ ext.
diuifione fua . 7 adjacuit NEVENTONE M qd ht intra

fua diuifione . 7 ibi ht . I . bord . Val 7 ualuit fep . LX . fot.

Wibtus ten dimid jugu   IN ESTREI HVND.

qd jacuit in gilda de DOVERE . 7 m defd fe cu tra Osbti
filii Letard . 7 ualet p annu . IIII . folid.

Osbn fili Letard ten de epo HAMA . p uno folin fe defd.

Tra . e.   In dnio . e . I . car . cu uno uillo 7 II . bord 7 II . feruis.

T.R.E. ualeb . L . fot . 7 poft: xx . fot . Modo . LX . fot.

Tres teigni tenuer de rege . E.

Ifde osbn ten de epo CILLEDENE . p uno folin 7 uno jugo

7 x . acris fe defd . Tra . e   In dnio nichil m . fed . IX.

uilli hnt ibi . II . car 7 dimid . T.R.E. ualeb . LX . fot . 7 poft:

xxx . fot . Modo: XL . folid . Goduin tenuit de rege . E.

7 alii . v . teigni.   Osbn miifit tras eoz in un M.

201   Ansfrid holds SOLES (Court) from the Bishop. It answers for 1
sulung. Land for ... In lordship 2 ploughs;
     8 villagers with ½ plough.
Value before 1066, 100s; later 20s; now £6.
     Aelmer held it from King Edward.

202   Ralph son of Robert holds HARTANGER from the Bishop.
It answers for 1 sulung. Land for ... In lordship 1 plough.
     5 villagers with 2 smallholders have 2 ploughs.
Value before 1066, 40s; later 10s; now 60s.
     Edith held it from King Edward.

203   Osbern holds 1½ yokes in the same Hundred from the Bishop.
He has
     7 smallholders.
Value before 1066 £10; later 10s; now 30s.
     Arnold held it from King Edward.

In BEWSBOROUGH Hundred   11 c

204   Hugh de Montfort holds 1 sulung of vacant land from the Bishop
outside his territory; it is attached to the manor of Newington.
which he has inside his territory. He has
     1 smallholder.
The value is and always was 60s.

In EASTRY Hundred

205   Wibert holds ½ yoke which lay in (the lands of) the guild of
Dover; now it answers with Osbern son of Ledhard's land.
Value, 4s a year.

206   Osbern son of Ledhard holds HAM from the Bishop. It answers
for 1 sulung. Land for ... In lordship 1 plough, with
     1 villagers, 2 smallholders and 2 slaves.
Value before 1066, 50s; later 20s; now 60s.
     3 thanes held it from King Edward.

207   Osbern also holds CHILLENDEN from the Bishop. It answers for
1 sulung, 1 yoke and 10 acres. Land for ... In lordship now
nothing, but
     9 villagers have 2½ ploughs.
Value before 1066, 60s; later 30s; now 40s.
     Godwin and 5 other thanes held it from King Edward.
Osbern put their lands into 1 manor.

Alured ten de epo *MIDELEA* . p . III . jugis 7 XII . acs

se defd . Tra . ē . III . car . In dnio . ē una car 7 dim . 7 v . uilli

cu . IX . bord hnt . I . car . Ibi æccla . 7 x . ac pti . Silua . x .

porc . T . R . E . ualeb . LX . sol . 7 post: XL . sol . Modo: LX . sol .

Godric tenuit de rege . E.   *IN SVMERDENE HVND.*

Rotbt Latin ten . VI . acs tre . 7 ibi ht dim car . Hanc

tra tenuit un socks . 7 De nouo dono epi ht in manu

regis de Ricardo filio Gislebti . x . uillos cu . III . car . 7 silua

. L . porc . 7 inde reddit Rotbt de firma . VI . lib .

Turstin ten de epo *TICHETESTE* . p uno solin 7 dim

se defd . Tra . ē   In dnio . ē : I . car . cu . IIII . bord . 7

7 parua siluula . T . R . E . ualeb . IIII . lib . 7 post . XL . sol . Modo:

c . sol . Edric de Alha tenuit de rege . E.

Isdē Turstin ten de . epo . I . jugu in *WANESBERGE*.

7 ibi sunt . II . bord .   Tochi tenuit de rege . E.

Isdē Turstin ten de epo . I . jugu in *ECE* . 7 ibi sun . IIII . bord .

Ĩ . II . juga T . R . E . ualeb . XV . sol . 7 post: x . sol . M . XX . sol .

Osbt ten de epo . I . jugu 7 x . acs . in *MASSEBERGE*.

7 ibi sunt . II . uilli cu dimid car . Goduin tenuit de rege . E.

Isdē osbt ten de epo . XV . acs . in *ESMETONE* : 7 ibi

manet un pbr . Hoc utrunq̃ . T . R . E . ualeb xxx . sol .

7 post: xx . sol . Modo . xxx . sol . Sired tenuit de rege . E.

                    IN ESTREI HVND.

Radulf de Curbespine ten de epo . II . solins in *WALWALESERE*.

Tra . ē   In dnio . I . car 7 dim . 7 XIIII . uilli cu . II .

car 7 dim . De hac tra ht Robt dimid solin . 7 una car

ibi . T . R . E . ualeb . VII . lib 7 x . sol . 7 post . L . sol . m . VII . lib .

Wluuard tenuit de rege . E.

Osbt fili Letard ten de epo . I . jugu in *ECE* . 7 ibi sun

III . uilli . T . R . E . ualeb . XII . sol . 7 post: VI . sol . Modo: XVI . sol .

Bernolt tenuit de rege . E.

208   Alfred holds MIDLEY from the Bishop. It answers for 3 yokes and 12 acres. Land for 3 ploughs. In lordship 1½ ploughs.
     5 villagers with 9 smallholders have 1 plough.
     A church; meadow, 10 acres; woodland, 10 pigs.
     Value before 1066, 60s; later 40s; now 60s.
       Godric held it from King Edward.

In SUMMERDENE Hundred

209   Robert Latimer holds 6 acres of land. He has ½ plough.
A Freeman held this land. He has it, by a new gift of the Bishop, in the King's hands, from Richard son of Count Gilbert and
     10 villagers with 3 ploughs.
     Woodland, 50 pigs.
Robert pays from it £6 in revenue.

210   Thurstan holds TICKENHURST from the Bishop. It answers for 1½ sulungs. Land for ... In lordship 1 plough, with
     4 smallholders.
     A small wood.
     Value before 1066 £4; later 40s; now 100s.
       Edric of Elham held it from King Edward.

211   Thurstan also holds 1 yoke in WOODNESBOROUGH from the Bishop.
     2 smallholders there.
     Toki held it from King Edward.

212   Thurstan also holds 1 yoke in EACH from the Bishop.
     4 smallholders there.
     Value of these 2 yokes before 1066, 15s; later 10s; now 20s.

213   Osbert holds 1 yoke and 10 acres in MARSHBOROUGH from the Bishop.
     2 villagers with ½ plough there.
     Godwin held it from King Edward.

214   Osbert also holds 15 acres in ELMTON from the Bishop.
     A priest lives there.
     Value of both of these before 1066, 30s; later 20s; now 30s.
       Sired held them from King Edward.

In EASTRY Hundred

215   Ralph of Courbépine holds 2 sulungs in WALDERSHARE from the Bishop. Land for ... In lordship 1½ ploughs, and
     14 villagers with 2½ ploughs.
     Robert has ½ sulung of this land. 1 plough there.
     Value before 1066 £7 10s; later 50s; now £7.
       Wulfward held it from King Edward.

216   Osbern son of Ledhard holds 1 yoke in EACH from the Bishop.
     3 villagers there.
     Value before 1066, 12s; later 6s; now 16s.
       Bernhold held it from King Edward.

Rad de curbespine ten de epo ESSEWELLE . p . iii . so
lins se defd . Tra . e̅   In d̅nio sunt . iii . car . 7 un
uitts cu̅ . vii . bord h̅nt dim car . Ibi un seru . Val . vi . lib.
·Molleue tenuit de rege . E.

11 d
Osb̅n ten de epo unu̅ M qd tenuer̅ , iii . libi ho̅c̅s
de rege . E . p uno solin 7 dimid se defd . Tra . e̅
In d̅nio . e̅ una car . 7 un uitts cu̅ uno bord h̅t dim car.
T . R . E . 7 post . 7 modo: ual . iiii . lib.

Radulf de Colu̅bers ten de epo SELINGES . p uno
solin 7 dimid se defd . Tra . e̅   In d̅nio . e̅ una car.
7 iiii . uitti cu̅ . iii . bord h̅nt dimid car . 7 i . car 7 dim
T . R . E . uale̅b . iiii . lib : 7 post: xl . sot . Modo: c . sot.
Vluuic tenuit de rege . E.

Radulf de curbespine ten DANETONE . p dimid
solin se defd . Tra . e̅ . iii . car . In d̅nio . e̅ una . 7 iiii . uitti cu̅
ii . bord h̅nt . i . car . Ibi æccta . 7 iiii . masuræ in cantuaria.
reddent . vi . sot un den min . T . R . E . uale̅b . lx . sot . 7 post:
xx . sot . Modo: lx . sot . Molleue tenuit de rege . E.

Isd̅e Radulf ten de epo . i . jugu̅ in Brochestele . Qd
Molleue tenuit de rege . E . 7 ibi . e̅ un uitts redd . xxx . den.

Radulf de curbespine ten . xl . ac̅s træ . IN BEVSBERGE HD.
quas tenuit Molleue de rege . E . 7 ibi . e̅ un uitts reddes
vi . solid . 7 tant ualet.

Rannulf de ualbadon ten dimid jugu̅ in· HAMESTEDE.
qd tenuer̅ . ii . libi ho̅c̅s de rege . E . in Bochelande . 7 dicit
m̅ Rannulf qd eps baiocsis dedit cuida̅ suo fri.
Ibi est un uitts reddens xxx . denar . IN NVNIBERG HD.

Anschitil de ros ten de feudo epi ACRES . qd tenuer̅
duo fr̅s . 7 q̅sq̅ habuit haula̅ . Modo . e̅ p uno M . 7 p una
solin se defd . Tra . e̅ . ii . car . In d̅nio . e̅ una car 7 dim.

217 Ralph of Courbépine holds EASOLE from the Bishop. It answers
for 3 sulungs. Land for ... In lordship 3 ploughs.
1 villager with 7 smallholders have ½ plough. 1 slave.
Value £6.
Molleva held it from King Edward.

218 Osbern holds a manor from the Bishop which 3 free men held   11 d
from King Edward. It answers for 1½ sulungs. Land for ...
In lordship 1 plough.
1 villager with 1 smallholder has ½ plough.
Value before 1066, later and now £4.

219 Ranulf of Colombières holds SHELVING from the Bishop. It answers
for 1½ sulungs. Land for ... In lordship 1 plough.
4 villagers with 3 smallholders have ½ plough and 1½ ploughs.
Value before 1066 £4; later 40s; now 100s.
Wulfwy held it from King Edward.

220 Ralph of Courbépine holds DENTON from the Bishop. It answers
for ½ sulung. Land for 3 ploughs. In lordship 1.
4 villagers with 2 smallholders have 1 plough.
A church; 4 dwellings in Canterbury which pay 6s less 1d.
Value before 1066, 60s; later 20s; now 60s.
Molleva held it from King Edward.

221 Ralph also holds 1 yoke in BOSWELL (Banks) from the Bishop, which
Molleva held from King Edward.
1 villager who pays 30d.

In BEWSBOROUGH Hundred
222 Ralph of Courbépine holds 40 acres of land which Molleva held
from King Edward.
1 villager who pays 6s.
The value is as much.

223 Ranulf of Vaubadon holds ½ yoke in HEMSTED which 2 free
men held from King Edward in Buckland; now Ranulf says that
the Bishop of Bayeux gave it to a brother of his.
1 villager there who pays 30d.
Value 10s.

In LONINGBOROUGH Hundred
224 Ansketel of Rots holds ACRISE from the Bishop's Holding; two
brothers held it and each had a hall. Now it is one manor; it
answers for 1 sulung. Land for 2 ploughs. In lordship 1½ ploughs.

7 .v . uitti cū . v . bord hnt . i . car̄ . Silua . x . porc̄ . 7 æccla.

T.R.E. ualeb̄ . xl . fol . 7 poft: xxx . fol . Modo: lx . fol.

Rogeri' fili' Anfchitil ten de   IN·BRICEODE HD̄.

feudo epi HASTINGELAI . qd̄ tenuit Vlnod de rege . E.

7 tc defd̄ fe p uno folin . 7 m̄ p . iii . jugis . q̄a Hugo

de montfort ten alia parte int diuifione fuam.

Tra . ē . iii . car̄ . In dn̄io funt . ii . 7 ii . uitti cū . vi . bord

hnt . i . car̄ . Ibi . iiii . ferui . 7 filua . i . porc̄.

T.R.E. ualeb̄ . lx . fol . 7 poft: xxx . fol . Modo.. lx . folid̄.

.VI. TERRA ÆCCLÆ DE LABATAILGE.

Abbas Sc̄i MARTINI de Loco belli| m̄ qd̄ uocat̄ WI.

qd̄ T.R.E. 7 m̄ fe defd̄ p . vii . folins . Tra . ē . lii . car̄.

In dn̄io . ix . car̄ funt . 7 cxiiii . uitti cū . xxii . bord hnt

xvii . car̄ . Ibi æccla . 7 vii . ferui . 7 iiii . molini de xxiii.

folid̄ 7 viii . den̄ . 7 cxxxiii . ac pti . 7 filua . ccc . porc̄ de

pafnagio.

T.R.E. ualeb̄ qt xx lib 7 . c . folid̄ . 7 vi . fol 7 viii . den̄ . Q̄do recep̄

cxxv . lib 7 x . fol de . xx . in ora . Modo: c . lib ad numerū

7 Si abb̄ habuiffet facas 7 foc̄as: xx . lib plus appciaret.

Radulf' de curbefpina una dena 7 un jugū de tra focho᷾

huj' Manerii . redd̄ de cfuetud̄ . vi . den̄ . 7 Adelulf' . ii . partes

uni folin . redd̄ . xii . denar̄ . 7 Hugo de montfort hr̄ . ii . juga.

redd̄ . ccc . Anguift 7 ii . folid̄ . 7 faca 7 foca . in T.R.E. reddebaN.

De . xxii . hund̄ ptin̄ ifti m̄ faca 7 foca . 7 om̄a forisfacta quæ

jufte ptin̄ regi.

5 villagers with 5 smallholders have 1 plough.
Woodland, 10 pigs; a church.
Value before 1066, 40s; later 30s; now 60s.

In BIRCHOLT Hundred

225 Roger son of Ansketel holds HASTINGLEIGH from the Bishop's
Holding; Wulfnoth held from King Edward. Then it answered
for 1 sulung, now for 3 yokes, because Hugh de Montfort holds
the other part in his territory. Land for 3 ploughs In lordship 2.
2 villagers with 6 smallholders have 1 plough.
4 slaves. Woodland, 1 pig.
Value before 1066, 60s; later 30s; now 60s.

6   LAND OF BATTLE CHURCH

1 The Abbot of St. Martin of the Battlefield holds a manor which
is called WYE, which answered for 7 sulungs before 1066 and now.
Land for 52 ploughs. In lordship 9 ploughs.
114 villagers with 22 smallholders have 17 ploughs.
A church; 7 slaves. 4 mills at 23s 8d; meadow, 133 acres;
woodland, 300 pigs from pasturage.
Value before 1066 £80 and 100s and 6s 8d; when acquired
£125 10s at 20 (pence) to the *ora*; now £100 at face value; if the
Abbot had had the full jurisdictions it would be assessed at £20
more.
Ralph of Courbépine holds 1 pig pasture and 1 yoke of
Freemen's land of this manor; he pays 6d as a customary due;
Aethelwulf (holds) 2 parts of 1 sulung; he pays 12d. Hugh de
Montfort has 2 yokes which pay 300 eels and 2s. Before 1066
they paid full jursidiction.

Full jurisdiction and all the penalties from 22 Hundreds
which rightly belong to the King belong to this manor.

TERRA ÆCCLÆ SCI AVGVSTINI

IN DIMIDIO LEST DE SVDTONE . IN LITELAI HVND.

.VII A BBAS SCI AVGVSTINI hत uñ ☠ nomine
PLVMSTÈDE . qđ defđ fe p . II . folins 7 uno jugo.

Tra . ē   In dñio ē . I . caŕ . 7 xvII . uiłłi cū
vi . cot hñt . vi . caŕ . Ibi filua . v . porc de pafnagio.

T . R . E . 7 poft: ualuit . x . lib . Modo: xII . lib . 7 tam
reddit xIIII . lib . 7 vIII . foliđ 7 III . deń.

IN LEST DE ELESFORT.   IN HAIHORNE HVND.

Ipfe abb teñ LERTHA . qđ fe defđ p . v . folins 7 dimiđ.
Tra . ē xvIII . caŕ . In dñio funt . II . caŕ . 7 xL . uiłłi cū
vII . borđ hñt xvi . caŕ . Ibi . I . feru . 7 II . molini de . vi .
foliđ 7 vIII . deń . 7 vIII . ac p̃ti . 7 Silua . xL . porc.

T . R . E . ualeb . xxvIII . lib . 7 poft: xvi . lib . Modo: xxvIII . lib.
De hoc ☠ teñ Robt Latiñ uñ jugū . qđ ualet . v . foliđ.

IN BOROART LEST.   IN BRIGE HVND.

Ipfe abb teñ BORNE . qđ fe defđ p uno folin . Tra . ē
II . caŕ . In dñio . ē una . 7 Ix . uiłłi cū uno borđ hñt . I . caŕ.
Ibi . II . molini de . Ix . foliđ 7 vi . deń . 7 III . ac p̃ti 7 dimiđ.
Silua de . v . porc . T . R . E . ualeb . c . fot . 7 poft: xL . foliđ.
Modo: c . foliđ.

Ipfe abb teñ ☠ LANPORT . 7 ibi . ē uñ folin 7 uñ jug.
7 fep q̃etū fuit . 7 fine c̃fuetudine . 7 uñ jugū jacet in alio
hunđ qđ p̃tiñ ifti ☠ . 7 Lxx . burgenfes erant in cantua
ria ciuit huic ☠ p̃tinent . In hoc ☠ funt . II . caŕ 7 dim
in dñio . 7 xx . vIII . uiłłi cū Lxiii . borđ hñt . vi . caŕ.
Ibi . xvII . ac p̃ti.

T . R . E . ualeb xx . lib . 7 poft: xvIII . lib . Modo: xxxv . lib
7 IIII . foliđ:

In the Half-Lathe of SUTTON
In LITTLE Hundred

1   The Abbot of St. Augustine's has a manor named PLUMSTEAD, which answers for 2 sulungs and 1 yoke. Land for ... In lordship 1 plough.
17 villagers with 6 cottagers have 6 ploughs.
Woodland, 5 pigs from pasturage.
Value before 1066 and later £10; now £12; however, it pays £14 8s 3d.

In the Lathe of AYLESFORD
In EYHORNE Hundred
The Abbot himself holds

2   LENHAM, which answers for 5½ sulungs. Land for 18 ploughs.
In lordship 2 ploughs.
40 villagers with 7 smallholders have 16 ploughs.
1 slave; 2 mills at 6s 8d; meadow, 8 acres; woodland, 40 pigs.
Value before 1066 £28; later £16; now £28.
Robert Latimer holds 1 yoke of this manor, value 5s.

in BOROUGH Lathe
in BRIDGE Hundred

3   BEKESBOURNE which answers for 1 sulung. Land for 2 ploughs.
In lordship 1.
9 villagers with 1 smallholder have 1 plough.
2 mills at 9s 6d; meadow, 3½ acres; woodland at 5 pigs.
Value before 1066, 100s; later 40s; now 100s.

4   the manor of LANGPORT. 1 sulung and 1 yoke. It was always exempt and without customary dues. 1 yoke which belongs to this manor lies in another Hundred. 70 burgesses (who) were in the City of Canterbury belong to this manor. In this manor are 2½ ploughs in lordship.
28 villagers with 63 smallholders have 6 ploughs.
Meadow, 17 acres.
Value before 1066 £20; later £18; now £35 4s.

Ipfe abb ten *Liteburne* . qd fe defd ꝑ . vii : folins.

Tra . e̅ . xii . car . In d̅n̅io funt . iii . car . 7 xxxv . uilli

cu̅ . xiiii . cot . h̅n̅t . vi . 7 dim . Ibi æccła . 7 xxxviii . ac̅ p̅ti.

Silua . iiii . porc̅ . T.R.E . ualeb . xx̆ . lib . 7 poſt : xx . lib.

Modo : xxxii . lib.

De iſto m̅ h̅r̅ eps baioc̅ in fuo parco tant qd ual . lx . fol.

Ipfe abb ten *Warwintone* 7 ded ei eps baioc̅fis

ꝑ excābio parci fui . ꝑ dimid folin 7 xlii . acris træ fe

defd . Tra . e̅ . i . car̅ . 7 ibi . e̅ in d̅n̅io . cu̅ . iii . cotar . 7 xvi.

ac̅ p̅ti . T.R.E . ualeb . iiii . lib . 7 poſt : xl . fol . Modo : iiii . lib.

Hoc m̅ tenuit Edric̅ de Sbern biga . 7 m̅ ten Radulf⁹

Ipfe abb ten *Estvrai* *In Estvrai Hvnd* . ꟊ de abbe.

qd fe defd ꝑ . v . folins q̇etis . Tra . e̅ . xii . car . In d̅n̅io

funt . ii . car . 7 xxxix . cu̅ xxxii . bord h̅n̅t . xii . car . Ibi

æccła . 7 x . molini de . viii . lib . 7 vii . pifcariæ de . v . fol.

7 xx.viii . ac̅ p̅ti . De pafnagio . xxx . porc̅.

T.R.E . ualeb . l . fol . Q̇do abb recep : xl.v . lib . Modo :

. l . lib . 7 tam redd . l.iiii . lib . *In Tanet Hvnd.*

Ipfe abb ten *Tanet* . m̅ . qd fe defd ꟊ S Mildredæ.

ꝑ . xlviii . folins . Tra . e̅ . lxii . car . In d̅n̅io funt . ii.

7 cl . uilli cu̅ . l . bord h̅n̅t . lxiii . car . Ibi æccła 7 un p̅br⁹

qui dat . xx . folid ꝑ ann̅ . Ibi una falina . 7 ii . pifcariæ.

de . iii . den : 7 un̅ molin̅.

T.R.E . ualeb q̇t . xx . lib . Q̇do abb recep : xl . lib . Modo . c . lib.

De iſto m̅ ten . iii . milites tant de tra uillanoꝛ . qd ual

ix . lib quando pax . e̅ in tra . 7 ibi h̅n̅t . iii : car̅

Ipfe abb ten *Cistelet* : qd ꝑ . xii . *In Cistelet Hvnd.*

folins fe defd . Tra . e̅ . xxx : car̅ . In d̅n̅io funt : v . car̅ . 7 lxxii.

uilli cu̅ . lxviii . bord h̅n̅t . xxxix . car̅ . Ibi æccła de . xii . folid.

7 xiiii . ferui . Ibi . l . ac̅ p̅ti . 7 xlvii : falinæ de . l . fumis falis.

in DOWNHAMFORD Hundred

5 LITTLEBOURNE, which answers for 7 sulungs. Land for 12 ploughs. In lordship 3 ploughs.

35 villagers with 14 cottagers have 6½ [ploughs].

A church; meadow, 38 acres; woodland, 4 pigs.

Value before 1066 £25; later £20 now £32.

The Bishop of Bayeux has in his park as much of this manor as is valued at 60s.

6 GARRINGTON. The Bishop of Bayeux gave it to him in exchange for his park. It answers for ½ sulung and 42 acres of land. Land for 1 plough. It is there, in lordship, with

3 cottagers.

Meadow, 16 acres.

Value before 1066 £4; later 40s; now £4.

Edric held this manor from Esbern Big; now Ralph holds it from the Abbot.

in STURRY Hundred

7 STURRY, which answers for 5 exempt sulungs. Land for 12 ploughs. In lordship 2 ploughs.

39 [villagers] with 32 smallholders have 12 ploughs.

A church; 10 mills at £8; 7 fisheries at 5s; meadow, 28 acres; from pasturage, 30 pigs.

Value before 1066, 50s; when the Abbot acquired it £45; now £50; however, it pays £54.

in the THANET Hundred of St. MILDRED

8 the manor of MINSTER, which answers for 48 sulungs. Land for 62 ploughs. In lordship 2.

150 villagers with 50 smallholders have 63 ploughs. A church and a priest who gives 20s a year.

A salt-house; 2 fisheries at 3d; a mill.   12 b

Value before 1066 £80; when the Abbot acquired it £40; now £100.

3 men-at-arms hold as much of the villagers' land of this manor as is valued at £9 when there is peace in the land; they have 3 ploughs there.

in CHISLET Hundred

9 CHISLET, which answers for 12 sulungs. Land for 30 ploughs. In lordship 5 ploughs.

72 villagers with 68 smallholders have 39 ploughs.

A church at 12s; 14 slaves. Meadow, 50 acres. 47 salt-houses at 50 packloads of salt; from pasturage, 130 pigs.

De paſnag̅ . cxxx . porc̅ . T.R.E. ualeƀ . L.IIII . liƀ ¡ 7 poſt.'
xL . liƀ . Modó.' Lxxviii . liƀ . Ibi ſunt . III . arpenni uineæ.

De iſto ꝳ ten̄ . IIII . francig̅ miłites . qđ uał p an̄n xII . liƀ.

Ipſe aƀƀ ten̄ unū paruū burgū *IN FOREVVIC HVND.*

qđ uocat̄ *FOREWIC* . Huj burgi . II ¡ partes deđ rex . E . ſc̄o

Auguſtino . T̄ciā ū parte quæ fuerat Goduini.' eꝑs baiocſis

c̄ceſſit eiđ ſc̄o annuente rege .W.

p uno ſe jugo defđ . Ibi fuer̄ . c . maſuræ træ . IIII . min̄.

reddı̄es . xIII . ſoł . Modo ſunt . Lxx1II . maſuræ . tn̄tđ reddı̄.

T.R.E. 7 poſt ualeƀ . c . ſolid . Modo.' xI . liƀ 7 II . ſolid.

Ibidē ſunt . xxIIII . ac̄ træ . quas ſe̅p habuit S̄ Auguſtin̄.

vbi fuer̄ 7 ſunt . vI . burg̅ſes reddı̄es . xxII . ſolid.

In iſto burgo ten̄ archieꝑs Lanfr̄ . vII ¡ maſuras træ ¡ quæ

T.R.E. ſeruiebaꝥ S̄ Auguſtino . m̄ arch̄ aufèrt ei ſeruitiū.

Juxta ciuitate cantuar̄ hī S̄ Augtin̄

dimiđ ſolin . qđ ſe̅p fuit quietū ¡ 7 ibi . ē . I . car̄ in dn̄io . cū

xv . borđ . 7 vII . acræ ꝑti . 7 ibiđ ſunt . IIII . ac̄ tre q̄s ten̄

.IIII . moniales in elemoſina de aƀƀe . 7 reddı̄ ¡ II . ſoł 7 unā

ſūmā farinæ . Totū hóc T.R.E. 7 poſt . 7 m̄.' uał . IIII . liƀ.

IN LEST DE WIWARLET . *IN FAVRESHANT HVND.*

Ipſe aƀƀ ten̄ *WIRENTONE* . qđ p uno ſolin ſe defđ.

Tra . ē . II . car̄ . In dn̄io . ē una . 7 ix . uiłłi cū . I . car̄ . Ibi . II.

ac̄ ꝑti . 7 v . porc̄ de paſnag̅ ſiluæ . T .R.E. ualeƀ . Lx . ſoł.

Q̄do recep.' xL . ſoł . Modo.' IIII ¡ liƀ .   *IN WI HVND.*

Ipſe aƀƀ ten̄ *ESMEREFEL* . 7 Anſchitil de eo . p uno ſolin

ſe defđ . Tra . ē . I . car̄ . 7 ibi . ē in dn̄io eū . v . borđ . 7 vI . ac̄ ꝑti.

Silua . x . porc̄ . T.R.E. xL . ſoł . 7 poſt.' xx . ſoł . Modo.' xL . ſoł.

In *DARENDEN* ten̄ Adā de aƀƀe dimiđ ſolin . Tra . ē dimiđ

car̄ . Ibi ſunt . II . ſerui . 7 vII , ac̄ ꝑti . Vał 7 ſe̅p ualuit . xx . ſoł.

Value before 1066 £53; later £40; now £78.

3 *arpents* of vines there.

Of this manor 4 French men-at-arms hold what is valued at £12 a year.

10 a small Borough which is called FORDWICH. King Edward gave two parts of this Borough to St. Augustine's; but the Bishop of Bayeux, with King William's assent, also assigned to St. Augustine's the third part, which had belonged to Earl Godwin.

It answers for 1 yoke. There were 100 measures of land less 4 there which paid 13s. Now there are 73 dwellings, which pay as much. Value before 1066 and later 100s; now £11 2s.

There also are 24 acres of land which St. Augustine's always had, where there were and are 6 burgesses who pay 22s.

In this Borough Archbishop Lanfranc holds 7 measures of land which served St. Augustine's before 1066; now the Archbishop takes (their) service from it.

11 Near the City of Canterbury St. Augustine's has ½ sulung which was always exempt. 1 plough there in lordship, with
15 smallholders.
Meadow, 7 acres.

There are also 4 acres of land which 4 nuns hold in alms from the Abbot; they pay 2s and 1 packload of flour.
Value of all this before 1066, later and now £4.

In the Lathe of WYE
In FAVERSHAM Hundred

12 The Abbot holds WILDERTON himself, which answers for 1 sulung. Land for 2 ploughs. In lordship 1;
9 villagers with 1 plough.
Meadow, 2 acres; 5 pigs from woodland pasturage.
Value before 1066, 60s; when acquired 40s; now £4.

In WYE Hundred

13 The Abbot holds ASHENFIELD himself and Ansketel from him. It answers for 1 sulung. Land for 1 plough. It is there, in lordship, with
5 smallholders.
Meadow, 6 acres; woodland, 10 pigs.
[Value] before 1066, 40s; later 20s; now 40s.

14 In DERNEDALE Adam holds ½ sulung from the Abbot. Land for ½ plough.
2 slaves.
Meadow, 7 acres.
The value is and always was 20s.

Ipſe abb ten SETLINGES ⊗   IN BOLTONE HVND.

ſine halla . qd ſe defd ,p . VI . ſolins . Tra . ē . XI . caſ.

Nichil in dnio . Ibi xxx . uitti hnt . x . caſ . Ibi æccta.

T.R.E . ualeb xv . lib . Qdo recep: VIII . lib . Modo: XIII . lib

Ipſe abb ten dimid jugū   IN CALEHEVE HVND.   ⌜ 7 . V . ſolid.

in Rotinge . qd T.R.E . ſe defd ,p dim ſolin . Ibi fuit 7 eſt

una caſ in dnio . Vat 7 ualuit ſep . xv . ſot . IN CERT HD.

Ipſe abb ten un jugū RAPENTONE . 7 Anſered de eo.

7 ,p uno jugo ſe defd . Tra . ē . II . caſ . In dnio . ē una . cū . IIII.

bord . Ibi . XI . ac pti . 7 qrta pars molini de . xv . den . 7 ſilua

.x . porc . 7 adhuc hr . II . juga quæ de ſuo dnio dedit ei abb.

7 ibi . II . uittos cū . VIII . bord . T.R.E . 7 póſt: ualuit . III . lib.

⌜ Modo . IIII . lib.

12 c

Anſfrid ten de abbe CHERINCHEHELLE . IN FERLEBERG HD.

,p dimid ſolin ſe defd . Tra . ē . I . caſ . In dnio ſunt . II . 7 VIII.

uitti hnt . I . caſ 7 dimid . T.R.E . 7 poſt . ualuit . xx . ſot . M . xxx . ſot.

IN LEST DE ESTREA.   IN CORNELEST HVND.

Ipſe abb ten NORBORNE . ,p xxx . ſolins ſe defd.

Tra . ē . LIIII . caſ . In dnio ſunt . III . 7 LXXIX . uitti cū

XL.II . bord hnt . xxxvII . caſ . Ibi XL . ac pti . 7 ſilua . x.

porc . T . |

T.R.E . ualeb qt xx . lib . Qdo recep: xx . lib . M: LXXVI . lib.

De tra uillanoƷ huj ⊗ ten Oidelard . I . ſolin . 7 ibi hr
.II . caſ . cū . XI . bord.   Vat . IIII . lib.

⌜ De ead tra uillanoƷ ten Gifflebt . II . ſolins . dimid jugū

min . 7 ibi hr . I . caſ . 7 IIII . uittos cū . I . caſ . Vat . VI . lib.

⌜ Wadard ten de iſto ⊗ . III . ſolins . LX . acs min de tra

uillanoƷ . 7 ibi hr . I . caſ . 7 VIII . uittos cū . I . caſ . 7 II . ſeruos.

Vat . IX . lib . Ipſe u nullū ſeruitiū reddit abbi . niſi . xxx . ſot

quos pſoluit in anno.

In BOUGHTON Hundred

15   The Abbot holds SELLING manor himself without a hall, which answers for 6 sulungs. Land for 11 ploughs. In lordship nothing.
      30 villagers have 10 ploughs. A church.
    Value before 1066 £15; when acquired £8; now £13 5s.

In CALEHILL Hundred

16   The Abbot holds ½ yoke in ROOTING himself, which answered for ½ sulung before 1066. There was and is 1 plough in lordship. The value is and always was 15s.

In CHART Hundred

17   The Abbot holds 1 yoke (in) RIPTON himself and Ansered from him. It answers for 1 yoke. Land for 2 ploughs. In lordship 1, with
      4 smallholders.
      Meadow, 11 acres. ¼ mill at 15d; woodland, 10 pigs.
Further, he has 2 yokes which the Abbot gave him from his lordship and
      2 villagers with 8 smallholders.
Value before 1066 and later £3; now £4.

In FELBOROUGH Hundred   12 c

18   Ansfrid holds SHILLINGHAM from the Abbot. It answers for ½ sulung. Land for 1 plough. In lordship 2.
      8 villagers have 1½ ploughs.
Value before 1066 and later 20s; now 30s.

In the Lathe of EASTRY
In CORNILO Hundred

19   The Abbot holds NORTHBOURNE himself. It answers for 30 sulungs. Land for 54 ploughs. In lordship 3.
      79 villagers with 42 smallholders have 37 ploughs.
      Meadow, 40 acres; woodland, 10 pigs.
    Value before 1066 £80; when acquired £20; now £76.
    Odilard holds 1 sulung of villagers' land of this manor; he has 2 ploughs, with
      11 smallholders.
    Value £4.
    Gilbert holds 2 sulungs less ½ yoke of the same villagers' land; he has 1 plough and
      4 villagers with 1 plough.
    Value £6.
    Wadard holds 3 sulungs less 60 acres of the villagers' land of this manor; he has 1 plough,
      8 villagers with 1 plough and 2 slaves.
    Value £9.
    But he himself renders no service to the Abbot except 30s which he pays in full in a year.

⌐Odelin⁹ ten⁷ de ead⁷ t̃ra uillanoᵹ . I . ſolin . 7 ibi ħt . I . cař.
cū . III . borđ.   Val . III . liƀ.

⌐Marcheri⁹ ten⁷ de ead⁷ t̃ra uillanoᵹ qđ ual . VIII . ſolid.

⌐Osƀn⁹ fili⁹ Letardi ten⁷ dimiđ ſolin 7 XI . aćs p̃ti . de t̃ra
uillanoᵹ . qđ ual . XXV . ſot . Ipſe redđ aƀƀi . XV . ſolid.

⌐Rannulf⁹ de colūbers ten⁷ uñ jugū.   Val . L . deñ.

⌐Rannulf⁹ de ualbadon ten⁷ uñ jugū . 7 redđ inde . L . deñ.

⌐It̃ ſup̃dict⁹ Oidelard ten⁷ de hoc M̃ . uñ ſolin . 7 uocaᷓ
BEVESFEL . 7 ibi ħt . II . cař . cū . X . borđ . Val . VI . liƀ.

Ipſe aƀƀ ten⁷ MVNDINGEHÃ . ꝑ duob⁹ ſolins 7 dimiđ
ſe defđ . T̃ra . ē . V . cař . In hoc M̃ t̃ra quã tenent
monachi nunᵹ geldauit . 7 Wadard ten⁷ ibi t̃ra
quæ T . R . E . ſ̃ep geldauit . 7 illo tp̃r erat M̃ inſimul.
Modo ħñt monachi in dñio . IIII . cař . 7 XX . borđ
cū una cař . 7 uñ moliñ de . XVI . ſolid . 7 ſiluã . IIII ᵒʳ . porc.
Ibi æccƚa . T . R . E . ualeƀ . XXII . liƀ . 7 poſt꞉ x . liƀ . Pars
aƀƀis꞉ XXVI . liƀ.

Wadard ħt in dñio ibi . I . cař . 7 VIII . uiƚƚos cū . II ᵇˢ.
borđ ħñtiƀ . IIII . cař . Val 7 ualuit . X . liƀ.
nullū ſeruitiū inde reddit niſi . XXX . ſolid ꝑ annū aƀƀi.

Ipſe aƀƀ ten⁷ SIBERTESWALT   IN BEVSBERG HVND⁷.
ꝑ duob⁹ ſolins ſe defđ . T̃ra . ē . IIII . cař . In dñio . ē una 7 dim⁷.
7 XI . uiƚƚi cū . VI . borđ . ħñt . II . cař 7 dim . Ibi æccƚa.
T . R . E . ualeƀ . VIII . liƀ . Ꝗdo recep꞉ XL . ſot . Modo꞉ VI . liƀ.
7 tam⁷ redđ . VIII . liƀ.

Ipſe aƀƀ ten⁷ PLATENOVT ꝑ uno ſolin ſe defđ . T̃ra . ē
         In dñio nichil . ſed . IIII . uiƚƚi cū . III . borđ ħñt
cař⁷ 7 dimiđ . Ibi ſilua minuta . Radulf⁹ de curbeſpina
ħt XXV . aćs de hac t̃ra . T . R . E . 7 poſt . 7 m̃ . ual . XX . ſolid.
tam̃ app̃ciaᷓ . XL . ſolid . eo qđ ſit ad firmã.

12 c

Odelin holds 1 sulung of the same villagers' land; he has 1 plough there, with
> 3 smallholders.

Value £3.

Marcher holds what is valued at 8s from the same villagers' land.

Osbern son of Ledhard holds ½ sulung and 11 acres of meadow of villagers' land, value 25s. He pays the Abbot 15s himself.

Ranulf of Colombières holds 1 yoke.

Value 50d.

Ranulf of Vaubadon holds 1 yoke; he pays 50d from it.

Also the above Odilard holds 1 sulung of this manor, called Beauxfield; he has 2 ploughs, with
> 10 smallholders

Value £6.

20 The Abbot also holds (Great and Little) MONGEHAM. It answers for 2½ sulungs. Land for 5 ploughs. In this manor the land which the monks hold never paid tax. Wadard holds land there which always paid tax before 1066. At that time the manor was all one. Now the monks have 4 ploughs in lordship, and
> 20 smallholders with 1 plough.
> A mill at 16s; woodland, 4 pigs. A church.

Value before 1066 £22; later £10; the Abbot's part £26.

Wadard has 1 plough in lordship, and
> 8 villagers with 2 smallholders who have 4 ploughs.

The value is and was £10.

He pays no service from it except 30s a year to the Abbot.

In BEWSBOROUGH Hundred

21 The Abbot holds SIBERTSWOLD himself. It answers for 2 sulungs. Land for 4 ploughs. In lordship 1½.
> 11 villagers with 6 smallholders have 2½ ploughs. A church.

Value before 1066 £8; when acquired 40s; now £6; however, it pays £8.

22 The Abbot holds WADHOLT himself. It answers for 1 sulung. Land for ... In lordship nothing, but
> 4 villagers with 3 smallholders have 1½ ploughs.
> Underwood.
> Ralph of Courbépine has 25 acres of this land.

Value before 1066, later and now 20s; however, it is assessed at 40s because it is at a revenue.

Ipſe abb̄ ten̄ PRESTETVNE .p̄. v . ſolins IN PRESTETVN

ſe defd̄ . Tra̅ . ē . viii . car̄ . In dn̄io ſunt . ii . car̄ . 7 xxv.

uitti cū . xvii . bord̄ . hn̄t ix . car̄ . Ibi parua ſiluula.

12 d

De hoc m̄ ten̄ Vital̄ . i . ſolin 7 dim̄ jugū . 7 ibi h̄t in dn̄io . ii . car̄.

7 xvii . bord̄ cū dim̄ car̄ . Totū m̄ T.R.E. ualeb̄ . x . lib̄.

Q̇do recep̄. vi . lib̄ . Modo ual̄ . xiiii . lib̄ . qd̄ h̄t abb̄.

Qd̄ Vitalis tenet. c . ſolid̄ ualet.

Ansfrid̄ ten̄ de abb̄e ÆLVETONE . p̄ dimid̄ ſolin 7 dim̄

jugo ſe defd̄ . Tra̅ . ē . In dn̄io . ē una car̄ . 7 iii.

uitti cū . iii . bobȝ in car̄.

In iſto m̄ ten̄ Ansfrid̄ dimid̄ ſolin de dn̄io monachoȝ.

7 reddit inde Ṡ Auguſtino . c . denar̄ p̄ annū.

Godeſſa tenuit in alodiū . 7 ded̄ inde Ṡ Auguſtino . xxv.

denar̄ in elemoſina . unoq̇qȝ anno.

T.R.E. ualeb̄ . xl . ſot . 7 poſt. x . ſot . Modo. lx . ſolid̄.

IN LEST 7 in hund̄ de ESTREI . h̄t Ṡ Auguſtin̄ . iii . uirḡ tre̅.

7 ibi . ē in dn̄io . i . car̄ . cū v . bord̄ . T.R.E. ualeb̄ . x . ſolid̄.

7 poſt. v . ſot . Modo. xx . ſolid̄.

IN LIMOWART LEST.   IN STOTINGES HVND.

Gaufrid̄ ten̄ BODESHĀ de abb̄e . p̄ uno ſolin ſe defd̄.

Tra̅ . ē . ii . car̄ . 7 ibi ſunt cū . viii . bord̄ . Silua . xv . porc̄.

T.R.E. ualeb̄ . iiii . lib̄ . 7 poſt. xx . ſot . Modo. iiii . lib̄.

Ipſe abb̄ ten̄ in LANPORT   ᚠQuidā uitts tenuit.

ii . ſolins 7 un̄ jugū . Tra̅ . ē . vi . car̄ . Ibi ſunt . ix . uitti cū

iiii . bord̄ . hn̄tes . vi . car̄ . Ibi . x . ac̄ p̄ti . 7 ſilua . ii . porc̄.

T.R.E. ualeb̄ . vi . lib̄ . 7 poſt. iiii . lib̄ . Modo. viii . lib̄.

IN LEST DE WIWARLET.   IN LANGEBRIGE HVND.

Ipſe abb̄ ten̄ CHENETONE . T.R.E. ſe defd̄ p̄ . iiii . ſolins.

7 jacuit in BORCHEMERES . Tra̅ . ē . x . car̄ . Ibi ſunt xxx.

uitti hn̄tes . x . car̄ . Ibi eccta.   Vitti tenuer̄ . T.R.E.

In PRESTON Hundred

23 The Abbot holds PRESTON himself. It answers for 5 sulungs.
Land for 8 ploughs. In lordship 2 ploughs.
25 villagers with 17 smallholders have 9 ploughs.
A small wood.
Vitalis holds 1 sulung and ½ yoke of this manor. He has   12 d
2 ploughs in lordship, and
17 smallholders with ½ plough.
Value of the whole manor before 1066 £10; when acquired £6;
now value of what the Abbot has £14; value of what Vitalis
holds 100s.

24 Ansfrid holds ELMSTONE from the Abbot. It answers for ½ sulung
and ½ yoke. Land for ... In lordship 1 plough, and
3 villagers with 3 oxen in a plough.
In this manor Ansfrid holds ½ sulung from the monks'
lordship; from it he pays St. Augustine's 100d a year. Godesa held
it in freehold; from it she gave St. Augustine's 25d in alms each year.
Value before 1066, 40s; later 10s; now 60s.

In the Lathe and Hundred of EASTRY

25 St. Augustine's has 3 virgates of land. 1 plough in lordship, with
5 smallholders.
Value before 1066, 10s; later 5s; now 20s.

In LYMPNE Lathe
In STOWTING Hundred

26 Geoffrey holds BODSHAM from the Abbot. It answers for 1 sulung.
Land for 2 ploughs. They are there, with
8 smallholders.
Woodland, 15 pigs.
Value before 1066 £4; later 20s; now £4.
A villager held it.

27 The Abbot holds 2 sulungs and 1 yoke in LANPORT himself.
Land for 6 ploughs.
9 villagers with 4 smallholders who have 6 ploughs.
Meadow, 10 acres; woodland, 2 pigs.
Value before 1066 £6; later £4; now £8.

In the Lathe of WYE
In LONGBRIDGE Hundred

28 The Abbot holds KENNINGTON himself. Before 1066 it answered
for 4 sulungs and lay in (the lands of) Burmarsh. Land for 10
ploughs.
30 villagers who have 10 ploughs. A church.
The villagers held it before 1066.

Cū his .IIII. folins h̄t ꝰ̃ S Auguſtin⁹. I .jugū q̃etū ab om̄i
ſcoto regio. 7 ibi tant̄ ſiluæ unde exeunt de paſnagio.
XL . porci. aut. LIIII. denar 7 uñ obol̄.

Totū hoc T.R.E. ualeb̄ . x. lib̄ . 7 poſt VIII . lib̄. Modo⸝
XII . lib̄ 7 x . ſol̄.   IN MARESS DE ROMENEL.

Ipſe abb̄ ten̄ BVRWARMARESC . p̄ . II . ſolins 7 III . jugis
ſe defd̄ . Tra . ē . XII . car̄. In dn̄io ſunt . IIII . 7 XL.IIII . uil̶li
cū . v . bord̄ hn̄t . x . car̄.

T.R.E. ualeb̄ . xx . lib̄ . 7 poſt⸝ x . lib̄. Modo⸝ xxx . lib̄.

Scȳra teſtificat̄ qd̄ Bedeneſmere fuit S Auguſtini
T.R.E. 7 de illo qui eā teneb̄ habeb̄ abb̄ ſacā 7 ſocā.

TERRA SC̃I PETRI DE GAND. IN GRENVIZ HVND̄.

.VIII Abbas de Gand ten̄ de rege LEVESHA . 7 de rege . E.
tenuit. 7 t̄c 7 m̄ p̄ . II . ſolins ſe defd̄ . Tra . ē . XIIII . car̄.
In dn̄io ſunt . II . car̄. 7 L . uil̶li cū . IX . bord̄ hn̄t XVII . car̄.
Ibi . III . ſerui . 7 XI . molini cū gablo ruſticoꝝ . VIII . lib̄ 7 XII .
ſolid̄ reddt̄. De exitu port⸝ XL . ſolid̄. Ibi . xxx . ac̄ p̃ti.
De ſilua⸝ L . porci de paſnag⸝.

Totū m̄ T.R.E. ualeb̄ . XVI . lib̄ . 7 poſt⸝ XII . lib̄. Modo⸝ xxx̄ . lib̄.

TERRA HVGONIS DE MONTFORT.

.IX Hvgo de montfort ten̄ uñ m̄ ESTWELLE . qd̄ tenuit Fre
deric de rege . E . 7 p̄ uno ſolin ſe defd̄ . Tria juga ſunt
infra diuiſionē Hugonis . 7 q̃rtū jugū . ē extra . 7 ē de feudo epi Baioc̄.
Tra . ē . III . car̄ int totū. In dn̄io ſunt . II . car̄. 7 v . uil̶li cū . v . bord̄
hn̄t . I . car̄ 7 dim̄. Ibi . x . ſerui . 7 XII . ac̄ p̃ti . 7 ſiluā
T.R.E. ualeb̄ LXX . ſol̄. 7 poſt⸝ xxx . ſol̄. Modo⸝ LXX . ſolid̄.

Ipſe Hugo ten̄ HAINTONE . de rege . qd̄ Vlſi prb̄r tenuit de rege . E.
7 p̄ uno ſolin ſe defd̄ . Tra . ē . I . car̄. 7 ibi . ē cū . I . uil̶lo 7 IIII . bord̄. 7 III.
ac̄ p̃ti. T.R.E. 7 poſt⸝ 7 modo . ual̄ . xx . ſolid̄.

With these 4 sulungs St. Augustine's has 1 yoke exempt from all royal levy, and as much woodland as produces an income from pasturage of 40 pigs or 54½d.
Value of all this before 1066 £10; later £8; now £12 10s.

In the MARSH of ROMNEY

29   The Abbot holds BURMARSH himself. It answers for 2 sulungs and 3 yokes. Land for 12 ploughs. In lordship 4.
    44 villagers with 5 smallholders have 10 ploughs.
Value before 1066 £20; later £10; now £30.

30   The Shire testifies that BADLESMERE was St. Augustine's before 1066. The Abbot had the full jurisdiction of its holder.

8   LAND OF ST. PETER'S OF GHENT

In GREENWICH Hundred

1   The Abbot of Ghent holds LEWISHAM from the King. He held it from King Edward. Then and now it answers for 2 sulungs.
Land for 14 ploughs. In lordship 2 ploughs.
    50 villagers with 9 smallholders have 17 ploughs.
    3 slaves; 11 mills with the countrymen's tribute pay £8 12s;
       from the income of the port 40s. Meadow, 30 acres;
       from the woodland 50 pigs from pasturage.
Value of the whole manor before 1066 £16; later £12; now £30.

9   LAND OF HUGH DE MONTFORT   13 a

1   Hugh de Montfort holds a manor, EASTWELL, which Frederick held from King Edward. It answers for 1 sulung. There are 3 yokes inside Hugh's territory; a fourth yoke is outside; it is of the Bishop of Bayeux' Holding. Land for 3 ploughs in total. In lordship 2 ploughs.
    5 villagers with 5 smallholders have 1½ ploughs.
    10 slaves; meadow, 12 acres; woodland ......
Value before 1066, 70s; later 30s; now 70s.

2   Hugh holds HAMPTON from the King himself. Wulfsi the priest held it from King Edward. It answers for 1 sulung. Land for 1 plough. It is there, with
    1 villager and 4 smallholders.
    Meadow, 3 acres.
Value before 1066 later and now 20s.

Maigno ten de Hug *Seivetone* . Bresibalt tenuit de rege . E.
7 ꝑ dimid solin se defd . Tra . e . i . car . 7 ibi . e in dnio . cu . i . uitto 7 vi.
bord . Ibi æccta 7 pbr . 7 un molin de . x . den . 7 viii . ac pti.

T.R.E.ualeb . xxx . sot . 7 post: xx . sot . Modo: xxx . solid.

Isde Maigno ten de Hugone *Estefort* . Turgisus tenuit de Goduino
7 ꝑ uno solin se defd . Tra . e dimid car . In dnio tam . e una car . 7 ii.
uitti hnt . i . car . Ibi . ii . serui . 7 viii . ac pti.

T.R.E. ualeb . xxv . solid . Qdo recep: xx . sot . Modo: xxx . solid.

Ipse Hugo ten *Essella* . Tres hoes tenuer de rege . E . 7 potuer ire
quolib₂ cu tris suis . ꝑ . iii . jugis se defd . Tra . e . i . car 7 dimid.
Ibi m . iiii . uitti cu . ii : bord hnt . i . car . 7 vi . acs pti.

Totu T.R.E. ualeb . xx . solid . 7 post: xv . solid . Modo: xx . solid.

Alia *Essetesford* ten Maigno de hugone . Wirelm tenuit
de rege . E . ꝑ uno solin se defd . Tra . e . iiii . car . In dnio suy . ii.
7 ii . uitti cu . xv . bord hnt . iii . car . Ibi æccta 7 pbr . 7 iii . serui.
7 ii . molin de x . solid 7 ii . den.

T.R.E. ualeb . lxx . sot . 7 post: lx . sot . Modo: c . sot.

Isde Hugo ten in Maresc de Romenel . i . jugu . Tra . e
Medietate huj træ tenuer . ii . sochi . 7 ii . uitti alia.
Ibi sunt m . iiii . uitti . hntes . i . car.

H tra ualuit 7 uat . xii . solid.

Isd Hugo ten dimid jugu . qd tenuit un socts . Ibi . ii . bord sunt m.
H tra appciat in Titentone . qa illuc arata . e cu dnicis carrucis.
Hoc testat hund 7 burgenses de Doure . 7 hoes abbis S Augustini.
7 Estrea lest: qd tra *Etretone* qua caluniant canonici S Martini
de Doure sup Hugone de montfort . qd Vluuile Wilde ea tenuit
in alodio . T.R.E. 7 defd se ꝑ uno jugo . 7 ibi ht . i . car in dnio . 7 v . bord
cu . i . car . 7 un molin de . xx . solid .   Vat 7 ualuit . x . lib.

In the Lathe of WYE
In LONGBRIDGE Hundred

3   Maino holds SEVINGTON from Hugh. Bresibalt held it from King
     Edward. It answers for ½ sulung. Land for 1 plough. It is there,
     in lordship, with
         1 villager and 6 smallholders.
         A church and a priest; a mill at 10d; meadow, 8 acres.
     Value before 1066, 30s; later 20s; now 30s.

4   Maino also holds (South) ASHFORD from Hugh. Thorgils held it
     from Earl Godwin. It answers for 1 sulung. Land for ½ plough.
     In lordship, however, 1 plough.
         2 villagers have 1 plough.
         2 slaves; meadow, 8 acres.
     Value before 1066, 25s; when acquired 20s; now 30s.

5   Hugh holds ESSELLA himself. Three men held it from King Edward;
     they could go wherever [they would] with their lands. It answers
     for 3 yokes. Land for 1½ ploughs.
         Now 4 villagers with 2 smallholders have 1 plough.
         Meadow, 6 acres.
     Value of the whole before 1066, 20s; later 15s; now 20s.

6   Maino holds the other ASHFORD from Hugh. Wirelm held it from
     King Edward. It answers for 1 sulung. Land for 4 ploughs.
     In lordship 2.
         2 villagers with 15 smallholders have 3 ploughs.
         A church and a priest, 3 slaves; 2 mills at 10s 2d.
     Value before 1066, 70s; later 60s; now 100s.

In LYMPNE Lathe
In NEWCHURCH Hundred

7   Hugh also holds 1 yoke in ROMNEY MARSH. Land for ... 2 Freemen
     held half of this land; 2 villagers the other.
         Now 4 villagers who have 1 plough.
     The value of this land was and is 12s.

8   Hugh also holds ½ yoke which a Freeman held.
         Now there are 2 smallholders.
     This land is assessed in Tinton, because it is ploughed with the
     lordship ploughs from there.

9   The Hundred and the Burgesses of Dover and the Abbot of St.
     Augustine's men and of Eastry Lathe testify this; that the land of
     ATTERTON which the Canons of St. Martin's of Dover claim from
     Hugh de Montfort which Wulfy Wilde held in freehold before 1066
     answers for 1 yoke. He has 1 plough in lordship, and
         5 smallholders with 1 plough.
         A mill at 20s.
     The value is and was £10.

Ipſe Hugo ten̅ *ESTBRIGE* . in d̅n̅io .   *IN WERDE HVND̅.*

Alſi tenuit de Goduino . 7 p̅ uno ſolin ſe deſd̅ . T̅ra . e̅ . vi . car̅.

In d̅n̅io ſunt . iii . car̅ . 7 ii . uiłłi cu̅ . xxxvi . bord̅ h̅n̅t . iiii . car̅ . Ibi . viii .

ſalinæ cu̅ t̅cia parte nouæ ſalinæ de . xx . ſolid̅ . Dimid̅ piſcaria . viii .

den̅ . Silua de . iii . porc̅ de paſnag̅ . Ibi . ii . æcclæ .

T . R . E . 7 po̅ſt̅: ualuit . x . lib̅ . Modo: xv . lib̅ .

Bertranń ten̅ de Hug̅ dimid̅ jug̅ 7 dimid̅ uirga̅ . p̅ tanto ſe deſd̅ .

Adelelm̅ tenuit de rege . E . T̅ra . e̅ ad . i . car̅ . T . R . E . ualeb̅ . xx . ſolid̅ .

Herueus ten̅ de Hugone *BLACHEMENESTONE* . Blacheman

13 b

tenuit T . R . E . 7 p̅ dimidio ſolin ſe deſd̅ . T̅ra . e̅ . ii . car̅ .

In d̅n̅io ſunt ibi . 7 iii . uiłłi cu̅ . x . bord̅ cu̅ . i : car̅ . Ibi æccła

7 un̅ ſeruus .

T . R . E . ualeb̅ . iiii . lib̅ . 7 po̅ſt̅: iii . lib̅ . Modo . vi . lib̅ .

Iſd̅ Hugo ten̅ in Mareſc de R̅omenel un̅ ſolin dimid̅

uirga min̅ . p̅ tanto ſe deſd̅ . T̅ra . e̅ . iii . car̅ . Ibi . xiiii . ſochi

h̅n̅t . iii . car̅ . T . R . E . ualeb̅ . iiii . lib̅ . 7 po̅ſt̅: iii . lib̅ . M̅: c . ſoł .

Rogeri ten̅ de Hugone un̅ jugu̅ in Mareſc de R̅omenel .

p̅ uno jugo ſe deſd̅ . Duo ſochi tenuer̅ . T̅ra . e̅ . i . car̅ . 7 ibi . e̅

cu̅ . iii . bord̅ . T . R . E . ualeb̅ . xxx . ſoł . 7 po̅ſt̅: xv . ſoł . Modo:

Rotbt̅ ten̅ de Hugone in eod̅ Mareſch   ʃ xxx . ſolid̅ .

ſexta̅ parte̅ uni̅ jugi . Vn̅ ſochis tenuit .

Vał 7 ualuit . v . ſolid̅ .   *IN HEN HVND̅.*

Rogeri ten̅ de Hugone *POSTINGES* . Sbern̅ tenuit .

p̅ duob̅z ſolins 7 dimid̅ ſe deſd̅ : T̅ra . e̅ . xiii . car̅ . In d̅n̅io

ſunt . iii . 7 xvi . uiłłi cu̅ . vii . bord̅ h̅n̅t . vii . car̅ .

Ibi . ii . æccleſiolæ . 7 ii . molini de . vi . ſolid̅ : 7 xl . ac̅ p̅ti .

Silua . xl . porc̅ .

T . R . E . ualeb̅ . x . lib̅ . 7 po̅ſt̅: c . ſolid̅ . Modo: xiiii . lib̅ .

De iſto m̅ ten̅ R̅adulf̅ de curbeſpine . iii . denas . exi̅

diuiſione̅ ſunt . 7 uał . xv . ſolid̅ .

10 Hugh holds EAST BRIDGE in lordship himself. Alfsi held it from Earl
Godwin. It answers for 1 sulung. Land for 6 ploughs. In lordship
3 ploughs.
2 villagers with 36 smallholders have 4 ploughs.
8 salt-houses with a third part of a ninth salt-house at 20s;
½ fishery, 8d; woodland at 3 pigs from pasturage. 2 churches.
Value before 1066 and later £10; now £15.

11 Bertram holds ½ yoke and ½ virgate from Hugh. It answers for as
much. Aethelhelm held it from King Edward. Land for 1 plough.
Value before 1066, 20s.

12 Harvey holds BLACKMANSTONE from Hugh. Blackman held it   13 b
before 1066. It answers for ½ sulung. Land for 2 ploughs. They
are there in lordship, and
3 villagers with 10 smallholders with 1 plough.
A church; a slave.
Value before 1066 £4; later £3; now £6.

13 Hugh also holds 1 sulung less ½ virgate in ROMNEY MARSH. It answers
for as much. Land for 3 ploughs.
14 Freemen have 3 ploughs.
Value before 1066 £4; later £3; now 100s.

14 Roger holds 1 yoke in ROMNEY MARSH from Hugh. It answers for
1 yoke. 2 Freemen held it. Land for 1 plough. It is there, with
3 smallholders.
Value before 1066, 30s; later 15s; now 30s.

15 Robert holds the sixth part of a yoke, also in the MARSH, from Hugh.
A Freeman held it.
The value is and was 5s.

In HAYNE Hundred

16 Roger holds POSTLING from Hugh. Esbern Big held it. It answers
for 2½ sulungs. Land for 13 ploughs. In lordship 3.
16 villagers with 7 smallholders have 7 ploughs.
2 small churches; 2 mills at 6s; meadow, 40 acres; woodland,
40 pigs.
Value before 1066 £10; later 100s; now £14.
Ralph of Courbépine holds 3 pig pastures of this manor; they are
outside his territory.
Value 15s.

Ifdē Hugo teń dimid folin . qd Aldret tenuit de

rege . E . fine halla . p dimid folin fe defd . Tra . ē . iii.

car . Ibi uñ uiłłs cū . iiii . bord man . nulla ibi car.

Vñ molin de . xxv . denar . 7 v . ãc p̄ti.

Ifdē Hugo teń BELICE . Turgis tenuit de rege . E.

7 p uno folin fe defd . Tra . ē   In dñio . ē una car ; 7 ii.

uiłłi cū uno bord hñt . i . car . Ibi . iii . ãc p̄ti.

Hæ duæ træ T . R . E . ualeb . lx . fol . 7 poft. xx . fol . M̃. lx . fol.

Ipfe Hugo teń unā trā quā   IN NEVVECERCE HD.

Azor tenuit de rege . E . fine halla ; p uno foliń fe

defd . Tra . ē . v . car . Ibi . viii . uiłłi cū . iii . bord hñt . ii.

car . T . R . E 7 poft. ualuit . viii . lib . Modo. ix . lib.

Ipfe Hugo teń dimid folin in Marefch dē Romenel.

p tanto fe defd . Tra . ē . iiii . car . Duodecī fochi te

nueř 7 tenent hñtes . iiii . car . Val 7 ualuit . lx . folid.

Ifdē Hugo teń in ipfo Marefch   IN ADELOVESBRIGE HD.

uñ jugū . p tanto fe defd . Tra . ē . ii . car . Ibi funt

xii . fochi cū . viii . bord hñtes . ii . car.

Hæ duæ træ T . R . E . ualeb . c . x . fol . 7 poft 7 m̃ fimilit.

              IN BLACHEBVRNE HD.

Ipfe Hugo teń TINTENTONE . Vlnod tenuit de

rege . E . 7 tc defd fe p uno folin . Modo p dimidio.

qa foris diuifione . ē . Tra . ē . v . car . In dñio funt

ii . car . 7 xxi . uiłłs cū . vi . bord hñt . vii . car.

Ibi æccła 7 ix . ferui . 7 iii . pifcariæ de . v . folid.

7 xxxviii . ãc p̄ti . Silua . xl . porc.

T . R . E . ualeb . xii . lib . 7 poft. vi . lib . Modo. vii . lib.

Ifdē Hugo teń dimid jugū qd tenueř . v . fochi

7 m̃ teneǵ . hñtes . i . car ibi cū . iiii . bord . Val 7 ualuit

                   ſ femp . v . folid.

17   Hugh also holds ½ sulung which Aethelred Bot held from King
     Edward, without a Hall. It answers for ½ sulung. Land for
     3 ploughs.
       1 villager with 3 smallholders lives there; no ploughs.
       A mill at 25d; meadow, 5 acres.

18   Hugh also holds *BELICE*. Thorgils held it from King Edward.
     It answers for 1 sulung. Land for ... In lordship 1 plough.
       2 villagers with 1 smallholder have 1 plough.
       Meadow, 3 acres.
     Value of these two lands before 1066, 60s; later 20s; now 60s.

In NEWCHURCH Hundred
19   Hugh holds a land himself which Azor Roote held from King
     Edward, without a Hall. It answers for 1 sulung. Land for 5
     ploughs.
       8 villagers with 3 smallholders have 2 ploughs.
     Value before 1066 and later £8; now £9.

20   Hugh holds ½ sulung in ROMNEY MARSH himself. It answers for
     as much. Land for 4 ploughs.
       12 Freemen who have 4 ploughs held and hold it.
     The value is and was 60s.

In ALOESBRIDGE Hundred
21   Hugh also holds 1 yoke in the MARSH. It answers for as much.
     Land for 2 ploughs.
       12 Freemen with 8 smallholders who have 2 ploughs.
     Value of these two lands before 1066, 110s; later and now
     the same.

In BLACKBURN Hundred
22   Hugh holds TINTON himself. Wulfnoth held it from King Edward.
     It answered for 1 sulung then; now for ½, because it is outside his
     territory. Land for 5 ploughs. In lordship 2 ploughs.
       21 villagers with 6 smallholders have 7 ploughs.
       A church; 9 slaves; 3 fisheries at 5s; meadow, 38 acres;
         woodland, 40 pigs.
     Value before 1066 £12; later £6; now £7.

23   Hugh also holds ½ yoke which 5 Freemen held, and now hold, who
     have 1 plough, with
       4 smallholders.
     The value is and always was 5s.

Herueus teñ de Hugoñe IN ESTRAITES HD.

SEDLINGES . Ofuuard tenuit de rege . E . ꝑ uno

folin fe defđ . Tra . ē . vii . car̄ . In dñio funt . iii . car̄.

7 viii . uiłłi cū . xxv . borđ hñt . iiii . car̄ . Ibi . ii . æcclæ.

7 uñ molin de . xxx . deñ . 7 xxxvi . ac̄ p̄ti . 7 filua

de . vi . porc̄.

T.R.E.ualeƀ . viii . liƀ . 7 poſt: c . foliđ . Modo: vii . liƀ.

Alnod teñ de Hugone HORTONE . IN STOTINGES HD.

Leuuiñ tenuit de rege . E . 7 ꝑ dimidio folin fe

defđ . Tra . ē . iii . car̄ . In dñio funt . ii . car̄ . 7 v.

uiłłi cū . vi . borđ hñt . i . car̄ 7 dimiđ . Ibi æccła.

7 uñ moliñ de . xxv . deñ . 7 xxiiii . ac̄ p̄ti . Silua.

x . porc̄ . T.R.E.ualeƀ . xl . foł . 7 poſt: xx . Modo: lx . foł.

Ibiđ teñ Alnod . i . jugū de Hugone . fed nil ibi eſt.

Ipfe Hugo teñ . iii . uirḡ 7 dimiđ in eođ LEST.

quas tenuer̄ . iii . fochi de rege . E.

Ibi m̄ uñ uiłłs hr̄ dimiđ car̄ cū . iii . borđ.

Vał 7 ualuit fep̄ . x . foliđ . IN HAME HVND.

Wiłłs teñ de Hugone . iii . juga 7 dimiđ uirga in

ORLAVESTONE . Hanc tr̄a tenuer̄ xi . fochi . Tra ē . iii . car̄.

Ibi m̄ . ii . car̄ in dñio . 7 xv . uiłłi cū . ix . borđ hñt . iii.

car̄ 7 dim̄ . Ibi . ii . æcclæ . 7 xx . ac̄ p̄ti . Silua . vi . porc̄.

T.R.E.ualeƀ . lx . foł . 7 poſt: xxx . foł . Modo: c . foliđ.

Radulf fili Ricardi teñ de Hugone dimiđ folin

in Rochinges . qđ Leuret tenuit de rege . E . ꝑ dimiđ

folin fe defđ . Tra . ē . ii . car̄ . Ibi m̄ . xii . uiłłi hñt unā

car̄ 7 dimiđ . de filua: i . porc̄.

T.R.E.ualeƀ . l . foł . 7 poſt: xxx . foł . Modo: l . foliđ.

Radulf teñ de huḡ HORTVN . IN STOTINGES HD.

Duo fochi tenuer̄ de rege . E . 7 ꝑ uno jugo 7 dim̄ fe defđ.

Tra i . car̄ 7 dim̄ . In dñio . ē una . cū . iiii . uiłłis . 7 uñ

In STREET Hundred

24   Harvey holds SELLINDGE from Hugh. Osward held it from King
      Edward. It answers for 1 sulung. Land for 7 ploughs. In
      lordship 3 ploughs.
           8 villagers with 25 smallholders have 4 ploughs.
           2 churches; a mill at 30d; meadow, 36 acres; woodland at
                6 pigs.
      Value before 1066 £8; later 100s; now £7.

In STOWTING Hundred

25   Alnoth holds (Monk's) HORTON from Hugh. Leofwin held it from
      King Edward. It answers for ½ sulung. Land for 3 ploughs. In
      lordship 2 ploughs.
           5 villagers with 6 smallholders have 1½ ploughs.
           A church; a mill at 25d; meadow, 24 acres; woodland, 10 pigs.
      Value before 1066, 40s; later 20[s]; now 60s.

26   There Alnoth also holds 1 yoke from Hugh; but there is nothing there.

27   Hugh holds 3½ virgates himself in the same Lathe, which 3 Freemen
      held from King Edward.
           Now 1 villager has ½ plough, with 3 smallholders.
      The value is and always was 10s.

In HAM Hundred

28   William holds 3 yokes and ½ virgate in ORLESTONE from Hugh.
      11 Freemen held this land. Land for 3 ploughs. Now 2 ploughs
      in lordship.
           15 villagers with 9 smallholders have 3½ ploughs.
           2 churches; meadow, 20 acres; woodland, 6 pigs.
      Value before 1066, 60s; later 30s; now 100s.

29   Ralph son of Richard holds ½ sulung from Hugh in RUCKINGE, which
      Leofred held from King Edward. It answers for ½ sulung. Land for
      2 ploughs.
           12 villagers have 1½ ploughs.
           From the woodland, 1 pig.
      Value before 1066, 50s; later 30s; now 50s.

In STOWTING Hundred

30   Ralph holds (Monk's) HORTON from Hugh. Two Freemen held it
      from King Edward. It answers for 1½ yokes. Land for 1½ ploughs.
      In lordship 1, with
           4 villagers.

molin de . xxx . den . 7 x . ac p̃ti . De filua . vi . porc.

T.R.E. ualeb . xl . fol . 7 poſt: xx . fol . Modo: xxx . foliđ.

Hugo de manneuile ten de Hug   IN ESTRAITES HĐ.

ESTRAITES . Vlnod tenuit de rege . E . p̃ . ii . folins fe

defđ . Tra . ē . viii . car . In dñio funt . ii . 7 xi . uiłłi cũ

xxv . borđ hñt . v . car . Ibi æccła . 7 vii . ferui . 7 xxx . ac

p̃ti . T.R.E. ualeb x . fol . 7 poſt: iiii . fol . Modo: viii . lib:

Ansfriđ ten de Hug . i jugũ qđ tenuit in eođ hunđ

uñ fochs de rege . E . 7 p̃ uno jugo fe defđ . Tra . ē . i . car.

Ibi . ē cũ uno uiłło 7 ii . borđ . 7 uñ molin de . xxvi . den.

7 viii . ac p̃ti . T.R.E. 7 m̃ ual . xl . fol.

Rotbt coc ten de Hugone . i . jugũ qđ tenuit uñ fochs

7 p̃ tanto fe defđ . Ibi . ē una car cũ uno borđ . 7 iiii . ac

p̃ti . T.R.E. 7 m̃ ual . xxx . foliđ.

Giſłebt ten de Hugone uñ jugũ IN LANGEBRIGE HĐ.

qđ tenuit q̃dā fochs de rege . E . Val 7 ualuit . iiii . fol.

Nil ibi fuit nec . ē.

De Etwelle q̃ ten Herbt fili Iuonis ext diuifionē Hugoñ.

ten ipfe Hugo . xiiii . acs træ . jnfra fuā diuifione . 7 ual . ii . fol.

IN ESTREA LEST.   IN BEVSBERGE HVND.

Ipfe Hugo de montfort ten ETWELLE . Molleue tenuit

p̃ . iii . folins fe defđ . 7 M: p̃ . i . folin.

Tra . ē . i . car . 7 ibi . ē in dñio . 7 xix . borđ hñt . i . car . Ibi

æccła . 7 iiii . molini | de . iiii . lib . 7 xvii fol 7 iiii . den . 7 iiii . ac

p̃ti . T.R.E. ualeb . xi . lib . 7 poſt: iiii . lib . Modo: viii . lib.

Ipfe Hugo ten NEVENTONE . Ederic tenuit de rege . E.

7 p̃ . ii . folins fe defđ tc . 7 m̃ p̃ uno q̃a alius . ē ext diuifionē.

Tra . ē . ii . car . 7 ibi funt in dñio . Ibi æccła 7 xxi . borđ . 7 iii.

ferui cũ . iii . car . Ibi . iii . molini 7 dimiđ de . c.v . foliđ.

Totũ T.R.E. ualeb . xii . lib . 7 poſt: iii . lib . Modo: xii . lib.

qđ h̃t Hugo int diuifionē fuā.

A mill at 30d; meadow, 10 acres; from the woodland, 6 pigs.
Value before 1066, 40s; later 20s; now 30s.

In STREET Hundred

31 Hugh de Mandeville holds (Court at) STREET from Hugh. Wulfnoth
held it from King Edward. It answers for 2 sulungs. Land for 8
ploughs. In lordship 2.
    11 villagers with 25 smallholders have 5 ploughs.
    A church; 7 slaves; meadow, 30 acres.
Value before 1066, 10s; later 4s; now £8.

32 Ansfrid holds 1 yoke from Hugh, which a Freeman held from King
Edward in the same Hundred. It answers for 1 yoke. Land for 1
plough. It is there, with
    1 villager and 2 smallholders.
    A mill at 26d; meadow, 8 acres.
Value before 1066 and now 40s.

33 Robert Cook holds 1 yoke from Hugh which a Freeman held. It
answers for as much. 1 plough there, with
    1 smallholder.
    Meadow, 4 acres.
Value before 1066 and now 30s.

In LONGBRIDGE Hundred

34 Gilbert holds 1 yoke from Hugh which a Freeman held from King
Edward.
The value is and was 4s.
    There was and is nothing there.

35 From (Temple) EWELL, which Herbert son of Ivo holds outside
Hugh's territory, Hugh holds 14 acres of land himself inside his
territory.
Value 2s.

In EASTRY Lathe   13 d
In BEWSBOROUGH Hundred

36 Hugh de Montfort holds (Temple) EWELL himself. Molleva held it.
It answered for 3 sulungs; now for 1 sulung. Land for 1 plough.
It is there, in lordship.
    19 smallholders have 1 plough.
    A church; 4½ mills at £4 17s 4d; meadow, 4 acres.
Value before 1066 £11; later £4; now £8.

37 Hugh holds NEWINGTON himself. Edric held it from King Edward.
Then it answered for 2 sulungs; now for 1, because the other is
outside his territory. Land for 2 ploughs. They are there, in lordship.
    A church; 21 smallholders and 3 slaves with 3 ploughs.
    3½ mills at 105s.
Value of the whole before 1066 £12; later £3; now what Hugh has in
his territory £12.

Intᵘ diuifionē hanc eſt uñ focħs tene⟍S . xvi . aĉs ᷣræ . 7 ipſe
idē tenuit de rege . E.

In eoð hund ten⁊ ið Hugo unā partē Jaonei . quæ nichil redð
nec reddið . nec ad ullū ꝏ jacuit . ſed . ē intᵘ diuifionē ſuā . 7 fuit
de dñio regis.   Aluuin pbr⁹ tenut

In eoð hund h� Fulbt de Hugone uñ moliñ . 7 redð . xxiiii . ſoł.

Herfrid ten⁊ de Hugone POLTONE . Vluuin⁹ tenuit de rege . E.
7 ꝓ uno folin ſe defð . Tra⁊ . ē . ii . caᷓ . Ibi ſunt . iii . uiłłi 7 æccleſiola.
T . R . E . ualeƀ . xl . ſoł . 7 poſt⁷ xv . ſoł . Mᷣ xxx . ſoł.

IN WIWART LEST.   IN BERISOVT HVND⁷.

Ipſe Hugo ten⁷ BREBVRNE . Godric⁹ de burnes tenuit de rege . E.
7 ꝓ . vii . folins ſe defð tĉ . 7 m̄⁷ ꝓ . v . folins 7 dimið . 7 dim⁷ jugo.
q̇a alia pars . ē ext diuifionē hug⁷ . 7 eā ten⁷ eꝑs baiocenſis.
Tra⁷ . ē . xv . caᷓ . In dñio ſunt . ii æ . 7 xxxi . uiłłs cū . x . borð
hn̄t . x . caᷓ . Ibi æccła 7 viii to . ſerui . 7 ii . molini de . vii . ſolið.
7 xx . aĉ ꝓti . Silua de . xxv . porĉ.
T . R . Eᷣ ualeƀ . xx . liƀ . 7 poſt⁷ viii . liƀ . Modoᷣ xvi . liƀ.

In Hund de Certh ten⁷ quædā femina de Hugone . i . uirgā.
quā uñ focħs⁹ tenuit de rege . E.   Vał . iii . folið.

Ipſe Hugo ten⁷ dimið jugū in TEPINDENE . IN BLACHEBVRNE HĎ.
qð tenuit Norman de rege . E . 7 ꝓ dim⁷ jugo ſe defð . Ibi ſu⟍
ii . uiłłi cū dim⁷ caᷓ . Valuit ſemꝑ 7 uał . c . denar⁷.

IN LIMOWART LEST.   IN ESTRAITES HĎ.

Ipſe Hugo ten⁷ SIBORNE . Oſiar tenuit de rege . E . 7 ꝓ uno
folin ſe defð tĉ 7 m̄ . Tra⁷ . ē . ii . caᷓ . In dñio . ē una . 7 uñ uiłłs
cū . iiii . borð hᷓ . i . caᷓ . 7 ibi uñ⁹ ſeruus.
T . R . E . ualeƀ . lx . folið . 7 poſt⁷ xx . ſoł . Modoᷣ iiii . liƀ.

Iſdē Hugo hᷓ   dimið folin SVANETONE . Tra⁷ . ē . i . caᷓ.
Norman tenuit de rege . E . ꝓ tanto ſe defð.
Ibi . iiii . uiłłi hn̄t . i . caᷓ . Ibi ſilua de . v . porĉ⁷.
T . R . E . ualeƀ . xxv . ſoł . 7 poſt⁷ xv . ſoł . Modoᷣ xxx . ſoł.

38   In this territory is a Freeman who holds 16 acres of land. He also held it himself from King Edward.

39   In the same Hundred Hugh also holds one part of *JAONEI* which pays and paid nothing, and did not lie in (the lands of) any manor, but it is in his territory and was of the King's lordship. Alwin the priest held it.

40   In the same Hundred Fulbert has a mill from Hugh which pays 24s.

41   Herfrid holds POULTON from Hugh. Wulfwin held it from King Edward. It answers for 1 sulung. Land for 2 ploughs.
     3 villagers and a small church.
   Value before 1066, 40s; later 15s; now 30s.

In WYE Lathe
In BIRCHOLT Hundred

42   Hugh holds BRABOURNE himself. Godric of (Bishops)bourne held it from King Edward. Then it answered for 7 sulungs; now for 5½ sulungs and ½ yoke, because the other part is outside Hugh's territory. The Bishop of Bayeux holds it. Land for 15 ploughs. In lordship 2.
     31 villagers with 10 smallholders have 10 ploughs.
     A church; 8 slaves; 2 mills at 7s; meadow, 20 acres;
       woodland, 25 pigs.
   Value before 1066 £20; later £8; now £16.

In the Hundred of CHART

43   A woman holds 1 virgate from Hugh which a Freeman held from King Edward.
   Value 3s.

In BLACKBURN Hundred

44   Hugh holds ½ yoke himself in TIFFENDEN which Norman held from King Edward. It answers for ½ yoke.
     2 villagers with ½ plough.
   The value always was and is 100d.

In LYMPNE Lathe
In STREET Hundred

45   Hugh holds *SIBORNE* himself. Osgeard held it from King Edward. Then and now it answered for 1 sulung. Land for 2 ploughs. In lordship 1.
     1 villager with 4 smallholders has 1 plough. 1 slave.
   Value before 1066, 60s; later 20s; now £4.

46   Hugh also has ½ sulung (in) SWANTON. Land for 1 plough. Norman held it from King Edward. It answers for as much.
     4 villagers have 1 plough.
     Woodland at 5 pigs.
   Value before 1066, 25s; later 15s; now 30s.

Nigellus teñ de Hugone uñ jugũ . 7 in Aia . vii . acræ.

Vñ focħs tenuit de rege . E . Tra . ẽ . 1 . cař.

In dñio . ẽ dimidia cař . 7 vi . borđ 7 ii . ferui . 7 v . ãc p̃ti.

T . R . E . ualeb . xx . foliđ . 7 poft: x . fot . Modo: xxv . fot.

Witts fili Groffę teñ de Hugone BONINTONE.

Norman tenuit de rege . E . 7 ᵽ uno folin fe defđ Tra . ẽ

.iiii . cař . In dñio . ẽ una . 7 ix . uitti cũ . iiii . borđ hñt . ii.

ᚠ cař.

Ibi æccła 7 viii . fcrui . 7 filua . viii . porc.

T . R . E . ualeb . iiii . lib . 7 poft: iii . lib . Modo: c . foliđ.

Herueus teñ de Hugone OBTREPOLE . Alrebot tenuit

de rege . E . 7 ᵽ uno folin fe defđ . Tra . ẽ . vi . cař . In dñio eft

una . 7 xi . uitti cũ . ii . cař . 7 uñ feru . 7 x . ãc p̃ti . 7 filua

redđ . v . denař de pafnagio . T . R.

T . R . E . ualeb . l . foliđ . 7 poft: xx . fot . Modo: iiii . lib.

IN BLACHEBVRNE HVND 7 IN NEVCERCE HVND.

Herald teñ dimiđ folin unã uirgã miñ

Sex focħi tenueř de rege . E . 7 ᵽ tanto fe defđ . Tra . ẽ . v . cař.

In dñio funt . ii . 7 xxxi . borđ hñt . iii . cař . Ibi uñ feruus.

T . R . E . ualeb . lx . fot . 7 poft: xxx . fot . Modo: iiii . lib . 7 xv . fot.

7 Adhuc ħt unã denã quæ jacuit in FANE manerio Adã.

Ibi funt . ii . borđ . redđtes . xxx . denař . Val 7 ualuit fep . v . fot.

Ipfe Hugo teñ dimiđ folin   *IN BERISCOLT HVND.*

in HASTINGELIE . Vlnod tenuit de rege . E . 7 ᵽ tanto fe defđ.

Modo teñ q̃dã homo de Hugone . 7 ħt ibi . ii . borđ . red

dentes . iiii . foliđ . Valuit fep 7 ual . x . fot.

ᚠ hđ.

Ipfe Hugo teñ in dñio uñ jugũ 7 dimiđ *IN LANGEBRIGE*

in TEVEGATE . God tenuit de rege . E . Ibi . ẽ m̃ uñ uitts

cũ . i . cař . 7 ibi . viii . ãc p̃ti.

T . R . E: ualeb . xx . fot . 7 poft: x . fot . Modo: xx . foliđ.

In eođ Hund eft una uirga træ in SVESTONE . quã te

nuit uñ focħs de rege . E . Ibi m̃ eft uñ borđ . xii . denař

redđ . T . R . E . ualeb xxx . den . 7 poft: xviii . Modo: iii . foliđ.

47 Nigel holds 1 yoke and 7 acres from Hugh in *AIA*. A Freeman held them from King Edward. Land for 1 plough. In lordship ½ plough;
    6 smallholders; 2 slaves.
    Meadow, 5 acres.
Value before 1066, 20s; later 10s; now 25s.

48 William son of Gross holds BONNINGTON from Hugh. Norman held it from King Edward. It answers for 1 sulung. Land for 4 ploughs. In lordship 1.
    9 villagers with 4 smallholders have 2 ploughs.
    A church; 8 slaves; woodland, 8 pigs.   14 a
Value before 1066 £4; later £3; now 100s.

49 Harvey holds OTTERPOOL from Hugh. Aethelred Bot held it from King Edward. It answers for 1 sulung. Land for 6 ploughs. In lordship 1;
    11 villagers with 2 ploughs; a slave.
    Meadow, 10 acres; woodland which pays 5d from pasturage.
Value before 1066, 50s; later 20s; now £4.

In BLACKBURN Hundred and in NEWCHURCH Hundred
50 Harold holds ½ sulung less 1 virgate. 6 Freemen held it from King Edward. It answers for as much. Land for 5 ploughs. In lordship 2.
    31 smallholders have 3 ploughs. 1 slave.
Value before 1066, 60s; later 30s; now £4 15s.

51 Further, he has a pig pasture which lies in (the lands of) Fanscombe, a manor of Adam's.
    2 smallholders there who pay 30d.
The value is and always was 5s.

In BIRCHOLT Hundred
52 Hugh holds ½ sulung in HASTINGLEIGH himself. Wulfnoth held it from King Edward. It answers for as much. Now a man holds it from Hugh. He has
    2 smallholders who pay 4s.
The value was and always is 10s.

In LONGBRIDGE Hundred
53 Hugh holds in lordship 1½ yokes in EVEGATE himself. Goda held it from King Edward.
    Now 1 villager with 1 plough.
    Meadow, 8 acres.
Value before 1066, 20s; later 10s; now 20s.

54 In the same Hundred 1 virgate of land in *SUESTONE* which a Freeman held from King Edward.
    Now 1 smallholder, who pays 12d.
Value before 1066, 30d; later 18[d] ; now 3s.

TERRA COMITIS EVSTACHII.

IN DIMIDIO LEST DE SVDTONE . IN OSTREHĂ HVND.

C.x. Comes EVSTACHIVS ten de rege OISTREHAM . Goduin coīn
tenuit de rege . E . 7 ṗ . IIII . ſolins ſe defđ tē 7 modo.
Tra . ē   In dñio ſunt . II . cař . 7 XLII . uitti cū . VII .
borđ hñt xxx . cař . Ibi . x . ſerui . 7 uñ moliñ de . v . ſoliđ.
7 xvi . ǎc ṗti . 7 de ſilua . c . porc.
T.R.E. ualeƀ . xxx . liƀ . Qdo recep . xxIIII . liƀ . Modo . xL . liƀ.

IN LEST DE WIWARLET.   *IN WI HVNDRET.*

Ipſe comes ten BOLTVNE . Goduin coīn tenuit . 7 ṗ . VII .
ſolins ſe defđ tē 7 m̃ . Tra . ē xxx.III . cař . In dñio ſunt . III .
7 LxvII . uitti cū . v . borđ hñt . xxx . cař . Ibi æccła . 7 xvII .
ſerui . 7 II . molini de . vII . ſoliđ 7 II . denar . 7 xxvI . ǎc ṗti .
Silua . cc . porc.
T.R.E. ualeƀ . xx . liƀ . 7 poſt . xxx . liƀ . Modo . xL . liƀ.

14 b

TERRA RICARDI . F . GISLEƀTI *IN TVIFERDE HVND.*

.XI. Ricard de Tonebrige ten HALLINGES . 7 Aldret
tenuit de rege . E . 7 tē 7 m̃ defđ ſe ṗ . II . ſolins . Tra . ē xvI .
cař . In dñio . ē una 7 dimidia . 7 xvI . uitti cū xII . borđ
hñt . vI . cař . Ibi . II . æcctæ . 7 xv . ſerui . 7 II . molini de xxv .
ſoliđ . 7 IIII . piſcariæ de mille 7 ſeptingent anguitt . xx min .
Ibi . v . ǎc ṗti . 7 Silua . c.L . porc.
.T.R.E. 7 poſt . ualuit . xxx . liƀ . Modo . xx . liƀ . eo qđ tra
uaſtata . ē a pecunia .   *IN MEDESTAN HVND.*

Iſđē Ricard . ten BERMELINGE . Alret tenuit de rege . E .
7 tē 7 m̃ ṗ uno ſolin ſe defđ . Tra . ē . IIII . cař . In dñio
II . cař . 7 v . uitti cū . vIII . borđ hñt . v . cař . Ibi . xIII . ſerui .
7 uñ moliñ de . v . ſoliđ . 7 IIII . ǎc ṗti . Silua . x . porc.
T.R.E. ualeƀ . IIII . liƀ . 7 poſt . c . ſoliđ . Modo . IIII . liƀ.

LAND OF COUNT EUSTACE

In the Half-Lathe of SUTTON

In WESTERHAM Hundred

1 Count Eustace holds WESTERHAM from the King. Earl Godwin held it from King Edward. It answered for 4 sulungs then and now. Land for ... In lordship 2 ploughs.

42 villagers with 7 smallholders have 30 ploughs.

10 slaves; a mill at 5s; meadow, 16 acres; from the woodland, 100 pigs.

Value before 1066 £30; when acquired £24; now £40.

In the Lathe of WYE

In WYE Hundred

2 The Count holds BOUGHTON (Aluph) himself. Earl Godwin held it. It answered for 7 sulungs then and now. Land for 33 ploughs. In lordship 3.

67 villagers with 5 smallholders have 30 ploughs.

A church; 17 slaves; 2 mills at 7s 2d; meadow, 26 acres; woodland, 200 pigs.

Value before 1066 £20; later £30; now £40.

11   LAND OF RICHARD SON OF GILBERT   14 b

In TWYFORD Hundred

1 Richard of Tonbridge holds YALDING. Aethelred held it from King Edward. It answered for 2 sulungs then and now. Land for 16 ploughs. In lordship 1½.

16 villagers with 12 smallholders have 6 ploughs.

2 churches; 15 slaves; 2 mills at 25s; 4 fisheries at 1,700 eels less 20. Meadow, 5 acres; woodland, 150 pigs.

Value before 1066 and later £30; now £20, because the land has been despoiled of livestock.

In MAIDSTONE Hundred

2 Richard also holds (East) BARMING. Alfred held it from King Edward. Then and now it answered for 1 sulung. Land for 4 ploughs. In lordship 2 ploughs.

5 villagers with 8 smallholders have 5 ploughs.

13 slaves; a mill at 5s; meadow, 4 acres; woodland, 10 pigs.

Value before 1066 £4; later 100s; now £4.

TERRA HAMONIS VICECOMITIS.

IN LEST DE WIWARLET.   *IN WIT HVND.*

.XII. **H**aimo uicecom ten de rege un Maner.

qd T.R.E. se desd p. ii. solins 7 dimid. 7 m p uno
solin 7 iii. jugis. Tra. e. viii. car. In dnio. v. bou arantes.
7 xvi. uilli cu. xv. bord hnt. x. car. Ibi æccla. 7 vii. serui.
7 un molin de. ix. solid. 7 lx. anguill. Ibi. xx. ac pti.
7 silua. xxx. porc.   £ 7. vi. den.
T.R.E. ualeb. x. lib. 7 post: vii. lib. Modo: xiiii. lib. 7 vi. solid
De isto co ten Hugo de montfort. iii. juga 7 dim. Val. lx. sol.

IN DIMIDIO LEST DE SVDTONE.   *IN GRENVIZ HVND.*

Ibi ht Haimo. lxiii. acs træ. quæ ptin in *HVLVIZ.*
Wills accipitrari tenuit de rege. E. Ibi sunt. xi. bord
reddtes xli. denar.   Totu ual. iii. lib.

IN LEST DE ELESFORD.   *IN LITEFEL HVND.*

Ipse Haimo ten *MAROVRDE*. Norman tenuit de rege. E.
7 tc 7 m p. ii. solins se desd. Tra. e. ix. car. In dnio sunt. ii.
7 xxviii. uilli cu. xv. bord hnt. x. car. Ibi æccla. 7 x.
serui. 7 ii. molini de. x. solid. 7 ii. piscar. de. ii. solid.
Ibi. xx. ac pti. 7 tant siluæ unde exeunt. lx. porc. de pasnag.
T.R.E. ualeb. xii. lib. 7 post: x. lib. Modo: xix. lib.

IN LEST DE BOROWART.   *IN WITESTAPLE HVND.*

Ipse Haimo ten *BLEHEM*. Norman tenuit de rege. E.
7 tc 7 m se desd p uno solin. Tra. e. iiii. car. 7 xii. uilli
hnt ibi. ii. car. In dnio. e una car. Ibi æccla. 7 ii. ac pti.
7 de pasnag. lx. porc. Ibi una piscaria.
T.R.E. ualeb. viii. lib. 7 post 7 modo: ual. vi. lib.

LAND OF HAMO THE SHERIFF

In the Lathe of WYE
In WYE Hundred

1 Hamo the Sheriff holds a manor from the King which answered
for 2½ sulungs before 1066; now for 1 sulung and 3 yokes. Land
for 8 ploughs. In lordship 5 ploughing oxen.
  16 villagers with 15 smallholders have 10 ploughs.
  A church; 7 slaves; a mill at 9s and 60 eels. Meadow, 20 acres;
    woodland, 30 pigs.
  Value before 1066 £10; later £7; now £14 6s 6d.
  Hugh de Montfort holds 3½ yokes of this manor.
  Value 60s.

In the Half-Lathe of SUTTON
In GREENWICH Hundred

2 Hamo has 63 acres of land which belong in WOOLWICH. William
the Falconer held them from King Edward.
  11 smallholders who pay 41d.
  Value of the whole £3.

In the Lathe of AYLESFORD
In LITTLEFIELD Hundred

3 Hamo holds MEREWORTH himself. Norman held it from King Edward.
Then and now it answered for 2 sulungs. Land for 9 ploughs. In
lordship 2.
  28 villagers with 15 smallholders have 10 ploughs.
  A church; 10 slaves; 2 mills at 10s; 2 fisheries at 2s.
    Meadow, 20 acres; as much woodland as produces
    60 pigs in pasturage.
  Value before 1066 £12; later £10; now £19.

In the Lathe of BOROUGH
In WHITSTABLE Hundred

4 Hamo holds BLEAN himself. Norman held it from King Edward.
Then and now it answered for 1 sulung. Land for 4 ploughs.
  12 villagers have 2 ploughs.
  In lordship 1 plough.
  A church; meadow, 2 acres; from pasturage, 60 pigs;
    a fishery.
  Value before 1066 £8; value later and now £6.

TERRA ALBERTI CAPELLANI.

IN DIMIDIO LEST DE MILDETONE . IN MILDETONE HD.

.XIII. ALBERTVS capellan ten de rege NEWETONE.

Sidgar tenuit de regina Eddid . 7 tc 7 m̃ ſe defd

p . vii . ſolins 7 dimid . Tra . e

Terra quæ fuit in dñio eſt ad firmã p . lx . ſolid.

In ipſo ꝏ̃ . x . uiłłi cũ . xlviii . bord hñt . v . car.

Ibi . xii . ac p̃ti . 7 iiii . denæ de ſilua reddt . xxx . porc.

de paſnag . Ibi una piſcaria ſeruieꝭ Hallæ . 7 ii . ſerui.

Siluula parua ad clauſurã.

Ad hoc ꝏ̃ p̃tin in cantuaria ciuitate . iiii . hagæ . 7 ii . in

Roueceſtre . quæ reddeb . lxiiii . denar.

7 de ꝏ̃ Mildentone reddit in Neuuetone una cſuetudo

ideſt . xxviii . penſæ caſeoȥ . 7 de xxviii . ſolins de Mi|dentone

p̃tin in Neuuetone . x . lib 7 x . ſot . 7 de alia parte de noue

ſolins de Middeltone p̃tin in Neutone xxviii . penſæ caſeoȥ.

7 dimidia . 7 lviii . ſolid de gablo ex his noue ſolins.

7 de his . ix . ſolins reddeb Sigar ap Mildetone Auerã.

De hoc ꝏ̃ ſunt foris . iii . denæ . quæ ibi fuer T.R.E. ſicut

hund teſtificat.

Tot ꝏ̃ T.R.E. ualeb xl . lib . 7 poſt: xxxvi . lib . Modo: xxxiiii . lib.

Archieps inde ht . vi . lib . 7 eps baioc . iii . denas ht . Vat . xl . ſot.

De tra huj ꝏ̃ ten Goisfrid unũ jugũ . 7 uat . x . ſot.

Adã fili Hubti tant ſiluæ unde exeunt . xl . den p ann.

In the Half-Lathe of MILTON

In MILTON Hundred

1   Albert the Chaplain holds NEWINGTON from the King. Sigar
held it from Queen Edith. Then and now it answered for 7½
sulungs. Land for ... The land which was in lordship is at a
revenue for 60s. In this manor

10 villagers with 84 smallholders have 5 ploughs.
Meadow, 12 acres; 4 woodland pig pastures pay 30 pigs
    from pasturage. A fishery which serves the Hall;
    2 slaves; a small wood for fencing.

To this manor belong 4 sites in the City of Canterbury and 2 in
Rochester which paid 64d. From the manor of Milton a customary
due is paid in Newington, that is 28 weys of cheeses; from the 28
sulungs of Milton £10 10s belong in Newington; from the other
part of 9 sulungs of Milton which belong in Newington 28½ weys
of cheeses; 58s of tribute from these 9 sulungs; from these 9 sulungs
Sigar paid cartage to Milton.

3 pig pastures of this manor which were there before 1066, as the
Hundred testifies, are outside it.

Value of the whole manor before 1066 £40; later £36; now £34.

The Archbishop has £6 from it; the Bishop of Bayeux has 3 pig
pastures.

Value 40s.

Geoffrey of Rots holds 1 yoke of the land of this manor;
value 10s.

Adam son of Hubert has as much woodland as produces 40d
a year.

NOTES

ABBREVIATIONS used in the notes. Birch ... *Cartularium Saxonicum*, ed. W. de G. Birch, 3 vols. (1885-93). Colvin, 'A list of the archbishop of Canterbury's tenants by knight service in the reign of Henry II', *Documents Illustrative of Medieval Kentish Society* (*Kent Archaeological Society*, xviii 1964). DB ... Domesday Book. DG ... H. C. Darby and G. R. Versey, *Domesday Gazetteer* (Cambridge 1975). Dom.Mon. ... *The Domesday Monachorum of Christ Church Canterbury* ed. David C. Douglas (1944). Excerpta ... 'An Eleventh-Century Inquisition of St. Augustine's Canterbury', Adolphus Ballard (ed), *The British Academy Records of the Social and Economic History of England and Wales*, iv (1920). Förstemann PN ... E. Förstemann, *Altdeutsches Namenbuch*, Band I, *Personennamen* (2nd ed. Bonn 1900). Hasted ... Edward Hasted, *The History and Topographical Survey of Kent*, 4 vols. (Canterbury 1778-1799). KPN ... J. K. Wallenberg, *Kentish Place Names* (*Uppsala Universitets arsskrift*, 1931). MS ... Manuscript. NoB ... *Namn och Bygd*. OEB ... G. Tengvik, *Old English Bynames* (*Nomina Germanica* iv, Uppsala 1938). PNDB ... O. von Feilitzen, *The Pre-Conquest Personal Names of Domesday Book* (*Nomina Germanica* iii, Uppsala 1937). PNK ... J. K. Wallenberg, *The Place-Names of Kent* (Uppsala 1934). Regesta ... *Regesta Regum Anglo-Normannorum 1066-1100* ed. H. W. C. Davis (1913). Sawyer ... P. H. Sawyer, *Anglo-Saxon Charters* (1968). VCH ... *The Victoria History of the County of Kent*, iii (1932), with Domesday and Domesday Monachorum translations by N. Neilson. WS ... *Winchester Studies*, I, ed. M. Biddle et al., (Winchester 1976).

The manuscript is written on either side of leaves, or folios, of parchment (sheepskin) measuring about 15 by 11 inches (38 by 28 cms.). On each side, or page, are two columns, making four to each folio. The folios were numbered in the 17th century, and the four columns of each are here lettered a, b, c, d. Red ink was used to emphasize words and to distinguish most chapters and sections. Underlining was used to indicate deletion.

KENT. In red, across the top of the page, spread above both columns, with the exception of 11 a,b, *CHENTH.*

ASSOCIATED TEXTS

In common with other counties a number of Domesday-like texts survive for Kent which appear to bear some relation to DB itself. The most notable are the *Domesday Monachorum* of Christ Church Canterbury, a Domesday-like account of some ecclesiastical estates, with a different order and different information to DB; and an eleventh-century Inquisition of St. Augustine's Canterbury, commonly referred to as the *Excerpta*, which likewise contains information presented in the fashion of DB and refers to the Survey in its own heading. Both texts omit much of the manorial detail to be found in DB.

The *Domesday Monachorum* is in reality a group of 4 texts, only one of which is claimed as a Domesday satellite. The manuscript survives in a hand of *c*. 1100 but is itself a copy of an earlier document, which its editor, David Douglas, argues was compiled in 1087 from the original returns of the Domesday Survey. Robert S. Hoyt ('A Pre-Domesday Kentish Assessment List'), *A Medieval Miscellany for Doris Mary Stenton*, Patricia M. Barnes & C. F. Slade (eds), *Pipe Roll Society*, New Series 36, 1960, 189-202) has more recently argued that part at least of another text is an assessment list independent of and earlier than the Domesday Survey itself.

The *Excerpta* survives only in an emended thirteenth-century copy but is derived from an independent compilation made in or before 1087. This compilation is likewise argued to have been based on the information of the original returns. The thirteenth-century heading of the document refers both to the *King's Domesday* and to an *account of the sulungs of the County of Kent*, perhaps an assessment list of the kind which appears as part of the *Domesday Monachorum*.

In recent years the significance of these texts and of the Kent folios in general has assumed a great importance in the debate dealing with the making of the Domesday Book. In outline the debate revolves around the question as to whether such texts as the *Excerpta* and *Domesday Monachorum* are to be seen as products of the Domesday Survey itself, the conclusion of the editors of both texts, or else as part of the framework of Anglo-Norman governance to which the Domesday Survey was the immediate heir. An account of the major theories is to be found in

V. H. Galbraith, *The Making of Domesday Book* (1961), 146–155; *idem, Domesday Book: Its Place in Administrative History* (1974); Sally Harvey, 'Domesday Book and its Predecessors', *English Historical Review*, lxxxvi (1971), 753–66 and *idem*, 'Domesday Book and Anglo-Norman Governance', *Transactions of the Royal Historical Society*, 5th Series, 25 (1975), 175–93. Since, however, both theories admit the contemporary eleventh-century nature of the information in these sources, full reference to variants and amplifications of the DB text is given in these notes.

D1	DOVER. *Excerpta* 23 adds 'is the King's Borough'.
D2	20 SHIPS. *Excerpta* 24 adds 'for the keeping of the sea'.
D7	ORA. Literally an ounce, in Scandinavia a monetary unit and coin still in use; in DB valued at 16 (assayed) or 20 (unassayed) pence, see S. Harvey, 'Royal revenue and Domesday terminology', *Economic History Review*, 2nd series, xx (1967), 221–8.
D8	WADARD. One of Odo of Bayeux's knights, named and depicted on the Bayeux Tapestry where he is shown during the foraging near Hastings, see *The Bayeux Tapestry*, ed. Sir Frank Stenton (2nd ed. 1965), plate 47.
	MODBERT'S SON. *Excerpta* 24–5 identifies him as Geoffrey son of Modbert.
D10	A MILL. From the description it would appear that this was a tidal mill.
D11	FOUR LATHES. See the Introduction to the Index of Places.
D17	DEATH DUTY. The *relevatio, relevum*, the 'relief' or 'heriot', was paid by the heir on taking up his inheritance. The scale of rates was laid down in the law codes, especially 2 Canute 71 and the 'Laws of King William' 20. The *villanus* paid an ox, cow or horse, the *censarius* a year's tribute.
D18	*SCHILDRICHEHAM.* An unlocated place which appears later in 5,146 as *Cildresham*. The first element is the personal-name *Cildric*, rare in Old English.
D23	PENENDEN Heath. The site of the Shire court and the scene of Lanfranc's claim against Odo of Bayeux in 1072 concerning the losses from the Canterbury estate sustained, it now appears, as a result of encroachments made by the Godwine family in the years before 1066, see David R. Bates, 'The Land Pleas of William I's Reign: Penenden Heath Revisited', *Bulletin of the Institute of Historical Research*, ii (1978), 1–19. DB refers to the claim at 2,5; 43.4,16. See also note 2,30.
M	LAND OF THE CANONS OF ST. MARTIN'S OF DOVER. Entered here as an appendix to the account of Dover, but interrupted by the account of the City of Canterbury on folio 2a. The account of the lands of the Canons of St. Martin's of Dover thus breaches the custom of beginning each County with the land of the King, and their name is omitted from the list of landholders on folio 2b. The information in these sections differs from the formula employed elsewhere in DB in omitting ploughlands and retaining, apparently, only the Edwardian assessment. Sally Harvey, 'Domesday Book and Anglo-Norman Governance', *Transactions of the Royal Historical Society*, 5th series, 25 (1975), 175–93, argues that these features are indicative of a pre-1085 date for the St. Martin's entries and suggests that Rannulf Flambard, who had been master of the house, had conducted a survey of the estate which, on the failure of the 1085 re-assessment, he recommended as a model for the Domesday Inquest.
M1	21 SULUNGS. Listed below in M2–24. The total here is 17 sulungs, 4½ yokes, 3 virgates and 235 acres. The 3 sulungs in Lympne Lathe are entered below in P2–4.
	PREBENDS IN COMMON. DB records that Bishop Odo of Bayeux had distributed the prebends individually, although in the following entries the former occupant is given.
M3	1 MONASTERY. *Excerpta* 26 calls it a church, *unam ecclesiam*.
M5	25 ACRES. See note M18.
M7	VALUE 60s AND 9s 2d. *Excerpta* 27 gives £3 10s 2d.
M9	VALUE 30s. *Excerpta* 27 gives 60s.
M10	WALTER. *Excerpta* 27 identifies him as Walter of Cambremer.
M11	ROBERT. *Excerpta* 27–8 has 'In the Hundred of Bewsborough and Cornilo Robert Trublet has 1 sulung in prebend which two men, Sigar and Goldstan, held before 1066'.
M13	85 ACRES. *Excerpta* 28 gives 80 acres.
	VALUE £3; BEFORE 1066, £4. *Excerpta* 28 gives 'Value then £12; now 60s'.
M14	ARCHDEACON ANSKETEL HOLDS. *Excerpta* 28 has 'In Cornilo Hundred the Archbishop of Canterbury has 1 sulung in prebend of St. Martin's. Value £6 10s'.
M15	½ SULUNG AND 12 ACRES. *Excerpta* 28 gives as '½ sulung and 12½ acres' and reduces the holding in Deal to '½ sulung less 11½ acres'.
M17	3 VIRGATES. Perhaps in error. *Excerpta* 29 renders as 3 yokes.
	THE VALUE IS AND ALWAYS WAS 60s. *Excerpta* 29, 'Value £4'.
M18	IN DEAL. *Excerpta* 29 places part of the holding in Guston, perhaps the 25 acres referred to in M5.

M20   VALUE 25s: BEFORE 1066, 35s. *Excerpta* 29, 'The value was 30s; now 25s'.
M21   1½ YOKES. *Excerpta* 29 gives 1 yoke.
       VALUE BEFORE 1066, 25s. *Excerpta* 29 gives it as 20s.
       SPIRITES. Favourite of Harold Harefoot (1037–40) and Harthacnut (*c.* 1040–42) who was banished by Edward the Confessor in 1065 and whose lands were forfeited, *Hemingi Chartularium* i, 254.
M23   EDWIN. *Excerpta* 29–30 identifies him as Baldwin's brother.
M24   GODRIC. *Excerpta* 30 identifies him as Godric Latimer, whose predecessor was Oswy Wild the priest.
       51 BURGESSES WHO PAID TRIBUTE. £3 7s 5d, *Excerpta* 7.
C1   212 BURGESSES. *Excerpta* 9 calls them free men (*liberi homines*) and adds 'The cobblers and drapers pay 30s, the porter 5s'.
       8 ACRES OF MEADOW. *Excerpta* 7 adds 'on which the King's horses graze, coming and going'.
       1000 ACRES OF UNPRODUCTIVE WOODLAND. '1000 acres of underwood where the men of the district (*patria*) and the burgesses of the City paid 20s to the King's Sheriff', *Excerpta* 7.
C2   TWO HOUSES. *Excerpta* 10 adds 'The monks of Holy Trinity destroyed one, and have forbidden the other to be repaired. They paid 16d in tribute to the King'.
C3   TRIBUTE. *Excerpta* 10 adds that it was worth 53s.
       THESE HOUSES. *Excerpta* 10 adds 'Now Ranulf of Colombières and Vitalis of Canterbury hold all these from the Bishop of Bayeux's Holding, but they only acknowledge 26'.
       5 ACRES. *Excerpta* 10 adds 'with a Church'.
C6   IF ANYONE DIGS. *Excerpta* 9 gives 'If anyone makes a ditch, or puts up a pigsty or narrows the King's highway'.
C8   BISHOP OF BAYEUX. *Excerpta* 7–8 adds 'and Hugh de Montfort and the Count of Eu and Richard son of Gilbert'. These were presumably the King's barons whom DB refers to as having tried the case.
P6   NORWOOD. Not entered under any Hundred. The place was later in the Hundred of Newchurch PNK 470. See also P18.
P11   MEDERCLIVE. Not entered under any Hundred, although geographcally within Bewsborough Hundred in Eastry Lathe.
P16   400½ ACRES, WHICH MAKE 2½ SULUNGS. The statement, taken literally, would make the Kentish sulung contain a little over 160 acres. Paul Vinogradoff, 'Sulung and Hide', *English Historical Review*, xix (1904), 282–6, argued that the Domesday clerk had meant 400 and ½ (a hundred) acres, which would give a sulung of roughly 180 acres. Comparison of the entries for Northbourne in DB and the *Excerpta* gives a much more precise figure of 200 acres. See note 7,19.
P19   MS. The manuscript omits the gallows-like section sign, added by Farley.
P20   HAWKHURST. A *dene* of Wye Lathe. The place was later in Great Barnfield Hundred which, it is argued, may have been in existence by 1086, PNK 335 and the Introduction to the Index of Places.
1,1   DARTFORD. Later in its own Hundred, PNK 31.
       PIG PASTURES. An area of woodland pasture located in the Weald but still dependent on its parent manor in the upland of north Kent. Identification of these Wealden settlements, which appear anonymously in DB, is often possible from later records. K. P. Witney, *The Jutish Forest* (1976) contains full reference to these identifications.
1,2   THE CASTLE. The original motte and bailey castle at Rochester, sited on Boley Hill outside the south-west angle of the city walls.
1,3   HUGH OF PORT HOLDS. *Excerpta* 3 adds 'from the Bishop of Bayeux. Edward held it'.
       THE ABBOT OF ST. AUGUSTINE'S HOLDS. *Excerpta* 3 adds 'From these sulungs (the Abbot of) St. Augustine has his part which was proved in the Hundred of Milton and in the County (court) of Kent in the time of William I'.
       CHURCHES AND TITHES. *Excerpta* 4 gives '8 prebends and a church'.
1,4   LATER £60. Farley error, *ix* for *lx*.
2,1   LATHE RUBRIC. In BOROUGH Lathe. Omitted in the MS.
       THE CLERGY OF THE TOWN. *Dom.Mon.* 82 adds '32 dwellings and a mill which the clergy of St. Gregory hold near their Church'. The Church was the Priory of Augustinian canons founded in 1084 by the Archbishop Lanfranc.
2,2   SANDWICH. *Dom.Mon.* 89 adds 'Sandwich is Holy Trinity's manor for the monks' clothing. It is in its own Lathe and Hundred'. There is no evidence that Sandwich was a

Lathe and the reference would seem to be an error. See the Introduction to the Index of Places. *Excerpta* 20 adds 'In this Borough St. Augustine's has 1 acre. In this acre St. Augustine's also has a Church'. Cf. 5,189.

2,3   LATHE RUBRIC. In the Half-Lathe of Sutton. Omitted in the MS.
VALUE £15 10s. *Dom.Mon.* 88 adds 'It is assessed at £15. Richard has 10s in his castle (*infra castellum*)'. The castle is that at Tonbridge, the centre of Richard of Tonbridge's territory. See note 2,4.

2,4   3 THANES. *Dom.Mon.* 87 identifies them and the value of their holdings. 'What Hamo holds is assessed at 60s and 10s. What Robert Latimer and Geoffrey of Rots hold at £8 10s'.
WHAT RICHARD OF TONBRIDGE HOLDS IN HIS TERRITORY. Richard of Tonbridge, son of Count Gilbert of Brionne held what was later to become the Lowy of Tonbridge. This was not a compact block of land and has no clear boundary. Its primary purpose was the maintenance of Tonbridge castle in the aftermath of the Conquest, an offensive role shared with other compact lordships such as the Sussex Rapes, and in Kent the *divisio* or territory of Hugh de Montfort, see note 5,130. Richard held the manors of Yalding, East Barming, Hadlow and Tudeley but the greater part of his holdings consisted of the *denes* of upland manors located in the Weald around the castle and manor of Tonbridge. DB surveys 24 of them in the accounts of the manors to which they were formerly dependent, usually prefacing the entry with the formula 'What Richard of Tonbridge holds in his territory'. See Richard Mortimer, 'The beginnings of the Honour of Clare', *Proceedings of the Battle Conference 1980*, ed. R. Allen-Brown (1981), 119–41 and Jennifer C. Ward, 'The Lowy of Tonbridge and the Lands of the Clare Family in Kent, 1066–1217', *Archaeologia Cantiana*, xcvi (1980), 119–31.

2,5   SUNDRIDGE. *Dom.Mon.* 87 adds 'which Godwin held unjustly before 1066. The Archbishop, that is Lanfranc, gained it justly by the King's grant in a plea against the Bishop of Bayeux'. See note D23.
SUNDRIDGE AND OTFORD. *Dom.Mon.* 87 adds 'these manors were in Codsheath Hundred'. The Hundred is not otherwise mentioned in DB.
13s 6d. MS *xiii solid. 7 dim.* interlined *id est vi d.*

2,7   CRAYFORD. *Dom.Mon.* 86 adds 'Osward held it from the Archbishop before 1066'.

2,10   WROTHAM. *Dom.Mon.* 87 gives the taxable value of the men-at-arms' holdings:
William the Bursar. 'It is assessed at £3'.
Geoffrey of Rots. 'It is assessed at £3'.
Farman. 'It is assessed at 100s'.
GEOFFREY HOLDS 1 SULUNG. Perhaps at Yaldham, Colvin 30.
1½ YOKES. *Dom.Mon.* 87 gives '1½ sulungs'.

2,11   3 MEN-AT-ARMS. *Dom.Mon.* 86 adds 'Ralph holds 1 sulung which is assessed at 50s. William, brother of Bishop Gundulf holds 2 sulungs. They are assessed at £10. Ansketel of Rots holds 1 sulung which is assessed at 60s'. The sulung belonging to Ansketel was perhaps at Cossington, Colvin 21.
2 MEN OF THIS MANOR. *Dom.Mon.* 86 adds '2 men have 1 sulung which pays 16s to the altar of Holy Trinity. Value of this sulung however, 20s'.
MAIDSTONE. *Dom.Mon.* 95 adds 'Wulfric and Cola hold *Burgericestune*. ½ sulung there. It pays 100d to the altar of Holy Trinity. This ½ sulung is from the 10 sulungs in Maidstone'.

2,12   TOTAL VALUE OF THIS MANOR. *Dom.Mon.* 85 gives 'What the Archbishop has in lordship is assessed at £18; what Ansketel of Rots and Robert Brutin hold, 40s; however, it pays the Archbishop £25 18s'.

2,13   LATHE RUBRIC. In BOROUGH Lathe. Omitted in the MS.
TOTAL VALUE OF THIS MANOR. *Dom.Mon.* 84 gives 'It is assessed at £42 5s less 3 farthings'. Farthing appears only once in DB, see DB Cheshire S3,2.

2,14   IT PAYS £50 14s 2d. 'It is assessed at £51 5s', *Dom.Mon.* 84.
VITALIS. Of Canterbury, *Dom.Mon.* 84. Named and depicted in the Bayeux Tapestry where he is shown being questioned by Duke William as to the location of Harold's army, see *The Bayeux Tapestry*, ed. Sir Frank Stenton (2nd ed., 1965), plate 56.
3 SULUNGS, 1 YOKE AND 12 ACRES. '1 sulung and 1 yoke and 1½ sulungs in Thanet. He also has 12 acres and ½ sulung in Makinbrook and Stourmouth from the Archbishop', *Dom.Mon.* 84.

2,15   GODFREY AND NIGEL HOLD 1½ SULUNGS. *Dom.Mon.* 83 adds 'From these sulungs Godfrey the Steward holds ½ sulung which belongs to the monks' clothing. That is Swarling. Nigel has 1 sulung and 1 yoke which is assessed at 40s'. *Dom.Mon.* 95 adds that Godfrey held Swarling '*at farm*'.

2,16	THERE ARE ONLY 25. *Excerpta* 12 and *Dom.Mon.* 81 add '25 burgesses who pay 10s in tribute'.
	NEW LODGING. MS *Inoua* for *In noua*, corrected by an interlined *n*.
	OF THIS MANOR 5 OF THE ARCHBISHOP'S MEN. *Dom.Mon.* 81-2 adds 'Godfrey the Steward holds 1 sulung from the Archbishop in Thanington. It is assessed at 100s. Vitalis has 1 yoke from the Archbishop. It is assessed at 20s. Robert of Hardres holds 1 yoke. It is assessed at 30s. Alfward holds 3 yokes in Nackington which before 1066 paid and still pays 12s to the altar of Holy Trinity. It is assessed at 40s. Aethelwold holds 1 yoke at *Wic*. It is from the land of the monks of Holy Trinity which is assessed at 30s'.
	HAMO THE SHERIFF HOLDS. *Dom.Mon.* 82 adds 'Hamo likewise holds ½ sulung which Alfred Big held from the Archbishop before 1066. It is assessed at 100s'. It was perhaps at Milton, near Canterbury, Colvin 2.
2,17	BARHAM HUNDRED. Later Kinghamford Hundred, PNK 552.
2,18	LATHE RUBRIC. In WYE Lathe. Omitted in the MS.
	5 SULUNGS. *Dom.Mon.* 84 gives '5½ sulungs'.
	TOTAL VALUE. *Dom.Mon.* 84 adds 'Before 1066 it was assessed at £10 and the Archbishop has 100s and 15 and 3d in tribute; now, however, the value is £20 but it pays £25 at a revenue and the Archbishop has his tribute as before'.
2,19	IT ANSWERS FOR 8 SULUNGS. *Dom.Mon.* 85 adds 'Before 1066 it answered for 8 sulungs, now for 7 because the Archbishop has the other for his plough'.
	TOTAL VALUE BEFORE 1066. *Dom.Mon.* 85 gives 'Value before 1066, £20; the Archbishop has £4 7s in tribute. Now the value is £30 but it pays £40 at a revenue and the Archbishop has tribute as before'.
2,21	VALUE OF THE WHOLE 40s. *Dom.Mon.* 83 gives 'Value £6'.
	5 OF THE ARCHBISHOP'S MEN. *Dom.Mon.* 83 identifies them: 'Vitalis has 1 sulung. Value 45s'. Probably Walmestone in Wingham, Colvin 14. 'Wibert and Arnold have 3 sulungs. Value £12'. Perhaps Ratling in Nonington, Colvin 23. 'Heringod has 1 sulung less 10 acres. Value 40s'. Probably Knell and Goss Hall in Ash, Colvin 25. 'Godfrey the Arblaster has 1½ sulungs. Value 100s'. Probably Overland in Ash, Colvin 26.
2,22	IT ANSWERED FOR 6 SULUNGS. MS *p vi . solins se defd.* Judging by the position of the full stop and a greyish patch it once read *vii.*, but the second minim has been scratched out. Farley renders as *p vii. solins se defd.*, although *Dom.Mon.* 91 supports a reading of the MS as corrected and suggests that the alteration was made by the Domesday copyist.
	LATHE RUBRIC. In WYE Lathe. Omitted in the MS.
	NOW FOR 3. *Dom.Mon.* 91 adds 'When the Archbishop acquired it for 5½. Hugh de Montfort has the moiety of them. Value £18'.
2,23	NOW FOR 15 SULUNGS. *Dom.Mon.* 83 gives '20'.
2,24	1½ SULUNGS. Probably in error for 1 sulung, as suggested by the value clause. *Excerpta* 14 and *Dom.Mon.* 82 give '1 sulung'. *Dom.Mon.* 82 adds that this land was part of the 7 sulungs of Westgate, in which case the DB entry would appear to duplicate information given earlier in 2,16 under the holdings of the Archbishop's men.
	RALPH. The Chamberlain, *Dom.Mon.* 82.
2,25	85 BURGESSES. *Dom.Mon.* 84, 'In Romney Marsh 25 burgesses who belong to Aldington'.
	STOWTING. *Dom.Mon.* 83 gives 'William of Argues has 1 manor, Stowting, which Alfhere held from the Archbishop. Then it answered for 1½ sulungs; now for 1. Value £10'.
2,26	3 OF THE ARCHBISHOP'S MEN. 'Robert son of Watson has 2 sulungs as a Holding; Robert of Hardres, ½ sulung and Osbern Paisforiere, ½ yoke', *Dom.Mon.* 84.
2,27	NEWENDEN. *Dom.Mon.* 92 refers to the Archbishop's manor of *Niuuendene* in Selbrittenden Hundred in Lympne Lathe which would seem to be this holding. On the basis of additional information given in the *Dom.Mon.* entry David Douglas' footnote raised the possibility that the entry referred to the holding of Hugh de Montfort in Newington (5,204; 9,37-8), although in the context this would seem less likely. The full *Dom.Mon.* entry is here reproduced: 'Newenden. In Lympne Lathe. In Selbrittenden Hundred. The Archbishop has 1 manor from the monks' land in lordship Newenden. Before 1066 Leofric held it from the former Archbishop. It answers for 1 sulung with Saltwood. Now it is assessed at £8 1s in gifts'.
2,28	LATHE RUBRIC. In the Half-Lathe of Sutton. Omitted in the MS.
	ANSGOT. Of Rochester, *Dom.Mon.* 95.
	FARNINGHAM. 'It is for the monks' clothing', *Dom.Mon.* 95.

2,29   RICHARD OF TONBRIDGE HOLDS. 'Richard has as much as is assessed at £3',
Dom.Mon. 88.

2,30   HUNDRED RUBRIC. In Ruxley Hundred. Omitted in the MS.
3 YOKES. 'These 3 yokes did not pay tax with this manor. They are from the pleading
which the Archbishop made against the Bishop of Bayeux with the King's agreement',
Dom.Mon. 94. See note D23.

2,31   BRASTED. 'This manor is in the Hundred of Westerham', *Dom.Mon.* 86, PNK 70.
ABBOT ALNOTH HELD THIS MANOR. 'Young Wulfnoth held Brasted from the
Archbishop before 1066', *Dom.Mon.* 86.

2,32   LATHE AND HUNDRED RUBRIC. In Aylesford Lathe. In Eyhorne Hundred. Omitted
in the MS.
VALUE NOW £9. 'It is assessed at £11', *Dom.Mon.* 88.

2,33   BOUGHTON (MALHERBE). 'Ratel held Boughton (Malherbe) from the Archbishop of
Canterbury before 1066', *Dom.Mon.* 91.

2,34   LATHE RUBRIC. In Wye Lathe. Omitted in the MS.
RICHARD. The Constable, *Dom.Mon.* 93.
LEAVELAND. 'The Deacon of Canterbury had and held this land', *Dom.Mon.* 93.

2,35   GRAVENEY. 'It is from the monks' clothing', *Dom.Mon.* 95.
RICHARD. The Constable, *Dom.Mon.* 95.

2,37   IN TEYNHAM HUNDRED. Not otherwise mentioned in DB. Teynham itself is not
surveyed, although the following detail appears in *Dom.Mon.* 85 as a preface to the
entry for Sheppey. 'Teynham is the Archbishop's manor. Before 1066 it answered for
5½ sulungs; now the same. It is assessed at £50.'
GODFREY. Of Malling, *Dom.Mon.* 85.
SHEPPEY. 'Osward held it from the Archbishop before 1066', *Dom.Mon.* 85.

2,38   LATHE RUBRIC. In Eastry Lathe. Omitted in the MS.

2,39   FINGLESHAM. Later in Cornilo Hundred, although the place lies close to the Hundred
boundary with Eastry, PNK 570. 'Leofnoth held it from the Archbishop before 1066.
Value 20s', *Dom.Mon.* 89.
STATENBOROUGH. 'Godwin held it from Archbishop Edsi before 1066. Value 30s',
Dom.Mon. 89. Edsi had been Archbishop from 1035 to 1050.

2,40   WILLIAM. Follet, *Dom.Mon.* 89.

2,41   SALTWOOD. 'Earl Godwin held it. It answered for 7 sulungs; now there are 5; however,
it is not taxed except for 3', *Dom.Mon.* 93.
225 BURGESSES. 'From whom Hugh de Montfort has nothing except 3 forfeitures',
Dom.Mon. 93. Probably robbery, breach of the peace and highway robbery.
IN THE BOROUGH OF HYTHE. *Dom.Mon.* 93 describes Saltwood as lying in Lympne
Lathe, in the Hundred of Hythe. DB nowhere refers to Hythe as a Hundred which, if it
existed in 1086, makes no further appearance in the records, PNK 459. It is possible
that the copyist of *Dom.Mon.* wrote *Hede* in error for *Hen*, Hayne Hundred, in which
Saltwood lay.
LATHE RUBRIC. In Lympne Lathe. Omitted in the MS.

2,42   BERWICK. 'Godric the Deacon held it', *Dom.Mon.* 92.

2,43   LANGPORT. 'Which the Archbishop proved against the Bishop of Bayeux. Earl Godwin
held it', *Dom.Mon.* 92. See note D23. *Dom.Mon.* 92 adds '1 yoke belongs elsewhere'.

3,1   LATHE RUBRIC. In the Half-Lathe of Sutton. Omitted in the MS.
ORPINGTON. 'A freeman held it before 1066', *Dom.Mon.* 94.
2½ SULUNGS. 'From these sulungs Derman has ½ sulung at Keston', *Dom.Mon.* 94.

3,2   ONE OF THE ARCHBISHOP'S MEN HOLDS ½ SULUNG. 'In Stokenbury which Edric
held from King Edward', *Dom.Mon.* 94. The place, now lost, is perhaps commemorated
by Stocking Lane in the adjoining parish of East Farleigh, PNK 166. The field-names
Stockenbury Meadows, Stockenbury Wood Field, Little Stockenbury Field and
Stockbury Wood are recorded in 1578 on the site of Borough's Oak Farm (TQ 671497)
in East Peckham. I am grateful to Mrs. Margaret Laurence for this reference. See also 5,61.

3,4   MEOPHAM. 'It is from the monks' food', *Dom.Mon.* 94.
WHAT IS VALUED AT 18s 6d. '18s 8d', *Dom.Mon.* 94.

3,5   WHAT ABEL NOW HOLDS. 'Loose is the monks' manor for their clothing. It answers for
1 sulung. Abel the Monk holds it and pays a revenue to the monks. This sulung lies in the
6 sulungs of Farleigh', *Dom.Mon.* 95.
WHAT GODFREY (HOLDS). 'Hunton is the monks' manor for their clothing. It answers
for ½ sulung which Godfrey the Steward holds and pays a revenue. This ½ sulung is from
the 6 sulungs of Farleigh', *Dom.Mon.* 95.

3,6	CLIFFE. 'It is from the monks' clothing. Before 1066 it answered for 2½ sulungs', *Dom.Mon.* 94.
3,7	MONKTON. 'For their food', *Dom.Mon.* 89.
3,8	WILLIAM. 'William of Adisham holds 1 sulung at Ruckinge. Value £7', *Dom.Mon.* 90.
3,9	NORTHWOOD. Thus DB and *Dom.Mon.* 88. *Excerpta* 12 gives *Norgate*, Northgate. 100 BURGESSES LESS 3. *Excerpta* 12 gives 100 burgesses less 19. WHO PAY £8 4s. *Dom.Mon.* 88 £8 0s 6d, *Excerpta* 12 £9 0s 6d.
3,10	BLIZE. *Blittaere, Dom.Mon.* 90. Perhaps a garbled Anglo-Norman attempt at the rare OE personal-name *Blithhere* (NoB 33 (1945), 75; WS I, 151 note 3), or OG *Blithgaer* (Förstemann PN 313). SEASALTER. *Dom.Mon.* 90 adds 'Land for 2 ploughs. This manor is in no Hundred'. It was later in Whitstable Hundred, PNK 100.
3,11	(SOUTH) PRESTON. 'For their clothing', *Dom.Mon.* 93.
3,12	CHARTHAM. 'For their clothing', *Dom.Mon.* 90.
3,13	GODMERSHAM. 'For their clothing', *Dom.Mon.* 90.
3,14	(GREAT) CHART. 'For their clothing', *Dom.Mon.* 90.
3,15	LITTLE CHART. 'For their food. Before 1066 it answered for 3 sulungs; now for 2½', *Dom.Mon.* 90. 2½ HIDES. Probably in error for 2½ sulungs as in *Dom.Mon.* 90. WILLIAM HOLDS. 'William son of Hermenfrid has ½ sulung in Pett from the Archbishop as a holding. It pays 25d to the altar of Holy Trinity for all customs', *Dom.Mon.* 90.
3,17	GIDDINGE. The DB entry would appear to locate this place in Eastry Hundred, although, like Denton, it was later in Kinghamford Hundred, similarly entered under Eastry in DB, see note 5,220. VALUE £36 10s 4¼d. *Dom.Mon.* 88 gives £37 10s 3d.
3,18	ADISHAM. Later in Downhamford Hundred in Borough Lathe. *Dom.Mon.* 89-90 records that 'This manor is itself a Hundred and is in Eastry Lathe'. The DB indentification is retained here. ADISHAM. 'Adisham is the monks' of Holy Trinity's manor for their food', *Dom.Mon.* 89. 2 MEN-AT-ARMS. 'Robert son of Watson has 2 sulungs. That is Eythorne. Value £7. Roger holds 1 sulung at Barham. Value £4', *Dom.Mon.* 90. IT PAYS £46 16s 4d. *Dom.Mon.* 90 gives £16 16s 4d.
3,19	LATHE RUBRIC. In Lympne Lathe. Omitted in the MS but added at 3,20.
3,21	LATHE RUBRIC. In Wye Lathe. Omitted in the MS. ONE MANOR. 'Robert of Romney holds one manor, Brook, at a revenue for the monks' food', *Dom.Mon.* 92.
3,22	LATHE RUBRIC. In Lympne Lathe. Omitted in the MS. ALMS-LAND. *Dom.Mon.* 84 associates this sulung with Lyminge but then adds, 'In Romney Marsh lies 1 sulung of *Aelmesland* from the alms of the monks of Holy Trinity. It is not from the above mentioned sulungs. From that sulung William Follet has 1 yoke, that is *Sturtune*. From that same sulung Robert has 3 yokes, that is Orgarswick, Castweazel and *Eadruneland*.' From this entry it is clear that DB *Asmelant, Dom.Mon. Aelmesland* is not a place-name, but a sulung of alms-land belonging to Holy Trinity, the four yokes of which lay in *Sturtune*, Orgarswick, Castweazel and *Eadruneland*. A reference to alms-land, OE *almeslond*, appears also in a charter of Athelstan to Milton abbey, Birch 738, Sawyer 391. In transcribing a minuscule *Almeslant*, the DB clerk clearly misread a false 's' for 'l'. The identification of *Asmelant* in DG as Gammons in Orgarswick is based on a misreading of KPN 267-9.
4,1	LATHE AND HUNDRED RUBRIC. In the Half-Lathe of Sutton. In Axton Hundred. Omitted in the MS. *Dom.Mon.* 96 assigns 4,1-4 to Axton Hundred. IN TONBRIDGE. In the territory of Richard of Tonbridge.
4,2	NOW FOR 4 SULUNGS. *Dom.Mon.* 96 gives it as 3 sulungs.
4,6	LATHE AND HUNDRED RUBRIC. In Aylesford Lathe. In Larkfield Hundred. Omitted in the MS. *Dom.Mon.* 97 assigns 4,6-9 to Larkfield Hundred. VALUE NOW £12. 'It is assessed at £13', *Dom.Mon.* 96.
4,10	VALUE NOW £10 10s. 'It is assessed at £10', *Dom.Mon.* 97.
4,11	VALUE NOW £7 15s. 'It is assessed at £6 10s', *Dom.Mon.* 97.
4,15	THEY PAY £11 13s 4d. *Dom.Mon.* 97 gives £11 13s 3d.
4,16	LANFRANC PROVED (HIS CLAIM). A reference to the land plea at Penenden Heath in 1072, see note D23. VALUE NOW £8 0s 20d. 'It is assessed at £8', *Dom.Mon.* 98.
5,2	OF THE WOODLAND. MS *De silva*. Farley renders it as *De Silva*.

5,2-3	MS. The manuscript leaves a gap in the value clause, probably for an intermediate value when acquired.
5,6	ADAM SON OF HUBERT. Adam of Ryes near Bayeux, brother of Eudo the Steward, D. Douglas (ed), *The Domesday Monachroum of Christ Church Canterbury* (1944), 29.
5,7	'SONNINGS'. A lost place, surviving as a field-name in the modern parish of Horton Kirby (TQ 580683), Zena Bamping, 'A Domesday Name Identified?', *Kent Archaeological Review*, 61 (1980), 6-7.
5,13	½ MILL AT 5s. MS *½ mill at 5 sulungs*, obviously in error. ANSKETEL. Of Rots, *Dom.Mon.* 101.
5,18	ALFWARD HELD IT FROM HAROLD. MS *tenuit de Heraldo. H.* The meaning of the *H.* is not apparent.
5,20	ANSGOT. Of Rochester. *Dom.Mon.* 103 associates this land with others held by Ansgot of Rochester. HOWBURY. A lost place surviving as Howbury Lane in Crayford. PNK 30.
5,24	(ST. MARY) CRAY. MS South Cray. The place was known as St. Mary Cray from at least the mid-thirteenth century, after the dedication of the parish church, PNK 20.
5,26	SEAL. Later in Codsheath Hundred, PNK 63.
5,27	(NORTH) CRAY. Thus PNK 19.
5,31	THOROLD OF ROCHESTER'S SON. Ralph son of Thorold, *Dom.Mon.* 102.
5,34	(FOOTS) CRAY. Thus PNK 18.
5,35	ANSKETEL. Of Rots, *Dom.Mon.* 107.
5,38	SANDLINGS. 'Alfgeat held Sandlings from the Archbishop before 1066', *Dom.Mon.* 94.
5.41	ANSKETEL. Of Rots, *Dom. Mon.* 107.
5,48	NASHENDEN. Entered by DB in Larkfield Hundred, although the place was later in Rochester Hundred, PNK 126. It lies close to the Hundred boundary.
5,53	MS *Rouecest.*, 'corrected' by Farley to *Roucest.*
5,56	ANSKETEL. Of Rots, *Dom. Mon.* 107.
5,61	'STOKENBURY'. See note 3,2.
5,62	IN THE LATHE OF AYLESFORD. The rubric would appear to be redundant, as that at 5,40 still applies. See note 5,90.
5,67	Farley error, *ten epo* for *ten de epo*. LEEDS. 'Earl Leofwin held Leeds from King Edward. It answered for 3 sulungs; now it answers for 2 sulungs. Aethelwold held it from the Bishop of Bayeux but now King William has it in his hand', *Excerpta 2*. BISHOP OF BAYEUX'S PARK. *Excerpta* 2 locates it at Wickhambreux (*Wicham*). 4 PIG PASTURES. 'Count Robert of Eu holds 4 pig pastures from this manor in Sussex', *Excerpta 2*.
5,70	Farley error, *ten de ALNOITONE* for *ten ALNOITONE*.
5,71	SUTTON (VALENCE). The identification here follows Hasted II, 409.
5,88	HUNDRED RUBRIC. In Chatham Hundred. Not entered in the MS until 5,89.
5,90	IN THE LATHE OF AYLESFORD. The rubric would appear to be redundant, as that at 5,40 still applies. See note 5,62.
5,94	PIMP'S COURT. Later in Maidstone Hundred but entered here under Twyford, PNK 138. The place is close to the Hundred boundary.
5,96	HAMO. The Sheriff, *Dom.Mon.* 103.
5,99-100	AETHELWOLD. The Chamberlain, *Dom.Mon.* 101.
5,103	HUNDRED HEADING. In Wrotham Hundred. Omitted in the MS.
5,104	HUNDRED HEADING. In Shamwell Hundred. Not entered in the MS until 5,107.
5,115	MS repeats *solins* at the start of the second line, corrected by Farley with the gap indicated by a line of dots.
5,117	STUPPINGTON. Interlined. Later in Faversham Hundred but entered here under Milton, PNK 289. The place lies close to the Hundred boundary.
5,121	STELLING. Later partly in Loningborough Hundred and partly in Stowting Hundred in Wye Lathe, but entered here under Bridge Hundred, PNK 437. The place is close to the Hundred boundary.
5,122	BEKESBOURNE. The place was also known as *Lyvyngisbourn*, after a descendant of the TRE holder, as late as the sixteenth century. The modern form commemorates a twelfth-century holder, PNK 540-1, P. H. Reaney, 'A Survey of Kent Place-Names', *Archaeologia Cantiana*, LXXIII (1959) 64.
5,124	ALFRED BIG HELD THIS MANOR FROM KING EDWARD. The MS originally read *Hoc M tenuit Alured' biga tenuit de rege.E.* but the second and redundant *tenuit* has been scratched out and is not reproduced by Farley.

5,124	ALFRED BIG. OE *Bigga*, used here as a byname. The personal-name appears in Surrey 5,22, PNDB 202, OEB 290.

5,124   ALFRED BIG. OE *Bigga*, used here as a byname. The personal-name appears in Surrey 5,22, PNDB 202, OEB 290.
GEOFFREY SON OF MALLETERRE. *Excerpta* 16 identifies him further as Geoffrey son of Roger of Malleterre, OEB 349.

5,126   NACKINGTON. Later in Bridge and Petham Hundred but entered here under Canterbury Hundred, PNK 544. The place is close to the Hu⟍dred boundary. The identification retained here and followed by VCH 233, DG and *Dom.Mon.* 103 note, and applied also to the 3 yokes which appear in *Dom.Mon.* 103 as dependent on Westgate, see note 2,16. Nackington was later in Bridge hundred. PNK 496-7 argued that this place was Hackington, as suggested by Hasted III, 594.
HAMO THE SHERIFF. 'Hamo the Steward holds Nackington from the Bishop of Bayeux. The Burgesses of the City claim this ½ sulung', *Excerpta* 14.

5,127   HAMO ALSO HOLDS ½ SULUNG. The location of this holding is not clear, although the lands which the Burgesses of Canterbury claimed from the Bishop of Bayeux would seem to have been between Westgate and Nackington, *Dom.Mon.* 82, *Excerpta* 14. See also note 2,16.

5,128   VALUE OF THE WHOLE OF FOLKESTONE. Farley adds the gallows-like section sign omitted in the MS.

5,130   HUGH DE MONTFORT'S TERRITORY. Some of Hugh de Montfort's holdings in Kent are described as lying either within (*infra*), or without (*extra*) his territory (*divisio*), see 5,130; 169; 182, 9,1; 22; 35; 37-39; 42. VCH 188-190 suggests that this was an arrangement, analogous to the Lowy of Tonbridge, which served to maintain the castle at Saltwood. Hugh's *divisio* was likewise not a compact block of lands, but its detail, as recorded in DB, suggests a significant re-organisation in the pattern of assessment in Kent in the years immediately after the conquest. DB also uses the same term to describe the holdings of the Bishop of Bayeux, Ralph of Courbépine and the Count of Eu on three occasions, see 5,171; 175, 9,16.

5,131   ANSFRID. Male the clerk, ... *Male* is a Norman French man's name, see OEB 351, s.v. *Masculus*; P. H. Reaney, *Dictionary of British Surnames*, 229.

5,133   1 YOKE. *Dom.Mon.* 101 assigns this holding to Ralph of Courbépine.

5,134   AETHELWOLD. The Chamberlain, *Dom.Mon.* 101.
EASOLE. Entered here and at 5,217 in Eastry Hundred but later in Wingham Hundred, PNK 534. The place lies close to the Hundred boundary.

5,135   1 SULUNG IN SHELVING. *Dom.Mon.* 102 gives '1 yoke'.

5,136   HUNDRED RUBRIC. In Bewsborough Hundred. Omitted in the MS but added at 5,137.
A MAN-AT-ARMS OF HIS. The Latin is equivocal and might refer either to Osbern or to Odo of Bayeux, although in the context the latter is perhaps more likely.

5,138   LATHE RUBRIC. In Borough Lathe. Omitted in the MS.
1 SULUNG TO OSBERN PAISFORIERE. *Dom.Mon.* 101 gives 1½ sulungs.

5,146-51   ANSFRID. Male the clerk, *Dom.Mon.* 101.

5,146   *CILDRESHAM. Dom.Mon.* 101, *Cyldresham*. See note D18.

5,149   BADLESMERE. 'Godric Wisce held the manor of Badlesmere from King Edward. It answers for 1 sulung. Now Ansfrid holds it from the Bishop of Bayeux. It is assessed at £4. The monks of St. Augustine claim back this manor through the charter and seal of King Edward', *Excerpta* 4-5. The claim is entered below at 7,30. Godric Wisce was undoubtedly the 1066 landholder, now dead, whose son provided evidence for the Domesday enquiry, see V. H. Galbraith, *The Making of Domesday Book* (1961), 153-5.

5,152   OSBERN. Paisforiere, *Dom.Mon.* 101.

5,156   NORTH EASTLING. *Dom.Mon.* 102 credits this land to Herfrid, see also 5,183.

5,159   30 VILLAGERS. The MS would seem to have been amended from *xxx* to *xxix* in heavy black ink. Farley retained what appeared to have been the original entry. Whether the alteration was a contemporary one is not apparent from close examination of the MS.

5,162   ANSFRID. Male the Clerk, *Dom.Mon.* 101.

5,163   IN [WYE] HUNDRED. The MS is damaged at this point. The following places were all in Wye Hundred.

5,166   HUNDRED RUBRIC. In Felborough Hundred. Omitted in the MS.

5,167   HUNDRED RUBRIC. In Calehill Hundred. Omitted in the MS.
WAUA. Probably from an OE *Wafa*, which may be associated with OE *wafian* 'to wave', PNDB 409. Farley misreads as *Wana*.

5,169   POSTLING. Entered here under Calehill Hundred in Wye Lathe, probably in error. It appears correctly under Hayne Hundred in Lympne Lathe at 9,16.

5,171   OSBERT. *Dom.Mon.* 101, makes it clear that this is Osbern Paisforiere.

5,171   ALDGLOSE. Now in Bircholt Hundred, KPN 425. DB associates it with Brabourne, also in Bircholt Hundred, see 9,42.
5,173   12 ACRES. *Dom.Mon.* 101 infers that these too, were at Palstre.
5,181   ½ YOKE. *Dom.Mon.* 103 places this in Benenden.
         A WIDOW WHO PAYS 22d. Farley error, *xiii* for *xxii*, apparently following the abbreviation *ci (tresdecim)* interlined. The figures in the MS are clearly *xxii*.
5,182   HUNDRED RUBRIC. In Blackburn Hundred. Omitted in the MS. Tinton is entered in Blackburn Hundred at 9,22. The name survives in Warehorne parish in Ham Hundred, parts of which are known to have lain in Aloesbridge and Blackburn Hundreds, PNK 474-5.
5,183   RINGLETON. *Dom.Mon.* 102 credits this land to Herfrid; see also 5,156.
5,185-188 HUGH. Of Port, *Dom.Mon.* 102.
5,189-90 ANSFRID. Male the Clerk, *Dom.Mon.* 101.
5,189   *LEUEBERGE.* Unidentified, Cf. 5,210-212 note. *Dom.Mon.* 101-102, *Endleueberga, Endleuaberga.* See PNK 561 where Wallenberg relates the DB form to the name of the TRE tenant *Leuuinus*, (OE *Leofwine*), and discounts the *Dom.Mon.* form as a subsequent rationalisation. However, in this section *Dom.Mon.* is independent of and antecedent to DB, and it shows the name to be OE *endleofan beorga* or *(æt) endleofan beorgum* '(at) eleven barrows'. Wallenberg *loc.cit.* may well be correct in supposing that DB *in leueberge* may represent a development of the OE place-name to **indlefenbeorga* > **inleueberge*, whence the metanalysis *in leueberge*, especially likely in a context where the Latin preposition *in* preceded the name.
5,192   A MAN-AT-ARMS. VCH 239 suggests that this is Hubert son of Ivo, who is recorded as holding land in Ewell at 9,35.
5,194   ASHRED. MS *Ascored*. Possibly from OE *Aescraed*, PNDB 165.
5,196   BUCK. OEB 359-60, PNDB 210.
5,197   ANSFRID. Male the Clerk, *Dom.Mon.* 101.
5,198   SANDWICH. 'It is in its own Lathe and Hundred', *Dom.Mon.* 89. See 2,2.
5,200   OSBERN SON OF LEDHARD. The MS calls him Osbert but refers in the same entry to *Osbern himself*. DB refers to Osbern son of Ledhard at 2,38; 5,135; 136; 200; 206-7. 7,19 and to Osbert son of Ledhard at 5,200; 205; 216, but they are clearly the same man as is made apparent in *Dom.Mon.* 102. The translation gives Osbern throughout.
5,201   ANSFRID. Male the Clerk, *Dom.Mon.* 101.
5,203   1½ YOKES IN THE SAME HUNDRED. VCH 240 suggests Buckland in Woodnesborough.
5,204   NEWINGTON. Entered here, and at 9,37-8, in Bewsborough Hundred in Eastry Lathe. The place was later in Folkestone Hundred in Lympne Lathe, PNK 453.
5,208   MIDLEY. Later in St. Martin's Hundred in Lympne Lathe, PNK 479.
5,209   IN SUMMERDENE HUNDRED. Taken literally the DB Hundred of Summerdene would include Robert Latimer's anonymous 6 acres and lands in Tickenhurst, Woodnesborough, Each, Marshborough and *Esmetone* in Eastry Lathe. Both Each (5,216) and Woodnesborough (5,197) are also entered by DB under Eastry Hundred, and all these places, with the exception of Robert Latimer's anonymous 6 acres, were later in that Hundred, PNK 574-88. Most authorities have therefore assumed that this entry refers to the Hundred of Somerden in the Half-Lathe of Sutton. K. P. Witney, *The Jutish Forest* (1976) 120, locates the 6 acres in Cowden (TQ 465404). That Robert held from Richard son of Count Gilbert might also be taken as circumstantial evidence that this holding lay in south-west Kent. The DB clerk, unfamiliar with this recent subinfeudation, was therefore unsure which Hundred the following five places were in and did not enter the next rubric until 5,215. Alternatively, it is possible that these places did lie in Summerdene Hundred in Eastry Lathe, although the Hundred was later absorbed into Eastry Hundred. The parish of Woodnesborough contains the place names Denne Court and Summer Field, PNK 587, 590. The translation and indices preserve the DB view of the situation for want of better evidence.
5,210-12 THURSTAN. Presumably Thurstan Tirel whom DB records as the holder of *LEUBERGE* 5,196 (cf. 5,189 note). *Dom.Mon.* 102 associates that holding with those at Tickenhurst, Woodnesborough and Each.
5,212   EACH. See note 5,209.
5,213-4 OSBERT. *Dom.Mon.* 101, makes it clear that this was Osbern Paisforiere.
5,214   ELMTON. DB *Esmetone*, *Dom.Mon.* 101 *Emmetune*. This place was identified by Hasted IV, 195, and followed by PNK 582-3 and DG, as Elmton in Eythorne. VCH and the editor of *Dom.Mon.* retained the eleventh-century form. *Esmetone* could represent a mis-copied minuscule script *Elmetone* OE *elmen-tune* 'village at the elms'; and *Emmetune* a poor translation of a mis-written form *elmne-tune*. Elmton is therefore a credible suggestion.

5,217   EASOLE. See note 5,134.
5,218   OSBERN. Son of Ledhard, *Dom.Mon.* 102.
5,220   DENTON. Entered here in Eastry Hundred, but later in Kinghamford Hundred, PNK 556.
5,221   HUNDRED RUBRIC. In Bewsborough Hundred. Not entered in the MS until 5,222.
5,222   40 ACRES. 'And near there (Boswell Banks) in a manor, 40 acres', *Dom.Mon.* 101.
5,223   LATHE AND HUNDRED RUBRIC. In Lympne Lathe. In Loningborough Hundred. Not entered in the MS until 5,224.
5,224   LATHE RUBRIC. In Lympne Lathe. Omitted in the MS.
6,1   LATHE AND HUNDRED RUBRIC. In Wye Lathe. In Wye Hundred. Omitted in the MS.
7,1   PLUMSTEAD. 'Sorag held it before 1066', *Excerpta* 1. The unintelligible personal-name of this *TRE* holder appears in a thirteenth-century MS copy of a 1087 text, so there is a possibility of scribal error. The origin may have been an OE by-name, *Strang* 'the strong' (not in OEB); or a variant form of the Anglo-Norman by-name *Sorz* 'the deaf' (*Winchester Studies* I (1976), 216).
       IT PAYS £14 8s 3d. 'It pays £14', *Excerpta* 1.
7,2   LENHAM. 'It is for the monks' food', *Excerpta* 2.
       1 YOKE OF THIS MANOR, VALUE 5s. 'St. Augustine has ½ yoke in *Bromfeld* which lies in this manor. It is assessed at 5s', *Excerpta* 2. Despite the discrepancy in the number of yokes this would appear to be the same holding.
7,4   LANGPORT. 'It lies in the Hundred of Canterbury', *Excerpta* 11.
       70 BURGESSES. '. . . who paid £4 10s in tribute. The villagers and smallholders who dwell outside the City pay £8 10s 8d in tribute and one sester of honey. 4 mills which pay 29s 4d', *Excerpta* 11.
       1 YOKE. 'Value 4s', *Excerpta* 11.
       VALUE NOW £35 4s. 'It is assessed at £35', *Excerpta* 11.
7,6   RALPH. Of St. Wandrille, *Excerpta* 16.
7,7   IT PAYS £54. 'It is assessed at £56', *Excerpta* 17.
7,9   IN CHISLET HUNDRED. 'In Blengate Hundred', *Excerpta* 17. See the Introduction to the Index of Places.
       12 SULUNGS. '6 are in Margate', *Excerpta* 17.
       WITH WILLIAM'S ASSENT. Odo's grant and King William's confirmation dated 1077, Regesta 99-100.
7,10   24 ACRES. 33 acres, *Excerpta* 17.
       SERVICE. 'At sea', *Excerpta* 18, *Dom.Mon.* 82.
7,11   VALUE NOW £4. 'It is assessed at £4 2s and one sester of flour', *Excerpta* 11.
7,12   WILDERTON. 'It is for the monks' food', *Excerpta* 4.
7,13   ANSKETEL. The Marshal, *Excerpta* 11. *Dom.Mon.* 101 adds 'of Rots'.
7,14   ADAM HOLDS ½ SULUNG FROM THE ABBOT. 'For a tribute', *Excerpta* 5.
7,15   ANSWERS FOR 6 SULUNGS. 'It answered for 7 sulungs', *Excerpta* 6.
7,16   ROOTING. 'Now a villager holds from the Abbot. It is assessed at 40s', *Excerpta* 6.
       1 YOKE IN RIPTON. *Excerpta* 5 and *Dom.Mon.* 100 give it as 1 sulung.
7,17   FURTHER, HE HAS 2 YOKES. 'Further, the Abbot gave him 3 villagers with 2 yokes. It is assessed at £4 5s', *Excerpta* 5-6.
7,18   ANSFRID. Male the clerk, *Excerpta* 5.
7,19   MS. *T.* probably for *T.R.E* which begins the next line.
       ODILARD. The Steward, *Excerpta* 21.
       VALUE £4. 100s, *Excerpta* 21.
       2 SULUNGS LESS ½ YOKE. '2 sulungs less 25 acres', *Excerpta* 21. On this evidence the Kentish yoke contained 50 acres, the sulung 200 acres, see note P16.
7,20   WADARD HOLDS LAND. 'Wadard holds all the villagers' land', *Excerpta* 22.
7,21   SIBERTSWOLD. 'It is for the monks' clothing', *Excerpta* 23.
7,23   PRESTON. 'It belongs to the monks' chamber', *Excerpta* 19.
       VITALIS HOLDS 1 SULUNG AND ½ YOKE. 'As a Holding', *Excerpta* 19.
7,24   ANSFRID. Male the clerk, *Excerpta* 19.
       IT ANSWERS FOR ½ SULUNG AND ½ YOKE. 'Before 1066 it answered for ½ sulung, 1 yoke and 20 acres', *Excerpta* 19.
7,25   3 VIRGATES. Probably in error for 3 yokes as in *Excerpta* 19, although *Dom.Mon.* 100 repeats 3 virgates.
       VALUE NOW 20s. 'Value 9s', *Excerpta* 19.
7,27   *LANPORT.* *Dom.Mon.* 100 renders as *Langeport* which David Douglas suggested might be Old Langport in Lydd, although the reference to Stowting Hundred would therefore be an error. In what is apparently the same entry *Excerpta* 30 places this holding at Elmsted and Monk's Horton.

7,29	BURMARSH. 'In the Hundred of Blackburn', *Excerpta* 30.
8,1	LATHE RUBRIC. In the Half-Lathe of Sutton. Omitted in the MS.
9,1	LATHE RUBRIC. In Wye Lathe. Omitted in the MS.
9,9	ATTERTON. DB enters Atterton with the rest of Hugh de Montfort's holding in Newchurch Hundred in Lympne Lathe but records the claim of the Canons of St. Martin's of Dover supported by the men of Eastry Lathe. The place was later in Bewsborough Hundred in Eastry Lathe, PNK 563.
9,10	MS. *'nove saline'*, corrected by Farley to *novae salinae*.
9,12	BLACKMANSTONE. Named after the pre-1066 holder, Blackman, PNK 461.
9,19	A LAND. *Dom.Mon.* 103 places this at *Belice*.
	BELICE. The name would appear to be identical in origin to that of Belce Wood, Sturry parish, PNK 514, although the hundred heading is an obstacle to its identification as that place.
9,27	IN THE SAME LATHE. *Dom.Mon.* 104 adds 'in Street Hundred'.
9,34	LATHE RUBRIC. In Wye Lathe. Omitted in the MS.
9,35	LATHE AND HUNDRED RUBRIC. In Eastry Lathe. In Bewsborough Hundred. Not entered in the MS until 9,36. The entry was perhaps added at the foot of column 13c.
9,41	POULTON. Later in Folkestone Hundred, PNK 454. The place lies close to the Hundred boundary.
9,44	LATHE HEADING. In Lympne Lathe. Not entered in the MS until 9,45. Farley omits *7 (et)* between *de rege.E.* and *p tanto*.
9,47	*AIA. Aie, Dom.Mon.* 104. VCH 250 suggests Hythe. DB places it in Lympne Lathe in Street Hundred, adjacent to Hythe. But *Aia, Aie* probably represent a name other than *Hythe*, identical with that represented by those spellings recorded by Wallenberg under the name *Hythe* in PNK 459–460 which are formally unlikely for *Hythe*, viz.: *Hee* 1199, *Hei* 1206, *Hea* 1206, *Heia*, *Heyā* 1224, *Heiā, Heyā* 1225. This other place-name was probably OE *(aet) Haege*, ME *Haye* from OE *hœg* 'hedged enclosure'. The spelling *Heiā, Heyā* are ambiguous; but read as *Heian, Heyan*, they would suggest comparison with the name Heane (Hundred meeting-place) in Saltwood parish, PNK 457, derived from the cognate OE *haegen* 'an enclosure'. However, the Hundred affiliation is an obstacle.
9,49	MS. *T.R.* Probably for *T.R.E.* which begins the next line. See note 7,19.
9,53	LATHE RUBRIC. In Wye Lathe. Omitted in the MS.
9,54	*SUESTONE*. Hasted iii, 388, followed by VCH and DG, identified this as Swetton in Cheriton in Folkestone Hundred. The DB reference to the same Hundred, that is Longbridge Hundred, would seem to militate against this suggestion, and the DB form is retained here. *Dom.Mon.* 103 gives *Westtune*, which may well represent the correct form.
10,1	IN WESTERHAM HUNDRED. MS *IN OSIREHA HUND* corrected by Farley *IN OSTREHA HUND.*
11,1	LATHE RUBRIC. In Aylesford Lathe. Omitted in the MS.
12,1	A MANOR. Hamo the Sheriff is recorded as holding 2½ sulungs at Trimworth in *Dom.Mon.* 103, probably the manor referred to here, see PNK 383 and Robert S. Hoyt, 'A Pre-Domesday Kentish Assessment List', in *A Medieval Miscellany for Doris Mary Stenton* ed. Patricia M. Barnes & C. F. Slade, *Pipe Roll Society*, New Series 36 (1960), 194.
13,1	2 IN ROCHESTER WHICH PAID 64d. *Excerpta* 4 gives 'which pay 2s to this manor'. £10 10s BELONG IN NEWINGTON. *Excerpta* 3 gives £11 10s. THE ARCHBISHOP HAS £6 FROM IT. From the customs of the Church, Regesta 176. 3 PIG PASTURES, VALUE 40s. *Excerpta* 4 gives 60s.

INDEX OF PERSONS

Familiar modern spellings are given where they exist. Unfamiliar names are usually given in an approximate late 11th century form, avoiding variants that were already obsolescent or pedantic. Spellings that mislead the modern eye are avoided where possible. Two, however, cannot be avoided; they are combined in the name 'Leofgeat', pronounced 'Leffyet', or 'Levyet'. The definite article is used before bynames where there is a probability that they described the individual, rather than one of his ancestors. While an attempt has been made, with the aid of additional information supplied by *Dom.Mon.* and the *Excerpta*, to differentiate individuals with the same name, there remain many individuals who cannot be so differentiated. Readers are therefore advised that a group of references given under a single name (e.g. Aethelwold) do not necessarily refer to the same individual. References are to persons named in the text of DB. All names or name-forms which are not contained in DB itself, but are supplied from *Dom.Mon.* and the *Excerpta*, are printed in italics, as are the chapter numbers of listed landholders.

William of Arques	2,21;*25*. 5,128
William of Poitou	M15
William of Thaon's son	5,90;171
William brother of Bishop Gundulf	*2,11*
William son of Geoffrey	D8. M22
William son of Gross	9,48
William *son of Hermenfrid*	3,15
William son of Odger	D8. M3. 5,33–34
William son of Robert	5,78
William son of Theodwald	D8. M19
William the Bursar	2,10
William the Falconer	12,2
William	9,28
William, see Hugh, Richard	
Wirelm	9,6
Wulfgeat	5,81–82;161
Young Wulfnoth	*2,31*
Wulfnoth	5,49;155;158;167;195;225. 9,22;31;52
Wulfric of Oxford	M13
Wulfric	M5. *2,11*. 5,41;56;137
Wulfrun	5,167
Wulfsi the Priest	9,2
Wulfsi	5,140
Wulfstan son of Wulfwin	M16
Wulfstan son of Wulfwin's father	M16
Wulfstan of Wateringbury	D25
Wulfstan	5,14;55
Wulfward White	D25. 5,114
Wulfward	5,215
Wulfwin	5,43;54;106–107. 9,41
Wulfwin, see Wulfstan	
Wulfwy Wilde	9,9
Wulfwy	5,150;219

Churches and Clergy

Archbishop ... of Canterbury 2. D19. C1;8. P15. 5,38;128. 13,1, see also Edsi, Stigand. **Bishop** ... of Bayeux. *5*. D7–8;10. M1–3;13–14. C3;5;8. P19. 3,3. 4,16. 7,5–6;10. 9,1;42. Lisieux ... 5,29. Rochester ... *4*. 1,1;2. 5,58. **Abbeys** ... Battle *6*. Ghent *8*. Holy Trinity C6;8. D19. 2,2. St. Augustine 7. D19. M18. C1;6;8. 1,3. 5,21;67;149. 9,9. St. Martin *6*. D1. 9,9. **Archdeacon** ... see Ansketel. **Chaplain** ... see Albert, Smelt. **Clerk** see Ansfrid Male. **Deacon** ... see Godric. **Monk** ... see Abel. **Priest** ... see Alwin, Ansketel, Edwy.

Secular Titles and Occupational Names

Arblaster (*archibalistarius*) ... Godfrey. **Bursar** (*dispensator*) ... William. **Chamberlain** (*camerarius*) ... Aethelwold, Ralph. **Concubine** (*concubina*) ... Harold's. **Constable** (*constabularius*) ... Richard. **Cook** (*cocus*) ... Robert. **Count** (*comes*) ... Robert of Eu, Eustace, Gilbert. **Doctor** (*medicus*) ... Nigel. **Earl** (*comes*) ... Godwin, Harold, Leofwin. **Falconer** (*accipitrarius*) ... William. **Interpreter** (*latinarius*) ... Godric, Robert. **Marshall** (*marescallus*) ... Anskell. **Queen** (*regina*) ... Edith. **Reeve** (*praepositus*) ... Alstan, Brunman. **Sheriff** (*vicecomes*) ... Hamo, Osward. **Steward** (*dapifer*) ... Alfred, Godfrey, Hamo, Helto, Odilard. **Young** (*cilt*) ... Alnoth, Brictsi.

INDEX OF PLACES

As in most counties some Hundred rubrics are missing. Others seem to be wrongly entered, as occasionally elsewhere, notably in Staffordshire. In most counties these omissions and errors are easily corrected, since the Hundreds were often geographical units, and their boundaries remained unchanged, apart from amalgamation, subdivision and the transfer of some monastic holdings to the Hundred of the Church concerned. In others, e.g. Buckinghamshire (see Bucks. note 1,1) the Hundred order is often the same within each chapter and throughout the County.

In Kent, however, the primary divisions of the County were the Lathes (see below) which were themselves subdivided into a large number of smaller Hundreds. DB frequently omits both Lathe and Hundred rubrics, or fails to refer to Hundreds which are known from other texts to have existed in 1086. The nature of Wealden settlement also ensured that many places there were annexed to Hundreds with which they had not a geographical connection. In the 13th century both the Lathes and the Hundreds were rearranged and renamed. Therefore, although it is possible that many of the anomalies are, as elsewhere, the result of errors and omissions in the MS, there is not always sufficient evidence to prove such errors. The authority of the MS in the location of places in their respective Lathes and Hundreds is therefore retained in the translation, and discussion of anomalies is reserved to the Notes. This index and the following maps do, however, reflect the incorporation of amendments to the MS as suggested in the Notes.

LATHES
The primary divisions of the County were the Lathes. These had originally been the provinces of the Jutish kingdom in Kent, each with its *villa regalis* at the centre and its share of Wealden forest. They first appear in written documents of the 6th century and have some parallels in the Sussex Rapes. DB mentions 7 in all: Aylesford, Wye, Lympne, Borough, Eastry and the half-Lathes of Sutton and Milton, although it is probable that there had once been several others. J. E. A. Jolliffe argued for the existence of two more, and K. P. Witney added another. The *Domesday Monachorum* of Christ Church Canterbury calls Sandwich a Lathe, but this is an isolated reference and would seem to be an error. The jurisdiction of the Lathe was originally comprehensive but its subdivision into Hundreds detracted from its judicial and administrative competence. At the time of the Domesday Survey, however, the men of the four east Kent Lathes, Borough, Eastry, Lympne, and Wye, were recorded as agreeing to royal laws (D11), although in the settlement of disputes the men of the Hundred gave evidence as was customary elsewhere in England (5,149. 9,9).

In the 13th century the number of Lathes in east Kent was reduced from 5 to 3: the half-Lathes of Milton and Wye were joined to form the Lathe of Scray, Borough and Eastry were joined to form the Lathe of St. Augustine, and Lympne was renamed as the Lathe of Shepway.

HUNDREDS
The division of the Kentish Lathes into Hundreds would seem to have been effected at some time after the kingdom lost its independence, probably during the 10th century (J. E. A. Jolliffe, 'The Origin of the Hundred in Kent', in J. G. Edwards, V. H. Galbraith & E. F. Jacob (eds.), *Historical Essays in Honour of James Tait* (1933), 155-68). The DB record of these Hundreds may, however, be in some respects incomplete. The *Domesday Monachorum* of Christ Church Canterbury refers to the Hundred of Codsheath in the half-Lathe of Sutton, and adds that Brook in Wye Lathe, Adisham in Eastry Lathe and the Borough of Hythe in Lympne Lathe were themselves Hundreds. The *Excerpta* of St. Augustine's Canterbury also contains a reference to the later Hundred of Blengate, although this would seem to be an interpolation by the 13th century copyist. In the Weald settlements were often dependent on parent manors elsewhere in the north of the County. They appear anonymously in DB as pig pastures or *denes*, although a number of places had been separated from their parent manors and are surveyed separately in DB and entered under an appropriate Wealden Hundred. Since reference to a Wealden Hundred in DB might be dependent on the chance that it contained some settlement which had been separated from its parent manor, it is conceivable that some of the later Hundreds in this area were in existence by 1086. An early date has been put forward for both Barclay Hundred and Great Barnfield Hundred in Wye Lathe (K. P. Witney, *The Jutish Forest* (1976), 124).

A number of Kentish Hundreds were reorganized, chiefly in the 13th century, and a few may have been created at the same time. At the time of DB Lympne Lathe contained the Hundreds of Stowting (Sw), Loningborough (Lo), Folkestone (F), Bircholt (Bi), Hayne (Ha), Street (St), Blackburn (Bl), Ham (Hm), Newchurch (N), Worth (Wo), Rolvenden (Rl), Selbrittenden (Se), Oxney (O), Aloesbridge (Al), and Langport (La). The Borough of Hythe lay within this Lathe and a number of places are described as being 'in Romney Marsh'. In the 13th century Blackburn, Rolvenden and Selbrittenden Hundreds were added to the Lathe of Scray, formerly Wye. Lympne Lathe, now Shepway, acquired the Hundreds of Felborough, Wye, Calehill, Chart and Longbridge. St. Martin's Hundred does not seem to have existed before the 13th century.

At the time of DB Eastry Lathe contained the Hundreds of Preston (P), Wingham (Wi), Sandwich (Sa), Eastry (E), Bewsborough (B), Cornilo (C), and perhaps also *Summerdene* (Su), see note 5,209.

At the time of DB Borough Lathe contained the Hundreds of Whitstable (Wh), Reculver (Re), Chislet (Ch), Sturry (Sy), Fordwich (Fo), Westgate (We), Bridge (Br), Petham (Pe), Barham (Ba), Downhamford (D), Thanet (Th) and Canterbury (Ca). In the 13th century Reculver, Sturry and Chislet Hundreds were joined to form the Hundred of Blengate; Bridge and Petham Hundreds were amalgamated, and the Hundreds of Barham and Thanet were renamed as Kinghamford and Ringslow respectively.

At the time of DB Wye Lathe contained the Hundreds of Teynham (T), Faversham (Fa), Boughton (Bo), Calehill (Ca), Chart (Ct), Longbridge (Lo), Wye (W), Felborough (Fe), and Bircholt (Bi). DB gives no authority for the existence of the 5 Wealden Hundreds of Marden, Cranbrook, Barclay, Great Barnfield and Tenterden, some or all of which may not have been created until the 13th century when Wye Lathe also acquired the Hundreds of Selbrittenden and Rolvenden.

At the time of DB the half-Lathe of Milton contained the Hundred of Milton (M).

At the time of DB Aylesford Lathe contained the Hundreds of Toltingtrough (To), Shamwell (S), Hoo (H), Rochester (R), Chatham (C), Eyhorne (E), Maidstone (M), Larkfield (La), Wrotham (Wr), Littlefield (Li), Twyford (Tw), and Washlingstone (Wa). Chatham Hundred was later known as Chatham and Gillingham Hundred. DB gives no authority for the existence of the Wealden Hundreds of Little Barnfield or Brenchley and Horsmonden which were probably not created before the 13th century.

At the time of DB the half-Lathe of Sutton contained the Hundreds of Greenwich (G), Bromley (Br), Ruxley (R), Little (Le), Axton (A), Westerham (Wm), and Codsheath (Co). Somerden Hundred, which was later part of this Lathe, may also have been in existence at the time of DB, see note 5,209. In the 13th century Greenwich Hundred was renamed as Blackheath, Bromley as Bromley and Beckenham, and Little as Little and Lesnes. At the same time Westerham Hundred was separated into the Hundreds of Brasted, and Westerham and Edenbridge; and Axton became the Hundreds of Axton, and Dartford and Wilmington.

The editor is grateful to Dr. Alexander Rumble for his advice on the place-names and Hundreds of Kent.

The name of each place is followed by (i) the initial of its Lathe and Hundred, and its location on the Map in this volume; (ii) its National Grid Reference; (iii) chapter and section reference in DB. Bracketed figures denote mention in sections dealing with a different place. Italic figures refer to places or information mentioned only in the notes. Unless otherwise stated the spellings of the Ordnance Survey are followed for places in England, of OEB for places abroad. Inverted commas mark lost places with known modern spellings; unidentifiable places are given in DB spelling, in italics. The National Grid reference system is explained on all Ordnance Survey maps, and in the Automobile Association Handbooks; the figures reading from left to right are given before those reading from bottom to top of the map. Places marked with (⁺) are in the 100 kilometre grid square lettered TR; all others are in square TQ.

	Map	Grid	Text
Acrise⁺	L Lo 4	19 42	5,224
Addington	A La 8	65 58	5,51
Adisham⁺	E E 8	22 54	3,18
Afettune	L La	—	5,176
Aia	L St	—	9,47
Aldglose⁺	W Bi 1	08 44	5,171
Aldington (near Hythe)⁺	L Bi 3	07 36	2,23;(25)
Aldington (in Thurnham)	A E 3	81 57	5,68
Allington (near Maidstone)	A La 19	74 57	5,41
Allington (in Hollingbourne)	A E 5	84 56	5,70
Appledore	L Bl 3	95 29	3,20
Appleton⁺	E B 9	34 47	5,194
Arnolton	W Fa 14	97 55	D18. 5,147
Ash	S A 18	60 64	5,7
Ashenfield⁺	W W 9	09 47	7,13
Ashford⁺	W Lo 2	01 42	9,6
Atterton⁺	E B 21	30 42	9,9
Aylesford	A La 13	72 58	1,2
Badlesmere⁺	W Fa 17	01 55	5,149. 7,30
Barfreston⁺	E E 17	16 50	5,132
Barham⁺	B Ba 2	20 50	*3,18.* 5,138
(East) Barming	A M 4	72 54	11,2
(West) Barming	A M 5	71 54	5,101
Beamonston⁺	W W 1	01 48	5,166
Beauxfield⁺	E C 4	30 45	*7,19*
Beckenham	S Br 1	37 69	5,39
Beckley	A S 5	70 74	5,107
Bekesbourne⁺	B Br 1	19 55	5,122. 7,3
Belice	L Rl	—	5,130
Belice	L Ha	—	9,18-19
Benenden	L Rl 1	80 32	5,180
Bensted	A Tw 6	70 49	5,100
Berwick⁺	L St 7	12 35	2,42
Betteshanger⁺	E E 15	31 52	5,200
Bexley	S R 1	49 73	2,6
Bilsington⁺	L N 1	04 34	5,175
Birling	A La 6	68 60	5,57
Bishopsbourne⁺	B Ba 1	18 52	2,17
Blackmanstone⁺	L W 2	07 29	9,12
Blean⁺	B Wh 4	12 60	12,4
Bochelande	L Sw	—	5,131
Bodsham⁺	L Sw 1	11 45	7,26
Bonnington⁺	L St 3	05 34	9,48
Borstall	A R 4	73 66	4,14-*15*
Boswell (Banks)⁺	E B 8	26 43	5,195;221-*2*
Boughton (Aluph)⁺	W W 4	03 48	10,2
Boughton (under Blean)⁺	W Bo 2	04 58	2,18
Boughton (Malherbe)	A E 27	88 49	2,33. 5,79
Bowley	A E 19	90 49	5,74
Boxley	A M 1	77 58	5,102
Brabourne⁺	W Bi 2	10 41	(5,171). 9,42
Brasted	S Wm 2	46 55	2,31
Brenzett⁺	L A 1	00 27	P5-6;18
Briseuuei	L	—	D24
Bromfeld	A E	—	*7,2*
Bromley	S Br 2	40 69	4,5
Brook⁺	W W 11	06 44	*3,21*
Broomfield	A E 16	84 52	5,85
Buckland (near Dover)⁺	E B 17	30 42	D18. M4. (5,223)
Buckland (in Luddenham)	W Fa 4	97 61	D18. 5,152;157
Buckwell⁺	W W 5	04 48	5,164

	Map	Grid	Text
Elmton[+]	E Su E	27 50	5,214
Eltham	S G 7	42 74	5,30
Essella	W Lo	–	9,5
Evegate[+]	W L 6	06 38	9,53
(Temple) Ewell[+]	E B 7	28 44	5,185;192. 9,35–36
Eynsford	S A 14	54 65	2,29
Eythorne[+]	E E 20	27 49	*3,18*
Fairbourne	A E 17	86 51	5,64;87
Fanscombe[+]	W W 8	08 47	5,163. 9,51
(East) Farleigh	A M 6	73 53	3,5
(West) Farleigh	A Tw 3	71 53	5,95
Farningham	S A 11	54 66	2,28. 5,10;13;15
Farthingloe[+]	E B 20	29 40	M22
Faversham[+]	W Fa 6	01 61	1,4
Fawkham	S A 12	59 68	4,3
Finglesham[+]	E E 13	33 53	2,39
Fleet[+]	E Wi 2	30 60	(2,21)
Folkestone[+]	L F 1	22 36	5,128
Fordwich[+]	B Fo 1	18 59	7,10
Frindsbury	A S 10	74 69	4,13;(15)
Frinsted	A E 7	89 57	5,66
Gara[+]	W	–	D24
Garrington[+]	B D 4	20 56	7,6
Giddinge[+]	E E 23	23 46	(3,17)
Gillingham	A C 2	78 68	2,12. 5,88
Godmersham[+]	W Fe 6	06 50	3,13
Goslaches	–	–	D18
Graveney[+]	W Bo 1	05 62	2,35
Gravesend	A To 2	64 74	5,54
Greenwich	S G 3	38 77	5,29
Guston[+]	E B 13	32 44	M5;(18)
Hadlow	A Li 3	63 49	5,60
Halling	A S 13	70 63	4,12
Ham[+]	E E 11	32 54	5,206
Hammil[+]	E E 4	29 55	5,184
Hampton[+]	W W 12	07 43	9,2
Harbilton	A E 11	86 52	5,84
(Lower) Hardres[+]	B Br 3	15 53	5,123;(133)
(Upper) Hardres[+]	B Br 4	15 50	5,120
Harrietsham	A E 12	87 53	5,63
Hartanger[+]	E E 19	26 49	5,202
Hartley	S A 13	61 66	5,3
Harty[+]	W Fa 1	01 66	D18
Hastingleigh[+]	L Bi 1	09 45	5,225. 9,52
Haven	A S 8	74 72	5,111–112
Hawkhurst	W	76 30	P20
Hawley	S A 4	54 71	(1,1). 5,1
Heane? see *Aia*			
Hemsted	L Lo 2	14 41	5,223
Henhurst	A S 11	66 69	5,109
Higham	A S 9	71 74	5,105
Hollingbourne	A E 4	84 55	(2,33). 3,3
Hoo	A H 1	78 71	5,93
Horton[+]	W Fe 1	11 55	D18. 5,162
Horton (Kirby)	S A 9	56 68	5,18
(Monk's) Horton[+]	L Sw 3	12 40	9,25–26;30
Hougham[+]	E B 19	27 39	M23. (5,138)
Howbury	S Le 3	53 76	5,20
Hunton	A M 8	72 49	*3,5*
Hurst (in Chilham)[+]	W Fa 21	06 51	D18. 5,153
Hythe[+]	L St 10	16 34	(2,26;41)
Ickham[+]	B D 3	22 58	3,8

	Map	Grid	Text
Offham	A La 14	65 57	5,47;56
Orgarswick	L Rm 3	09 30	*3,22*
Orlestone	L Hm 2	00 34	9,28
Orpington	S R 9	46 66	2,30. 3,1
Oslachintone	–	–	D18
Ospringe[+]	W Fa 10	00 60	D18. 5,145
Otford	S Co 1	52 59	2,4
Otham	A E 9	78 54	5,83
Otterden	A E 14	94 54	5,76
Otterpool[+]	L St 6	10 36	9,49
Paddlesworth	A La 4	68 62	5,45
Palstre (Court)	L O 1	88 28	5,172–173
Patrixbourne[+]	B Br 2	18 55	5,119
(East) Peckham	A Li 4	66 49	3,2
(West) Peckham	A Li 2	64 52	5,59
Penenden	A M 2	76 57	D23
Perry (Court)[+]	W Fa 7	01 60	D18. 5,151
Perry (Wood)[+]	W Fa 20	03 55	D18. 5,150
Petham[+]	B Pe 1	13 51	2,15
Pett	W Ca 3	96 48	*3,15*
Pimp's (Court)	A Tw 7	75 52	5,94–(95)
Pinden	S A 7	59 69	5,11
Pineham[+]	E B 10	31 45	5,174
Pising[+]	E B 11	32 45	5,174
Pivington	W Ca 7	91 46	5,168
Pluckley	W Ca 8	92 45	2,20
Plumstead	S Le 1	45 78	5,21. 7,1
(North) Ponshall[+]	E B 3	28 47	5,136
(South) Ponshall[+]	E B 4	28 46	5,137
Postling[+]	L Ha 1	14 39	5,169. 9,16
Poulton[+]	E B 16	27 41	9,41
Preston (near Fordwich)[+]	E P 1	24 60	7,23
(South) Preston[+]	W Fa 9	02 60	3,11
Reculver[+]	B Re 1	22 69	2,13
Ridley	S A 19	61 63	5,6
Ringlestone	W Fa 19	88 55	5,161
Ringleton[+]	E E 3	29 57	5,183
Ripe[+]	L La 2	03 19	P6;17
Ripton	W Ct 2	99 44	7,17
Rochester	A R 1	74 68	R. *1,2.* (2,3.) 4,15. (5,44;53; 56;70;93;97;104. 13,1)
Romney[+]	L Rm 2	03 25	2,25;(43). 5,178
Rooting	W Ca 9	94 45	7,16
Ruckinge[+]	L Hm 3	02 33	*3,8.* 9,29
Ruxley	S R 4	48 70	5,22
Ryarsh	A La 9	67 59	5,46
St. Margaret's at Cliffe[+]	E B 15	35 44	M6–13;(14); 21. P8
St. Martin's[+]	B We 3	15 57	*2,16*;24
Saltwood[+]	L Ha 2	15 35	2,41
Sandlings	S R 7	46 66	5,38
Sandwich[+]	E S 1	33 58	D22;24. 2,2. 3,23. 5,198
Schildricheham, see *Cildresham*			
Scortebroc	–	–	P14
Seal	S R 14	55 56	5,26
Seasalter[+]	B Wh 2	09 64	3,10
Sellindge[+]	L St. 4	09 38	9,24
Selling[+]	W Bo 3	03 56	7,15
Sevington[+]	W Lo 4	03 40	9,3
Shalmsford (Street)[+]	W Fe 5	09 54	5,170
Shelborough	A E 18	88 52	5,65
(New) Shelve	A E 21	91 51	5,78
(Old) Shelve	A E 22	92 51	5,77;82

	Map	Grid	Text
Shelving[+]	E E 2	29 54	5,135;219
Sheppey	W T 1	90 72	2,37
Sibertswold[+]	E B 1	26 47	M15-16;20. P12. 7,21
Siborne	L St	–	9,45
Siffleton	A La 18	71 58	5,43
Snodland	A La 3	70 61	4,9
Soles (Court)[+]	E E 16	25 50	5,201
Solton[+]	E B 12	33 45	5,187
'Sonnings'	S A 10	58 68	(5,7)
Sophis	W	–	D24
South Ashford[+]	W Lo 3	00 41	9,4
Southfleet	S A 6	61 71	4,1
Stalisfield	W Fa 18	96 52	5,142
Stansted[+]	L Bi 2	06 37	P4
Stansted[+]	L St 2	06 37	P3
Statenborough[+]	E E 7	31 55	(2,39)
Stelling[+]	B Br 5	14 48	5,121
Stockbury	A E 1	84 61	5,69
Stoke	A H 2	82 75	4,16. 5,92
'Stokenbury'	A Li 5	67 49	3,2. 5,61
Stone	S A 2	57 74	4,2
Stourmouth[+]	B Re 3	25 62	*2,14*
Stowting[+]	L Sw 2	12 41	(2,25)
Stuppington	M M 6	96 59	5,117
Sturry[+]	B Sy 1	17 60	7,7
Sturtune	L Rm	–	*3,22*
Suestone	L F		9,54
Sundridge	S Co 2	48 54	2,5
Sutton (Valence)	A E 24	81 49	5,71
East Sutton	A E 25	82 49	5,73
Swalecliffe[+]	B Wh 3	13 67	5,139
Swanscombe	S A 3	60 73	5,2
Swanton (in Bilsington)[+]	L St 1	02 35	9,46
Swanton (in Lydden)[+]	E B 6	24 44	5,193
Swarling[+]	B Pe 2	12 52	*2,15*
Teston	A Tw 2	70 53	5,99
Thanington[+]	B We 2	13 56	*2,16*
Throwley	W Fa 15	99 55	D18. 5,155
Thurnham	A E 2	80 57	5,86
Tickenhurst[+]	E Su 3	29 54	5,210
Tiffenden	L Bl 1	91 36	9,44
Tilmanstone[+]	E E 18	30 51	2,40
Tinton	L Bl 2	98 31	5,182. 9,8;22
Tonbridge	A Te 1	59 46	4,1
Tonge	M M 4	93 64	5,118
Tottington	A La 12	73 59	5,49-50
Trimworth	W W 2	06 49	12,1
Trottiscliffe	A La 7	64 60	4,8
Tudeley	A Wa 1	62 45	5,62
Tunstall	M M 5	89 61	5,115
Ulcombe	A E 26	84 49	2,32
Upchurch	M M 1	84 67	5,116
Wadholt[+]	E B 5	29 46	7,22
Waldershare[+]	E E 21	29 48	5,215
Warehorne	L Hm 1	98 32	3,19
Wateringbury	A Tw 1	68 53	5,97-98
West Cliffe[+]	E B 14	35 44	5,186
Westerham	S Wm 1	44 54	10,1
Westgate (in Canterbury)[+]	B We 1	14 57	2,16;(24)
Westwell	W Ca 4	99 47	3,16
(West) Wickham	S R 10	38 64	5,25

	Map	Grid	Text
Whitstable[+]	B Wh 1	10 66	2,14
Wic	B We	–	*2,16*
Wichling	A E 8	91 55	5,81
Wickhambreux[+]	B D 1	22 58	(5,67);124
Wilderton	W Fa 12	99 56	7,12
Wingham[+]	E Wi 1	24 57	2,21
Woodnesborough[+]	E E 5	30 56	5,197
Woodnesborough[+]	E Su 4	30 56	5,211
Woolwich	S G 1	43 78	12,2
Wormshill	A E 6	88 57	5,80
Wouldham	A La 2	71 64	4,6
Wricklesmarsh	S G 6	41 76	5,31
Wrotham	A Wr 1	61 59	2,10
Wrotham (Heath)	A Wr 2	63 58	5,103
Wye[+]	W W 7	05 46	D24. 6,1
Yalding	A Tw 5	69 50	11,1

Places not named

P2. 5,140;181;203;205;209;218. 7,25. 9,7-8;11;13-15;17;20-21;23;27;32-34;38;40;43;50. 12,1

Places not in Kent

Elsewhere in Britain

ESSEX ... 5,104.   LONDON ... Alstan.   OXFORDSHIRE ... Oxford, Wulfric.   SUSSEX ... *5,67*. Battle 6.

Outside Britain

Abbeville ... Walter.   Arques ... William.   Barbes ... Robert.   Bayeux ... Bishop.   Brébouef ... Hugh. Cambremer ... Walter.   Colombières ... Ralph, Ranulf.   Courbépine ... Ralph.   Douai ... Walter. Eu ... Robert.   Ghent ... Abbey.   Gironde ... Thurstan.   Hesdin ... Arnulf.   Le Marais ... Richard. Mandeville ... Hugh.   Montfort ... Hugh.   Poitou ... William.   Port ... Hugh.   Rots ... Ansketel. St. Ouen ... Bernard,   St. Samson ... Ralph.   St. Wandrille ... Ralph.   Thaon ... William. Vaubadon ... Ranulf.

MAP AND MAP KEYS

The County Boundary and the boundaries of the Lathes are shown in thick lines, broken where uncertain; Hundred boundaries by thin lines, dotted where uncertain.

The boundaries of the Lowy of Tonbridge, Romney Marsh and *Summerdene* Hundred are not mapped.

The letters of National Grid 10-kilometre squares are shown on the map border. Each four-figure square covers one square kilometre (5/8ths of a square mile).

WEST KENT
Half-Lathe of Sutton
Greenwich (G)
1 Woolwich
2 Charlton
3 Greenwich
4 Lewisham
5 Lee
6 Wricklesmarsh
7 Eltham

Bromley (Br)
1 Beckenham
2 Bromley

Ruxley (R)
1 Bexley
2 North Cray
3 Foots Cray
4 Ruxley
5 St. Pauls Cray
6 St. Mary Cray
7 Sandlings
8 Crofton
9 Orpington
10 West Wickham
11 Keston
12 Chelsfield
13 Cudham
14 Seal

Little (Le)
1 Plumstead
2 Lessness
3 Howbury
4 Crayford

Axton (A)
1 Dartford
2 Stone
3 Swanscombe
4 Hawley
5 Darenth
6 Southfleet
7 Pinden
8 Longfield

9 Horton Kirby
10 'Sonnings'
11 Farningham
12 Fawkham
13 Hartley
14 Eynsford
15 Lullingstone
16 Maplescombe
17 Idleigh
18 Ash
19 Ridley
Eddintone

Westerham (Wm)
1 Westerham
2 Brasted

Codsheath (Co)
1 Otford
2 Sundridge

Aylesford Lathe
Toltingtrough (To)
1 Northfleet
2 Gravesend
3 Milton
4 Nurstead
5 Meopham
6 Luddesdown

Shamwell (S)
1 Cliffe
2 Cooling
3 Denton
4 Chalk
5 Beckley
6 Oakleigh
7 Merston
8 Haven
9 Higham
10 Frindsbury
11 Henhurst
12 Cuxton
13 Halling

Hoo (H)
1 Hoo
2 Stoke

Rochester (R)
1 Rochester
2 Great Delce
3 Little Delce
4 Borstal

Chatham (C)
1 Chatham
2 Gillingham

Eyhorne (E)
1 Stockbury
2 Thurnham
3 Aldington
4 Hollingbourne
5 Allington
6 Wormshill
7 Frinsted
8 Wichling
9 Otham
10 Leeds
11 Harbilton
12 Harrietsham
13 Marley
14 Otterden
15 Langley
16 Broomfield
17 Fairbourne
18 Shelborough
19 Bowley
20 Lenham
21 New Shelve
22 Old Shelve
23 Chart Sutton
24 Sutton Valence
25 East Sutton
26 Ulcombe
27 Boughton Malherbe
Bromfeld

Maidstone (M)
1 Boxley
2 Penenden
3 Maidstone
4 West Barming
5 East Barming
6 East Farleigh
7 Loose
8 Hunton
Burgericistune

Larkfield (La)
1 Nashenden
2 Wouldham
3 Snodland
4 Paddlesworth
5 Burham
6 Birling
7 Trottiscliffe
8 Addington
9 Ryarsh
10 Leybourne
11 Eccles
12 Tottington
13 Aylesford
14 Offham
15 West Malling
16 East Malling
17 Ditton
18 Siffleton
19 Allington

Wrotham (Wr)
1 Wrotham
2 Wrotham Heath

Littlefield (Li)
1 Mereworth
2 West Peckham
3 Hadlow
4 East Peckham
5 'Stokenbury'

Twyford (Tw)
1 Wateringbury
2 Teston
3 West Farleigh
4 Nettlestead
5 Yalding
6 Bensted
7 Pimp's Court

Washlingstone (Wa)
1 Tudeley

The Lowy of Tonbridge (Te)
1 Tonbridge

Half-Lathe of Milton
Milton (M)
1 Upchurch
2 Newington
3 Milton Regis
4 Tonge
5 Tunstall
6 Stuppington

EAST KENT
Wye Lathe
Teynham (T)
1 Sheppey

Faversham (Fa)
1 Harty
2 Luddenham
3 Oare
4 Buckland
5 Norton
6 Faversham
7 Perry Court
8 Macknade
9 South Preston
10 Ospringe
11 North Eastling
12 Wilderton
13 Eastling
14 Arnolton
15 Throwley
16 Leaveland
17 Badlesmere
18 Stalisfield
19 Ringlestone
20 Perry Wood
21 Hurst
Cildresham

Boughton (Bo)
1 Graveney
2 Boughton under Blean
3 Selling

Calehill (Ca)
1 East Lenham
2 Charing
3 Pett
4 Westwell
5 Dean Court
6 Little Chart

7 Pivington
8 Pluckley
9 Rooting

Chart (Ct)
1 Great Chart
2 Ripton

Longbridge (Lo)
1 Kennington
2 Ashford
3 South Ashford
4 Sevington
5 Mersham
6 Evegate
Essella

Wye (W)
1 Beamonston
2 Trimworth
3 Eastwell
4 Boughton Aluph
5 Buckwell
6 Dernedale
7 Wye
8 Fanscombe
9 Ashenfield
10 Coombegrove
11 Brook
12 Hampton

Felborough (Fe)
1 Horton
2 Chartham
3 Shillingham
4 Chilham
5 Shalmsford
6 Godmersham

Bircholt (Bi)
1 Aldglose
2 Brabourne

Hundred not known
Gara
Hawkhurst
'Northborough'
Sophis

Borough Lathe
Whitstable (Wh)
1 Whitstable
2 Seasalter
3 Swalecliffe

Whitstable (Wh) cont'd.
4 Blean

Reculver (Re)
1 Reculver
2 Makinbrook
3 Stourmouth

Chislet (Ch)
1 Chislet

Sturry (Sy)
1 Sturry

Fordwich (Fo)
1 Fordwich

Westgate (We)
1 Westgate
2 Thanington
3 St. Martins
Wic

Bridge (Br)
1 Bekesbourne
2 Patrixbourne
3 Lower Hardres
4 Upper Hardres
5 Stelling

Petham (Pe)
1 Petham
2 Swarling

Barham (Ba)
1 Bishopsbourne
2 Barham

Downhamford (D)
1 Wickhambreux
2 Littlebourne
3 Ickham
4 Garrington

Thanet (Th)
1 Monkton
2 Minster in Thanet
3 Margate

Canterbury (Ca)
1 Canterbury
2 Nackington
3 Northgate
4 Langport

Lympne Lathe
Stowting (Sw)
1 Bodsham
2 Stowting
3 Monks Horton
Bochelande
Lanport

Loningborough (Lo)
1 Elham
2 Hemsted
3 Lyminge
4 Acrise

Folkestone (F)
1 Folkestone
Suestone

Bircholt (Bi)
1 Hastingleigh
2 Stansted
3 Aldington

Hayne (Ha)
1 Postling
2 Saltwood
Belice

Street (St)
1 Swanton
2 Stansted
3 Bonnington
4 Sellindge
5 Court at Street
6 Otterpool
7 Berwick
8 Lympne
Aia
Siborne

Blackburn (Bl)
1 Tiffenden
2 Tinton
3 Appledore

Ham (Hm)
1 Warehorne
2 Orlestone
3 Ruckinge

Newchurch (N)
1 Bilsington
2 Norwood

Worth (W)
1 Eastbridge
2 Blackmanstone

Rolvenden (Rl)
1 Benenden
Belice

Selbrittenden (Se)
1 Newenden

Oxney (O)
1 Palstre

Aloesbridge (A)
1 Brenzett

Langport (La)
1 Langport
2 Ripe
3 Dengemarsh
Afettune

The Borough of Hythe
1 Hythe

In Romney Marsh (Rm)
1* Burmarsh
2* Romney
3* Orgarswick
4* Castweazel
Eadruneland
Sturtune

Hundred not known
Brisewei

Eastry Lathe
Preston (P)
1 Preston
2 Elmstone

Wingham (Wi)
1 Wingham
2 Fleet

Sandwich (Sa)
1 Sandwich

Eastry (E)
1 Each
2 Shelving
3 Ringleton
4 Hammil

Eastry (E) cont'd.

5 Woodnesborough
6 Buckland
7 Statenborough
8 Adisham
9 Chillenden
10 Eastry
11 Ham
12 Easole
13 Finglesham
14 Knowlton
15 Betteshanger
16 Soles Court
17 Barfreston
18 Tilmanstone
19 Hartanger
20 Eythorne
21 Waldershare
22 Denton
23 Giddinge
24 Midley

Bewsborough (B)

1 Sibertswold
2 Coldred
3 North Ponshall
4 South Ponshall
5 Wadholt
6 Swanton
7 Temple Ewell
8 Boswell Banks
9 Appleton
10 Pineham
11 Pising
12 Solton
13 Guston
14 West Cliffe
15 St. Margaret's at Cliffe
16 Poulton
17 Buckland
18 Charlton
19 Hougham

20 Farthingloe
21 Atterton
22 Dover
23 Mederclive
24 Newington
Jaonei
Leueberge

Cornilo (C)

1 Deal
2 Northbourne
3 Great & Little Mongeham
4 Beauxfield

Summerdene **(Su)**

A Each
B Marshborough
C Tickenhurst
D Woodnesborough
E Elmton

WEST KENT

EAST KENT

SYSTEMS OF REFERENCE TO DOMESDAY BOOK

The manuscript is divided into numbered chapters, and the chapters into sections, usually marked by large initials and red ink. Farley did not number the sections and later historians, using his edition, have referred to the text of DB by folio numbers, which cannot be closer than an entire page or column. Moreover, several different ways of referring to the same column have been devised. In 1816 Ellis used three separate systems in his indices: (i) on pages i–cvii, 435–518, 537–570; (ii) on pages 1–144; (iii) on pages 145–433 and 519–535. Other systems have since come into use, notably that used by Vinogradoff, here followed. The present edition numbers the sections, the normal practicable form of close reference; but since all discussion of DB for two hundred years has been obliged to refer to folio or column, a comparative table will help to locate references given. The five columns below give Vinogradoff's notation, Ellis's three systems, and that used by Welldon Finn and others. Maitland, Stenton, Darby, and others have usually followed Ellis (i).

Vinogradoff	Ellis (i)	Ellis (ii)	Ellis (iii)	Finn
152 a	152	152 a	152	152 ai
152 b	152	152 a	152.2	152 a2
152 c	152 b	152 b	152 b	152 bi
152 d	152 b	152 b	152 b2	152 b2

In Kent the relation between the Vinogradoff column notation, here followed, and the chapters and sections is

1 a	D1 – D10	6 a	5,1 – 5,8	11 a	5,178 – 5,192		
b	D11 – D24	b	5,9 – 5,18	b	5,192 – 5,203		
c	D25 – M10	c	5,18 – 5,24	c	5,204 – 5,217		
d	M11 – M16	d	5,25 – 5,34	d	5,218 – 6,1		
2 a	C1 – R1	7 a	5,34 – 5,43	12 a	7,1 – 7,8		
b	P1 – P20	b	5,43 – 5,51	b	7,8 – 7,17		
c	1,1 – 1,3	c	5,52 – 5,59	c	7,18 – 7,23		
d	1,3 – 1,4	d	5,60 – 5,70	d	7,23 – 8,1		
3 a	2,1 – 2,7	8 a	5,70 – 5,78	13 a	9,1 – 9,11		
b	2,7 – 2,11	b	5,80 – 5,88	b	9,12 – 9,23		
c	2,12 – 2,16	c	5,88 – 5,95	c	9,24 – 9,35		
d	2,16 – 2,22	d	5,95 – 5,104	d	9,36 – 9,48		
4 a	2,23 – 2,27	9 a	5,104 – 5,115	14 a	9,48 – 10,2		
b	2,28 – 2,35	b	5,115 – 5,124	b	11,1 – 12,4		
c	2,36 – 2,40	c	5,124 – 5,128	c	13,1		
d	3,1 – 3,7	d	5,129 – 5,138				
5 a	3,7 – 3,15	10 a	5,139 – 5,146				
b	3,16 – 3,23	b	5,147 – 5,156				
c	4,1 – 4,9	c	5,157 – 5,166				
d	4,10 – 4,16	d	5,167 – 5,178				

TECHNICAL TERMS

Most of the words expressing measurements have to be transliterated. Translation may not, however, dodge other problems by the use of obsolete or made-up words which do not exist in modern English. The translations here used are given below in italics. They cannot be exact; they aim at the nearest modern equivalent.

AVERA. Provision of draught-horses or mules for the King's use; sometimes commuted to a money payment. *cartage*

BEREWICA. An outlying place, attached to a manor. *outlier*

BORDARIUS. Cultivator of inferior status, usually with a little land. *smallholder*

CARUCA. A plough, with the oxen who pulled it, usually reckoned as 8. *plough*

COTARIUS. Inhabitant of a *cote*, cottage, often without land. *cottager*

DENA. An area of woodland pasture, in Kent mostly associated with land in the Weald belonging to upland manors. *pig pasture*

DOMINIUM. The mastery or dominion of a lord (*dominus*); including plough, land, men, villages, etc., reserved for the lord's use; often concentrated in a *home farm* or *demesne*. *lordship*

FEUDUM. Continental variant, not used in England before 1066, of *feuum* (the Latin form of Old English *feoh*, cattle, money, possessions in general); either a landholder's holding, or land held under the terms of a specific grant. *Holding*

FIRMA. Old English *feorm*, provisions due to the King or lord; a fixed sum paid in place of these and of other miscellaneous dues. *revenue*

GABLUM. Old English *gafol*, tribute or tax to the King or a lord. *tribute*

GELDUM. The principal royal tax, originally levied during the Danish wars, normally at an equal number of pence on each *sulung* of land. *tax*

HIDA. A unit of land measurement, reckoned in DB at 120 fiscal acres; rarely used in Kent, probably in error for *sulung*. *hide*

HUNDREDUM. An administrative district within a shire, whose assembly of notables and village representatives usually met once a month. *hundred*

INUUARD. Provision of a mounted man for the King's use, originally to escort the King when he visited the shire; sometimes commuted to a money payment. *escort*

IUGUM. A unit of land measurement, one quarter of the sulung. *yoke*

LEUGA. An area of jurisdiction, originally a league outside a fixed place; in Kent used of land assigned to the maintenance of Tonbridge castle. *territory*

LEST. A division of the shire peculiar to Kent and containing several hundreds (cf. introduction to the Index of Places). *Lathe*

MANERIUM. A territorial and jurisdictional holding. *manor*

SACA. German *Sache*, English *sake*, Latin *causa*, 'affair', 'lawsuit'; the fullest authority normally exercised by a lord. *full jurisdiction*

SOCA. '*Soke*', from Old English *socn*, seeking, comparable with Latin *quaestio*. Jurisdiction, with the right to receive fines and other dues; also the district in which such *soca* was exercised. *jurisdiction*

SOCHEMANNUS. 'Soke man', liable to attend the court of a *soca* and serve its lords; before 1066 often with more land and higher status than villagers; bracketed in the Commissioners' brief with the *liber homo* (free man); see Bedfordshire, Appendix. *Freeman*

SOLIN. The Kentish unit of land measurement, usually reckoned at 200 acres (see note 7,19). *sulung*

TEIGNUS. Person of superior status; originally one of the King's military companions, later often in his service in an administrative capacity. *thane*

T.R.E. *tempore regis Edwardi*, in King Edward's time. *before 1066*

VILIA. Translating Old English *tun*, estate, town, village. The later distinction between a small *village* and a large *town* was not yet in use in 1066. *village* or *town*

VILLANUS. Member of a *villa*, usually with more land than a *bordarius*. *villager*

VIRGATA. A quarter of a hide (40 fiscal acres in DB), rarely used in Kent, often in error for *yoke*. *virgate*